About Island Press

Island Press is the only nonprofit organization in the United States whose principal purpose is the publication of books on environmental issues and natural resource management. We provide solutions-oriented information to professionals, public officials, business and community leaders, and concerned citizens who are shaping responses to environmental problems.

In 1999, Island Press celebrates its fifteenth anniversary as the leading provider of timely and practical books that take a multidisciplinary approach to critical environmental concerns. Our growing list of titles reflects our commitment to bringing the best of an expanding body of literature to the environmental community throughout North America and the world.

Support for Island Press is provided by The Jenifer Altman Foundation, The Bullitt Foundation, The Mary Flagler Cary Charitable Trust, The Nathan Cummings Foundation, The Geraldine R. Dodge Foundation, The Charles Engelhard Foundation, The Ford Foundation, The Vira I. Heinz Endowment, The W. Alton Jones Foundation, The John D. and Catherine T. MacArthur Foundation, The Andrew W. Mellon Foundation, The Charles Stewart Mott Foundation, The Curtis and Edith Munson Foundation, The National Fish and Wildlife Foundation, The National Science Foundation, The New-Land Foundation, The David and Lucile Packard Foundation, The Pew Charitable Trusts, The Surdna Foundation, The Winslow Foundation, and individual donors.

About the Natural Lands Trust

The Natural Lands Trust (NLT), located in Media, Pennsylvania, is a nonprofit regional land trust dedicated to working with people to conserve land in the greater Philadelphia region and nearby areas. Created in 1961, the Trust maintains approximately 47 preserves and has approxmately 23,000 acres under conservation easement. During the late 1970s, the Trust began a significant shift in its operations by providing professional planning assistance to conservation-minded landowners and becoming actively involved in "limited development" projects. By the late 1980s, the Trust began to work closely with communities to help them apply new approaches for managing growth and conserving land. The concept for conversation subdivisions has evolved from the Trust's effort to help municipalities add significant land protection standards to their existing land-use ordinances, so that conservation approaches will become institutionalized within the local planning framework.

For more information on NLT, visit <www.natlands.org>.

About the Pennsylvania Department of Conservation and Natural Resources

Growing Greener is a collaborative effort of the Pennsylvania Department of Conservation and Natural Resources (DCNR), the Natural Lands Trust, the Pennsylvania State University Cooperative Extension, and an advisory board of state agency, local government, nonprofit, and private sector officials.

The mission of the DCNR is to maintain, improve, and preserve state parks; to manage state forest lands to assure their long-term health, sustainability, and economic use; to provide information on Pennsylvania's ecological and geologic resources; and to administer grant and technical assistance programs that will benefit rivers conservation, trails, and environmental education programs across Pennsylvania.

For more information on DCNR, visit <www.dcnr.state.pa.us> or access DCNR through the Pennsylvania home page at <www.state.pa.us>.

GROWING GREENER

"The advantage of land around a growing town being laid out on a plan prepared with forethought and care to provide for the needs of the growing community seems self-evident; and yet it is only within the last few years that any general demand for such powers of town planning have been made. The municipal governing bodies have looked on helplessly while estate after estate around their towns has been covered with buildings, without any provision having been made for open spaces, school sites, or any other public needs. . . . The community . . . having watched the value of land forced up to its utmost limit, has been obliged to come in at this stage and purchase at these ruinous values such scraps of land as may have been left, in order to satisfy public needs."

— Raymond Unwin, *Town Planning in Practice,* 1909

"It is not a choice of either the city or the countryside; both are essential, but today it is nature, beleaguered in the country, too scarce in the city, which has become precious. . . . Let us abandon the self-mutilation which has been our way and give expression to the potential harmony of man–nature. The world is abundant, we require only a deference born of understanding. . . . Man must become the steward of the biosphere. To do this he must design with nature."

— Ian McHarg, *Design with Nature,* 1969

"When we lose our ability to contact the common species (of plant and animal), . . . the ordinary everyday species in our immediate vicinity, they might as well be extinct, in one sense. These humble little places where a kid can go and not do damage can have an enormous impact in creating a national character that cares for the land."

— Robert Pyle, *Thunder Tree,* 1993

"Conservation begins with an understanding of the significance of the natural world."

— David Attenborough

"Planning is more than a tool or technique; it is a philosophy for organizing actions that enable people to predict and visualize the future of any land area. Moreover, planning gives people the ability to link actions on specific parcels of land to larger regional systems. It is up to us to plan with vision. Our responsibility is to retain what we treasure, because we are merely guests on those spaces of the earth that we inhabit. We should leave good impressions about our visit."

— Frederick Steiner, *The Living Landscape,* 1991

"The idea of using development as an engine to protect open space, strengthen communities, reduce automobile use and even restore damaged ecosystems is an exciting one. . . . It will require a paradigm shift to move society 'from thinking the best it can do is to minimize negative impact, toward a view in which development is seen as both contributing to the growth of healthy human communities, while simultaneously restoring (not merely sustaining) the natural environment.'"

— Alex Wilson, *Green Development,* 1998

"All sustainability is local."

— William A. McDonough, FAIA
   Architect, planner, product designer
   Dean, School of Architecture, University of Virginia

GROWING GREENER

Putting Conservation into Local Plans and Ordinances

Randall Arendt

With Site Plans and Perspective Sketches
by Holly Harper, Stephen Kuter, and Diane Rosencrance

*Natural Lands Trust, American Planning Association,
and American Society of Landscape Architects*

ISLAND PRESS

Washington, D.C. • Covelo, California

Library of Congress Cataloging-in-Publication Data
Arendt, Randall.
      Growing greener : putting conservation into local plans and
ordinances / Randall Arendt
         p.   cm.
      Includes bibliographical references and index.
      ISBN 1–55963–742–0 (pbk.)
      1. City planning—Environmental aspects—United States. 2. Land
subdivision—United States—Planning. 3. Conservation of natural
resources—United States. 4. Land use—United States—Planning.
I. Title.   99–33885
HT167.A83   1999   CIP
333.7'2'0973—dc21

Printed on recycled, acid-free paper

Manufactured in the United States of America
10 9 8 7 6 5 4 3

CONTENTS

Chapter 5: Conservation Subdivisions: Application Documents, Design Process, and Conservation Land Design Standards   53

Chapter 7: Examples of Subdivisions with Substantial Conservation Areas   91

Design Exercise 1: Community-Wide Map of Potential Conservation Lands   115

FOREWORD:
THE GROWING GREENER PROGRAM

Communities across Pennsylvania and in other states are realizing that they can conserve their farmland, wooded habitat, and natural areas at the same time they accommodate inevitable development.

These critical elements of the community's "green infrastructure" are just as important as the more conventional "gray infrastructure" of roads, wires, pipes, and drains. What tools do local residents and officials need to protect the special resources in their community? This book describes two: conservation zoning and conservation subdivision design, an approach we call Growing Greener.

Growing Greener enables communities to reach as high as their ideals, putting the greener vision of their Comprehensive Plans into practice through conservation zoning and subdivision ordinances that set new standards for more creative development design.

The approaches described in this book combine some of the most effective ways yet conceived to protect interconnected networks of conservation lands at the local level because they are relatively easy to implement, do not involve large public costs, do not diminish landowner equity, and are not onerous to developers.

What is Growing Greener? It began as a statewide community planning initiative in Pennsylvania, a collaborative partnership effort of the Pennsylvania Department of Conservation and Natural Resources (DCNR), Natural Lands Trust, and the Pennsylvania State University Cooperative Extension Service. Growing Greener is designed to help communities use the development regulation process to their advantage to protect interconnected networks of permanent open space. The program offers multimedia educational material and technical assistance to communities so that conservation and development objectives may be achieved simultaneously, in a manner that is fair to all parties concerned.

The Growing Greener concept is introduced to local officials primarily at countywide workshops in which the techniques are described and illustrated by Natural Lands Trust staff in a dual-image slide presentation that is followed by questions and answers, a buffet dinner, and a participatory hands-on design exercise in which attendees themselves lay out a residential development following the principles introduced in the slide lecture. This helps people internalize what they have seen and heard, allowing them to translate these concepts into a specific plan for conservation and development on a particular property following the special four-step design approach described in this book. Additional workshops of this nature are frequently cosponsored by statewide and regional associations of township supervisors, land surveyors, realtors, and home builders, often in conjunction with local land conservancies. The unusual breadth of interest in the Growing Greener technique is perhaps due to the fact that this approach is fair, easy to understand and implement, and beneficial to all parties (as further detailed in Chapter 6).

Following the county-wide workshops, Trust staff offer to conduct evaluations or "audits" of local zoning and subdivision ordinances, producing a detailed report critiquing the codes in a constructive manner, pointing out areas where the regulations inadvertently thwart conservation objectives, and specifically detailing the ways in which the model ordinance provisions in Appendix 3 of this book could be incorporated into that community's regulatory framework. This evaluation and set of recommendations enables local officials and residents to readjust their course in the Growing Greener direction. Technical assistance in adapting the model code language to local conditions and needs is the next step, provided either by Trust staff or by consultants in the private or public sectors. Ongoing help is also available to review the first subdivisions submitted under the new regulations and to provide design services that make it easier for applicants to meet the new conservation standards contained in the community's updated requirements.

Interest in Growing Greener is increasing in states other than Pennsylvania as well, and Trust staff have assisted communities in Delaware, Ohio, Indiana, Illinois, Michigan, Wisconsin, Minnesota, Virginia, North Carolina, Georgia, Florida, Massachusetts, Maine, Connecticut, and Utah in adapting the Pennsylvania model ordinances for application in their areas. In addition, strong interest in this program has been expressed by planners in South Carolina, Rhode Island, Montana, Iowa, Missouri, and Texas.

This program has virtually been cloned for use in Michigan by the Michigan State University Co-operative Extension Service, which has modified these ordinances for use in that state, with help from the Trust. And in North Carolina the state's Association of County Commissioners worked with Trust staff to produce a primer on conservation design techniques, illustrating it with case studies of three properties in the Albemarle-Pamlico watershed. The Growing Greener technique has been featured at national conferences of the American Planning Association, the American Society of Landscape Architects, the National Home Builders Association, the National Association of Counties, the National Association of Towns and Townships, the U.S. Environmental Protection Agency, and the Urban Land Institute, where it has been promoted as one of the approaches communities can follow to achieve "Smart Growth" objectives.

As an example of the magnitude of success that can be achieved in this way, one Pennsylvania community has conserved more than 500 acres of prime farmland through this technique alone, in only six years. This equates to $3.5 million worth of land conservation at no cost to the township, no dependence on public bond funds, no sacrifice to local landowners, and no "takings" from developers. And in

Michigan, one township has protected more than 1,000 acres in the last eight years in a very similar way, at virtually no public cost, simply by implementing the Growing Greener principles it learned about in a slide workshop conducted by the author in that community in the early 1990s. In both cases the community's conservation acreage continues to increase with each new subdivision that is approved, so that the ultimate area protected with this technique undoubtedly will be much larger than the acreage figures reported here. Figures F-1 through F-6 illustrate the diversity of conservation areas protected in six subdivisions designed according to our Growing Greener principles in southeastern Pennsylvania, and Chapter 7 contains ten additional examples from eight states in various parts of the country. If your community does not yet have any similarly designed developments, the techniques in this book could help you reverse past trends and create a greener future.

Figure F-2. Woodlands: Homes abutting open space at Garnet Oaks, in Bethel Township, Delaware County, sold faster and at premium prices because buyers recognized the value added by proximity to protected lands. Installing the trail system before sales began, and making it a special marketing feature, enhanced the development's success.

Figure F-1. Farmland: More than 500 acres of prime farmland have been preserved through Growing Greener techniques over the past six years in Lower Makefield Township, Bucks County. Farmview, illustrated here, was the first such development and demonstrated the profitability of this approach to other local developers who later copied this example.

Figure F-3. Hayfield Buffer: Although the hayfield in this 16-acre subdivision in Buckingham Township, Bucks County, is not very big, its larger significance is that it provides a 300–500-foot buffer between the new homes and the farmland on the other side of the hedgerow to the left, creating enough separation to maintain good relationships between the farmer and the new residents.

Figure F-4. TREE NURSERY: A commercial tree nursery occupies most of the conservation land at Indian Walk, also in Buckingham Township. This noncommon open space yields a continuing income because the former farmland, which was too small after development for conventional agriculture, is planted with longer term crops.

Figure F-6. HORSE PASTURES: Converting cornfields to pastures for an equestrian facility produced a very workable solution to the challenge of maintaining former cropland as open space at Summerfield, in Elverson Borough, Chester County. Instead of adding to maintenance costs, this land now generates income as a boarding stable. Common open space for residents has also been provided in the form of playing fields and playgrounds.

Figure F-5. NEIGHBORHOOD GREEN: The village green at Plumsock in Willistown Township, Chester County, is but one-half acre in area, yet it provides an attractive community focal point along the street leading into the development, two-thirds of which has been designated as a woodland preserve.

Within Pennsylvania the Growing Greener program is supported principally by DCNR and by generous multi-year grants from the William Penn Foundation, with supplemental funding from the Department of Environmental Protection and the Governor's Center for Local Government Services. Funding for collateral work in Maryland and Virginia has been made available through the Chesapeake Bay Program of the U.S. Environmental Protection Agency and also through that agency's Green Communities program.

An instructional manual has been prepared recently for use in training Pennsylvania's generalist land-use planners in these regulatory and design techniques so that they may in turn teach local planning commissioners and township supervisors about this approach. This "Train the Trainers" program is scheduled to begin in late 1999.

And a 55-minute learning video entitled *Creating Open Space Networks Through Conservation Subdivision Design* has been produced by the author as a supplemental educational tool for viewing by small groups of residents and officials or for broadcast on local cable television channels. Developer education was institutionalized eight years ago by one Vermont town that amended its subdivision ordinance to require that all applicants borrow its copy of an earlier version of this video before submitting any proposed development plans.

Education, or simply information exchange, lies at the heart of all progress. It is hoped that this book will help your community progress beyond conventional land-use regulations to achieve the kind of conservation gains experienced by other municipalities that have implemented the Growing Greener principles.

Secretary John Oliver
Pennsylvania Department of Conservation and Natural Resources

PREFACE:
DESIGNING LAND DEVELOPMENT FROM
A BIRD'S PERSPECTIVE (AMONG OTHERS)

The significance of the bird's-eye perspective drawings (see Fig. P-1, for example) that have appeared in all my books is twofold. Their principal virtue lies in their ability to convey to laypersons what a particular site looks like in its natural or current state and how that would change after employing either of two alternative design approaches to laying out a residential development.

The second reason I use this form of illustration is because I feel it is important to design developments partly from an avian viewpoint. Development designers should be considering numerous aspects of their projects, among them whether a bird (or other wild creature) would want to continue living there after their design has been implemented. This simple and fairly basic idea is not original with me; it is a philosophy shared by many site designers who strive to walk in balance with nature. It has been eloquently expressed by Dean William McDonough of the University of Virginia School of Architecture who suggests that one measure of a project's success should be the increase in the number of songbird species inhabiting a site after it has been developed.

In that context I am privileged to have had the opportunity to design a 1,000-acre conservation development in North Oaks, Minnesota, where one of the desires of my client was to create a bio-preserve within 700 acres of permanent open space that we "greenlined" on detailed resource maps from the very outset. After taking that first critical step, laying out the actual development areas was

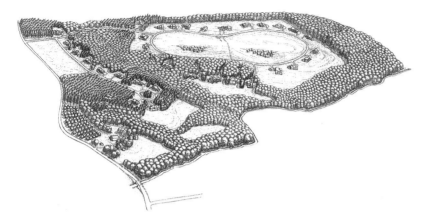

Figure P-1. Bird's-eye perspective sketch of a conservation subdivision design in Currituck County, North Carolina.

fairly straightforward, guided by the principle of including attractive community open space within each neighborhood unit. Recognizing the enormous advantages of this design approach, local officials readily agreed to amend their zoning to allow the same number of houses that would have fit onto the land under a conventional build-out to be located on less than one-third of the property. And within that developed one-third, nearly half has been designated as neighborhood green space in the form of squares, commons, and playing fields. A wildlife biologist has been added to the development company staff to enhance habitat and to monitor species distribution, with longer term goals including possible tree canopy studies. The company has already received recognition by the state Department of Natural Resources for its work in restoring water quality in one of its lakes and bringing back a healthy fisheries situation.

Relatively few conservation subdivisions offer opportunities of this magnitude, but some larger and more complex eco-developments are likely to accomplish even more. Twelve examples of various kinds of simpler conservation subdivisions are featured in Chap-

ter 7, all of which tread far more lightly on the land than development would have under the conventional large-lot mentality. A few of these examples even rise above the level of being "less injurious" to the environment than standard layouts and can therefore claim to have actually improved the preexisting situation by enhancing formerly natural areas that had been cleared of their native vegetation and degraded by decades of agrichemical use. Among these are Prairie Crossing and the Fields of St. Croix, where many acres of prairie habitat have been reclaimed and restored, and where organic farming has replaced chemical-intensive "industrial agriculture." Streambank restoration and water quality improvements were undertaken by the developer of the Ranch at Roaring Fork, and conservation meadows filled with native grasses and wildflowers grace much of the unwooded open space at Ringfield.

William McDonough and the AIA Roundtable on Sustainable Development challenge us to discard the mindset that measures success by how much we minimize negative impacts and replace it with a more positive approach that asks instead how much we are enhancing the current situation and making it better. Our goal, McDonough argues, should be more than "getting down to zero."

In reminding us that "design is the first signal of human intent," McDonough implicitly asks those who propose insensitive conventional developments whether they truly intend to contribute to increased deforestation (gradually depleting local wildlife habitat), increased runoff volume (gradually depleting local aquifers), or increased nitrogen loading in our waterways (gradually degrading local fisheries). Sadly, most local codes allow such projects to be undertaken because their standards are often that low.

In declaring that "All sustainability is local," McDonough helps us to understand that our sustainable development designs are essentially local in their impacts but that the cumulative, positive effect of many such projects will ultimately produce community-wide and regional benefits over the long term.

To be sure, designing a development mostly on the basis of an avian perspective would be as bird-brained as designing it mostly on the basis of an engineering perspective (as commonly happens). Many important viewpoints must be considered, and it is the purpose of this book to weigh them and to recommend a design approach that establishes an intelligent balance. This balance begins with a thorough assessment of each site's natural and cultural resources (in relation to those in the immediate vicinity) and then evaluates the most appropriate location for houses before proceeding to the lesser matters of aligning streets and fixing lot lines. Such a sequence places the resource specialist and landscape architect at the head of the process where they properly belong and then brings in the engineer only when his or her unique skills to fit the streets and drainage systems within the broad conceptual framework of conservation lands and development areas are needed.

In designing developments partly from an avian perspective, developers will discover collateral benefits because sales experience has clearly shown that the very same enhancements that birds (or butterflies, or honeybees . . .) find attractive also add to any development's desirability in the real estate marketplace. Man is part of nature, and home buyers consistently rate the conservation of natural areas and the provision of such simple amenities as trails and playing fields more highly in national surveys than they rate large lawns or fancy fairways.

So growing in a greener way is also growing in a smarter way, for it is greener both environmentally and economically. And that's certainly much smarter than the way we have been growing as a society for decades.

INTRODUCTION:
HOW THIS BOOK CAN HELP YOU

This illustrated volume was written to make it relatively easy for local officials to learn the basic steps involved in designing residential developments that maximize land conservation in a way that also avoids the political and legal problems often associated with "downzoning." Because landowner equity is thereby respected, and because developers continue their ability to build at full legal density, the risk of a serious "takings" challenge is greatly reduced.

This book also shows how communities can employ state-of-the-art zoning and subdivision standards to preserve large, interconnected networks of permanent open space, using the protected lands within individual "conservation subdivisions" as basic building blocks to create this "green infrastructure."

The essence of this book is a three-pronged municipal strategy for shaping growth around the special natural and cultural features found in each community. The three basic elements of this strategy are the municipal Comprehensive Plan, its Zoning Ordinance, and its Subdivision Ordinance. All of these documents can be modified to include a strong conservation focus so that open space protection becomes the central organizing principle around which new residential development is designed and built. Accordingly, extensive model language is included for just such ordinances. Although written originally for Pennsylvania communities, these model regulations can be adapted by planners and land-use attorneys in your state for consistency with the enabling legislation and case law prevailing where you live.

Thus, the basic message is that, *through the Growing Greener approach, the open space that is conservable in nearly every new residential development can be required to be laid out so that it will ultimately coalesce to form an interconnected system of protected lands running across your community.* This is an uplifting concept that goes well beyond current practice in much of this country today and challenges both planners and developers to incorporate the tools of the landscape architect and the conservation biologist, which have generally been overlooked and neglected.

In addition to the designated wetlands, floodplains, and steep slopes that are often the only lands protected under existing codes, the types of open space that can easily be conserved through the simple design approaches illustrated here include upland woodlands, meadows, fields, and historic, cultural, or scenic features of local or greater significance.

Although many of the principles advocated in this workbook are not particularly new, they have been articulated and illustrated in a way that makes them understandable to the majority of participants in the subdivision process—most of whom are typically not designers. Experience has shown that this kind of information is most accessible and usable for such participants when it is presented in a simplified manner that brings the various elements down to their fundamentals.

One of the more exciting aspects of this approach is the possibility it holds for land-use planners to work much more closely with conservation professionals—with developers and landscape architects being the principal bridging members of an emerging "greenspace alliance" in which all these parties could collaborate to produce a more balanced pattern of conservation and development. The current imbalance is related directly to the fact that conventional suburban zoning and subdivision ordinances are essentially legal instruments for approving unimaginative, land-hogging development without any significant conservation components (except for unbuildable wetlands, floodplains, and steep slopes).

This book is unique because it links natural resource conservation, historic preservation, land development, and real estate interests through a common method of preserving such resources: conservation zoning and conservation subdivision design, a variation of the "clustering" technique with some very important distinctions. It is also unique because its original development in Pennsylvania involved the cooperative efforts of state and federal agencies, the state university, and a private conservation organization to produce a document that could benefit many different kinds of growing communities.

Another reason for the preparation of this book is that until now there did not exist a practical "how-to" publication explaining just how resource-conserving development techniques could be put into practice by municipal officials, residential developers, and site designers. This publication is meant to fill that void as an easy-to-read user's manual. It builds on and expands the basic ideas presented in an earlier volume titled *Conservation Design for Subdivisions,* published by Island Press in 1996. That book focused almost exclusively on subdivision design, whereas this book broadens the scope to include more detailed sections on the comprehensive planning process and particularly on methods for updating zoning ordinances to incorporate the concept of conservation design. In addition to providing extensive model language for comprehensive plans, subdivision ordinances, and zoning ordinances, this book includes case studies of eleven conservation developments in nine states, in which the protected lands are the most salient feature, as well as two exercises suitable for group participation.

Although a conscious effort has been made to write this book in a clear and friendly style that will engage the reader's interest, it is expected that many users will thumb to particular sections that are most relevant to their needs. In fact, many readers might choose to turn to the illustrated examples in Chapters 4, 5, and 7 first, before delving into the other sections for additional background information and implementation tips.

Whether you choose to read the chapters in sequence or to skip around a bit, the central message of the text and pictures should come through clearly—that there are better ways of designing new residential developments and that the approach recommended in this book is really quite simple and straightforward. The trick is to re-arrange density on each development parcel as it is being planned so that only half (or less) of the buildable land is consumed by house lots and streets. Without controversial "down-zoning," the same number of homes could easily be built in a less land- and resource-consumptive manner, allowing the balance of the property to be permanently protected and added to an interconnected network of green spaces and green corridors criss-crossing the community.

The approach advocated in this book:

- respects private property rights,
- respects the ability of developers to create new homes for an expanding population, and
- accommodates newcomers without unduly impacting the remaining natural areas and cultural resources that make our communities such special places to live, work, and recreate.

In so doing, this approach provides a *fair* and *equitable* way to balance opportunities for developers and conservationists to meet in the middle, creating more livable communities in the process.

Chapter I

Context

Growth and Development Trends

Although the techniques in this book were originally devised to deal with growth problems experienced by communities in Pennsylvania, they are applicable in most other parts of the country as well. Zoning laws throughout the United States are based on the same original source: the Zoning Enabling Act passed by Congress in 1926, proposed by Herbert Hoover during his tenure as commerce secretary in the Coolidge administration.

Even though the scale and rate of development vary among the different regions of the country, a fairly constant and relatively unchanging aspect of this growth is its *pattern* as it sits upon the land, consuming important natural resources and converting them into bland, unproductive suburban lawns, streets, and parking lots. That pattern is one of geographically dispersed growth, typically occurring in a sporadic, haphazard fashion.

Whatever the rate of growth may be in a particular state, county, or locality, of far greater significance is its physical manifestation in the explosive increase in land consumption relative to population growth.

For example, in the 30-year period from 1960 to 1990, the population in Pennsylvania's ten largest metropolitan regions grew by 12 percent while its developed land area mushroomed by 80 percent. In other words, the amount of resource land taken for urban and suburban development grew six to seven times faster than population. Unfortunately, this trend is not unusual. Similar but less extreme trends have been reported in many other parts of the country. In Florida, for example, developed land grew twice as fast (by 80 percent) as did total population (38 percent) between 1974 and 1984. The experience was even worse in four metropolitan-area counties around Puget Sound, where total acreage of developed land grew two and one-half times faster than population growth (87 percent versus 36 percent). The habit of zoning for ever-lower densities in new development is a sad but common phenomenon, one that afflicts nearly every state in the union.

The situation in Pennsylvania has been strikingly illustrated by a simple graph produced for the report of the Governor's 21st Century Environmental Commission (see Fig. 1-1).

Recognizing the huge societal and economic costs imposed by the land-consumptive results of implementing outdated local land-use policies, the Governor's Environmental Commission has identified sprawl as the commonwealth's most basic underlying problem.

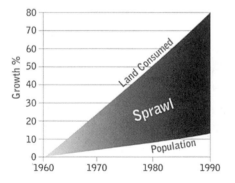

Figure 1-1. Growth of developed land versus population in Pennsylvania, 1960–1990. Results of a study of the ten largest metropolitan areas in Pennsylvania by David Rusk, Washington, D.C., 1997.

Yesterday's techniques for coping with the challenge are insufficient to the task. For example, while 115,000 acres of farmland were protected through expensive buy-back programs from 1982 to 1992, Pennsylvania lost more than one million acres of cropland and pastureland during that same time period. Significantly, the American Farmland Trust has ranked south-central and southeastern Pennsylvania as the nation's second most threatened agricultural area. Although traditional buy-back programs should continue and be expanded, they must be supplemented with more creative approaches that are capable of conserving more land than can possibly be saved through the expenditure of tax dollars. Among the key recommendations of the Governor's Commission is that local governments must begin to implement more innovative land-use practices, with conservation subdivision design specifically mentioned in its final report.

Similar stances and actions—some considerably stronger—have been adopted by other states around the country, including Maryland, New Jersey, Vermont, Florida, and Hawaii, and the Growing Greener approach could be used to good effect in all these states and in most others as well. The exception to this rule of general applicability is Oregon, whose strict Urban Growth Boundary (UGB) program limits suburban land consumption far more effectively. However, even in such situations the illustrated design guidelines for hamlets, villages, and traditional small-town neighborhoods contained in Appendix 3 could be of significant value to planners, site designers, and local officials, where new development within the UGBs would otherwise tend to be simply a denser version of the standard cookie-cutter design.

The accelerating loss of critical resource lands to inefficient low-density sprawl development will almost certainly lead to greater conflicts among resource users. While environmentalists work to preserve woodland habitats and farmland preservationists seek to protect productive fields and orchards, developers must find sites for new subdivisions. Many of these new developments will be served by central sewage treatment facilities that discharge into nearby waterways. Downstream, fishermen will suffer from declining or diseased catches. Individuals may feel that their actions have only insignificant impacts on the environmental resources of their region, but every part of the natural system is related. The cumulative effects of these individual actions can be profound, especially over the longer term, and sound planning will be essential to conserve and protect your community's natural and cultural heritage.

In this regard, the remarks of Representative Tayloe Murphy of the Virginia State Legislature on the problems of the Chesapeake Bay are relevant—if only as one example of actions that produce indirect, cumulative impacts beyond those imagined by the people most directly and immediately involved:

> Every individual and seemingly isolated action has consequences. Most activities that affect the bay and other public resources are of little apparent consequence in themselves: a subdivision here, a road there, a filled wetland, a new field cleared from a forest—but as they are added together, they have the effect of an avalanche that starts with a few pebbles rolling down a hillside. . . . There are simply too many of us doing too many things in the bay's vicinity to continue with the notion that our individual actions make no difference.

Our Natural and Cultural Heritage

Every state embodies a wide expanse of ecosystems that endow it with a rich natural heritage. These areas provide habitat for wildlife, protection for rare plant and animal species, and natural water quality buffers for streams and rivers. Wetlands serve a variety of important functions such as protecting water quality, preventing floods, and providing wildlife habitat (e.g., nursery areas for fisheries), in addition to giving us areas of natural beauty to enjoy and places in which to recreate.

Maintaining our common natural heritage requires a special emphasis on the protection of diverse plant and animal communities, some of which are rare or endangered. The Keystone State's rarest and most significant ecological features are tracked in a database known as the *Pennsylvania Natural Diversity Inventory* (PNDI), a partnership between the state Bureau of Forestry, The Nature Conservancy, and the Western Pennsylvania Conservancy. As of May 1997, the state species lists classified 290 plant species and 155 animal species as endangered and 87 plant species and 84 animal species as threatened. In addition, the PNDI has identified 103 different kinds of natural communities across the state. Many other states have conducted similar inventories, and some others (such as Michigan) have produced sets of maps showing presettlement vegetation patterns that are invaluable to those interested in ecological restoration on properties that have been cleared, drained, or otherwise significantly altered since European settlers arrived.

Wetland habitats include freshwater marshes, bottomland hardwood forests, and nonalluvial wetland forests. Once regarded as wastelands, wetlands are now regarded as ecologically and economically productive ecosystems. Wetlands cover about 2 percent of Pennsylvania, yet more than 80 percent of the state's endangered and threatened species depend on wetlands during their life cycle. The U.S. Fish and Wildlife Service estimates that wetland area in Pennsylvania decreased by more than one-half from the 1780s to the 1980s. The percentage loss of wetlands is even higher in other states, especially in those with longer coastlines or with larger expanses of farmland, much of which occupies land drained generations ago to increase its suitability for cultivation (such as in many of the Great Plains states). Records maintained between 1956 and 1979 indicate that, in Pennsylvania, conversion to ponds, lakes, and reservoirs constituted the leading cause of wetland losses (46 percent), followed by farmland conversion (17 percent) and urbanization (14 percent). Peat mining in the Pocono Mountains region, where peat is removed and the wetland area is commonly converted to a pond or a lake, also contributes to wetland loss. Similar historic trends were experienced in other peat-rich areas in Maine, Michigan, Wisconsin, and Minnesota.

Pennsylvania's historic and cultural heritage is inextricably linked to the natural environment. While many residents recognize the national significance of the Gettysburg Battlefield and Independence Hall, few realize the vastness of resources in their own back yards. A wealth of history may be found in the working landscape of vernacular homes and industrial buildings in riverbank communities around the state. And many of our small downtowns provide local models for new "neo-traditional" development. Nearly the same can be said for every other state in the union.

While the quantity and significance of historic resources varies from one community to another, the importance of public and/or private initiatives in protecting our common heritage of historic sites and cultural landscapes is clear. Only when a community identifies its resources in a Comprehensive Plan can new growth respect the integrity of the community's history and culture.

Growing Greener Applicability in a Wide Variety of Density Situations

As further described on pages 31–34, the Growing Greener techniques may be applied across a broad spectrum of base density situations—from rural districts where density is expressed in acres per dwelling to more urban districts where density is noted as dwellings per acre. The principal difference between these situations lies in the percentage of minimum required open space, typically varying from 50–70 percent in the former to 25–40 percent in the latter.

In other words, the basic techniques described and illustrated in this book can be applied effectively and successfully whether the goal is to conserve broad expanses of important resource lands in the countryside or to provide formal squares and informal neighborhood parks and greenways in and around established towns. In both applications, the Growing Greener approach helps build better communities, where the quality of life is enhanced appreciably. The environmental, social, recreational, and economic benefits of conservation planning and subdivision design are detailed in Chapter 6.

Reasons for Updating Plans and Codes to Include a Conservation Focus

Readers might wonder why they should bother updating their Comprehensive Plans and their zoning and subdivision ordinances to expand the options available to landowners and increase the opportunities for conserving land through the development process. Here are several reasons:

- *Simply put, existing conventional approaches to subdivision development ultimately produce nothing more than house lots and streets.* This process eventually "checkerboards" rural and suburbanizing areas into a seamless blanket of "wall-to-wall subdivisions" with no open space, except for perhaps a few remnant areas that are too wet, steep, or floodprone to build on. Few people, whether they are landowners, developers, realtors, planners, engineers, surveyors, landscape architects, or local officials, can take a great deal of professional pride in helping to create just another conventional subdivision, converting every acre of natural land within a site to lawns, driveways, and streets.

- *Alternative methods of designing for the same overall density while also preserving 50 percent or more of the site are not difficult to master, and they create more attractive and pleasing living environments that sell more easily and appreciate faster than conventional "house lot and street" developments.* This is particularly true for three large and growing sectors of the housing market—young households, single-parent families, and "empty-nesters."

- *The significant land protection achievable through "conservation subdivision design" should help smooth the local review and approval process* by responding to many environmental concerns even before they are raised by county and local officials or by members of the public interested in preserving wildlife habitat and protecting water quality in neighborhood streams, ponds, and aquifers.

- *Conservation subdivisions are simply better places in which to live.* When well designed, the majority of lots in these subdivisions abut or face onto a variety of open spaces, from formal "greens" or "commons" to wildflower meadows, farm fields, mature woodlands, tidal or freshwater wetlands, and/or active recreational facilities. At present, only golf course developments offer comparable amounts of open space. But those green areas are managed for only one kind of activity and typically convert all previously natural areas (except wetlands and steep slopes) into intensively managed lawns that are off limits to everyone but golfers and are uninviting to most forms of wildlife (except the more tolerant animals, such as geese).

One measure of the demand for open space among home buyers is the fact that nearly 40 percent of people living in golf course developments do not even play the game. According to published reports, these people are buying "the park-like views of open space, views that can command a premium in a home's initial sale price and its resale value."

This book will show how virtually any community can adapt and improve on the basic technique used for decades by the designers of golf course communities. Briefly stated, that technique is to outline the open space first and to let its size and location become the central organizing elements driving the rest of the design. The next three steps are to locate the houses around the open space, to trace in street alignments and trail corridors, and finally to set the lot lines.

It is almost as simple as it sounds. Naturally, a number of resource base maps are required (typically pertaining to soils, slopes, wetlands, floodplains, existing vegetation, wildlife habitats, and historic resources), and several elemental principles relating to physical layout and neighborhood design should be observed. These are illustrated and described in later chapters.

Of course, this book does not reduce the need to engage a team of professionals, including a landscape architect or physical planner, in addition to a surveyor and an engineer. It can, however, make everyone's role clearer by articulating a "greener vision" for residential developments of nearly every size, shape, and variety.

Frequently Asked Questions About Conservation Subdivision Design

For a quick overview of the questions most often asked about this approach by local residents and officials, and for helpful answers to those queries, readers are referred to Appendix 1. The information contained in that appendix has been gleaned from the text of this book and assembled in a format that is easy to photocopy (with the publisher's permission) for distribution at public meetings where this approach is being discussed.

Chapter 2

How Your Community
Can Choose Its Own Future

There is no particular future that is preordained for any community. To a greater extent than many people believe, the future is a matter of choice. A wide range of alternative futures exists and, realistically, "staying the same" is usually not one of them.

In regions experiencing population growth, change is inevitable. The real choice facing communities in such areas is whether to try to actively shape those internal and external forces bringing change or to passively accept unplanned, haphazard development patterns and try to cope with the results in the best way possible.

For those communities that have adopted some type of land-use plan and regulation to control growth, additional choices face local residents and officials. Those choices run the gamut from relying on conventional zoning and subdivision codes to turning to newer conservation-based tools that can effectively protect the community's most valued resources and its most special places, while still accommodating full-density growth.

The future that faces most communities that have adopted standard land-use regulations is to witness the systematic conversion of every acre of buildable land into a developed use. As long as such standard regulations remain on the books, the future will inevitably consist of one development after another, each consisting entirely of house lots and streets.

However, for those who desire a future comprising something more than lawns and cul-de-sacs and who would like to see substantial acreages of open space conserved each time a tract is subdivided, real practical alternatives do in fact exist. The most promising of these alternatives, which are the focus of this book, are based on a community-wide conservation plan and are known as "conservation zoning" and "conservation subdivision design."

How does a community determine what kind of future is likely to unfold if it maintains its current zoning and subdivision regulations? The answer can be foreseen by engaging in any of three complementary processes, as described in this chapter. Although the results of these various "auditing" procedures are frequently not pleasant to hear or read, such exercises are an extremely effective tool in helping local residents and officials understand exactly where they are headed if their community remains on its current course. The most common response to the audit is for people to question the effectiveness of present plans and land-use regulations in their community and to be motivated to explore other tools and techniques that hold the promise of a brighter, greener future. The most effective of those tools and techniques are the principal subjects of Chapters 3, 4, and 5.

The Community Audit Process

The community audit process enables municipalities to predict their likely futures in light of:

- the continuation of past development trends,
- recent land-use patterns, and
- the community's current package of plans and ordinances that affect the density and layout of new subdivisions.

It also takes into account the level of public funding that is likely to be available to acquire land for conservation purposes and the degree of success that private conservation efforts might reasonably be expected to have in terms of encouraging donations of land and/or easements to limit new development.

The principal purpose of an audit is to evaluate the probable effectiveness of a community's regulatory and nonregulatory tools in achieving its land conservation goals as expressed in its Comprehensive Plan.

An important component of the audit is that it encourages public dialogue among different community interests. It gives everyone the opportunity to understand the assumptions used in the analysis and helps them appreciate the implications of continuing on the present course charted by the community's current ordinances, as supplemented by private conservation efforts (such as the donation of land or restrictive easements by the landowner). If, after reviewing the results of the audit, residents and officials are satisfied that the future will shape up in an acceptable manner, they can resume business as usual with settled minds. However, as is typically the case, if the results cause them to question the wisdom of proceeding exactly as before, the audit will have served a very useful purpose as a wake-up call.

All too often, local residents and officials lack any clear idea of the kind of "wall-to-wall" development that will ultimately result from carefully and diligently implementing their existing codes over the long term. This is quite understandable because it is extremely difficult for anyone other than highly experienced planners to read the dry, legal provisions of an ordinance and then be able to mentally project the kind of development patterns they are likely to produce. Lay members of local boards and commissions cannot be expected to translate zoning texts into concrete imagery and be able to visualize, in their own minds' eyes, the results of many new subdivisions built in the conventional manner, nearly covering the countryside after several decades of sustained growth. One element of the audit process, the build-out map, accomplishes this task in a way that no previous planning tool has ever done. It enables community leaders and others "to see the future before it happens."

The choice of evaluation methods will differ somewhat by the type of community with respect to the following variables: (1) the percentage of unprotected land that is not yet developed, (2) the permitted zoning densities, and (3) the range of mapped data available in formats that are consistent and readily usable. Audits generally take one or more of three forms, which may be seen as three consecutive steps:

- *Numerical Analysis.* The first form or step involves a numerical analysis of growth projections, in terms of both the number of dwelling units and the number of acres that will probably be converted to house lots and streets to accommodate that growth, under present-day codes.
- *Written Evaluation.* The second form or step consists of a written evaluation of the land-use regulations that are presently on the books, identifying their strengths and weaknesses and offering constructive recommendations about how they might be improved. It should also include a realistic appraisal of the extent to which private conservation efforts are likely to succeed in protecting lands from development through various nonregulatory approaches such as purchases or donations of easements or fee title interests. Local officials tend to respond best to this type of audit because it provides them with a specific critique of their existing ordinances and spells out exactly what kind of changes would be needed if the Growing Greener promise of protecting an interconnected network of conservation lands is to be fulfilled.
- *Build-Out Maps.* The third form or step entails a mapping exercise in which future development patterns are displayed visually on a map of the entire municipality or in selected areas where the likely development pattern under current codes is of the greatest imme-

diate interest, perhaps due to the presence of resources or special features identified in the Comprehensive Plan or particular vulnerability to development pressures.

Numerical Analysis

The purpose of a numerical analysis is to project the number of acres that are likely to be converted from farmland or woodlands to suburban uses over the next 10 to 20 years in the community being evaluated. To accomplish this goal, various types of numerical data are analyzed. To better understand and anticipate the larger growth trends at work, this analysis should be undertaken on an area-wide basis, identifying the acreage and percentage of the community's developed and undeveloped land and comparing these figures with parallel data from the surrounding municipalities. A similar kind of comparative analysis should be performed with regard to recent and projected growth trends, in terms of population increase, new home construction, and land conversion to developed uses.

Written Review of Ordinances and Private Conservation Efforts

The second step entails a thorough review of the community's present land-use plans and ordinances and an evaluation of nonregulatory efforts by the municipality and private conservation organizations. The purpose of this ordinance review is to determine how well or poorly the municipality is being served by its current codes — in terms of its resource land conservation objectives. In other words, the auditor's primary goal is to identify shortcomings or limitations of the regulations that would inhibit or restrict good conservation design and to constructively offer specific suggestions for improved wording.

Although zoning and subdivision ordinances have traditionally focused almost exclusively on development-related issues (such as lot dimensions, street geometry, and stormwater management), there is no reason they cannot be overhauled and adjusted to place an equal emphasis on conserving a variety of environmental, cultural, historic, and scenic features. It is precisely those features that typically give a community its special character. Under conventional zoning and subdivision regulations, these features are frequently at great risk of being swept away by new checkerboard developments that are simply not required to be designed in a sensitive way to enable those special elements to be conserved.

The ordinance aspects that are typically examined fall into several broad categories pertaining to *substance* and *procedures*. Both the zoning and the subdivision ordinances are considered under each of these broad categories, in turn.

SUBSTANTIVE PROVISIONS OF ZONING ORDINANCES

Zoning requirements to be examined by the community auditor under the heading of "substance" are listed below, with a brief description of their relevance to the ordinance's ability to foster community land conservation objectives.

- *Density Standards—Separating Lot Size from Density.* Density should never be regulated through a minimum lot size requirement, which is an indirect and counterproductive method. Instead, density should be regulated directly as "the maximum number of dwellings permitted for the buildable acreage involved," or as "the buildable acres required per dwelling, including common, undivided conservation land." When minimum lot sizes are used to govern development density, there is no possibility for conserving undivided open space because all land must be allocated either to house lots or to streets. For example, two-acre lots in a two-acre district are totally land-consumptive, just as are half-acre lots in a half-acre density district. If land-conserving designs are desired, lot sizes should generally be no more than about one-half the density figure (to allow or require one-acre lots in a two-acre district, for

example) within the context of an overall density limitation. Ordinances that do not separate lot size from density and do not allow smaller lots provided that density remains "neutral," produce "mandatory sprawl," and suffer from a fundamental defect that essentially prohibits conservation subdivision design.

- *Density Standards—Accounting for Environmental Constraints.* When ordinances allow density to be calculated simply by dividing total land area by the "land area per dwelling unit," commonsense adjustments should be made to discount lands that are inherently unbuildable due to physical constraints such as steepness, wetness, or proneness flood. These commonsense adjustments are the heart of Bucks County's nationally acclaimed "performance zoning," which introduced the idea of "site capacity analysis" to the planning profession 25 years ago. (This concept is described in detail on pages 41–43.) Ordinances that fail to discount the buildability of land tend to permit more development than would otherwise occur. Even lots in conventional subdivisions can be subject to minimum criteria for buildability so that no more than a certain percentage of land within the minimum-sized lot would be so constrained. For example, many ordinances require that at least half of any minimum-sized building lot be free of such basic limitations. Carrying this principle over to conservation subdivision design is prudent and in fact sometimes necessary to prevent unintended density bonuses to applicants whose development parcels contain a large proportion of land that is clearly unfit for house sites, yards, or streets.

- *Minimum Permitted Lot Sizes.* The opportunity for land conservation through the subdivision process is directly proportional to the permitted difference between maximum density and minimum lot size. For example, in a two-acre district where the minimum lot size is *not* two acres but rather "one acre of unconstrained land," the remaining unconstrained land that is not needed for house lots, plus all the constrained land, would constitute the open space. When ordinances require that the land occupied by house lots be limited to just one-half of the unconstrained land on the development parcel (so that at least half of the required open space will be reasonably flat and dry), the open space ratio would be 50 percent. And in cases where a developer might voluntarily reduce lot sizes to one-half acre, this ratio would rise to 75 percent. In conservation subdivisions where overall density is held at a certain level, the smaller the permitted lot size, the greater the percentage of undivided open space.

This approach can confer various advantages to developers by reducing their street construction costs and providing them with a greater marketing advantage where the open space is advertised as a special amenity for home buyers. In fact, some Pennsylvania communities have entirely eliminated their minimum lot size standards in certain districts where conservation subdivision design has become a basic requirement, relying instead on density controls (supplemented by "net-outs" for steep, wet, and floodprone land) and a minimum (50 percent) requirement for open space. Ordinances with the largest differential between density and lot size would therefore achieve the highest grade in the audit process.

- *Minimum Frontages and Setbacks.* The same thinking described above with regard to minimum lot size also pertains to minimum frontages and setbacks. The larger these dimensional requirements are, the more land-consumptive is the ordinance. More modest frontage and setback requirements not only save land, they also help to produce walkable neighborhoods with a real sense of community, such as can readily be found in the traditional residential areas of many nineteenth-century villages and boroughs.

- *Minimum Required Open Space.* One must examine the ordinance standards for both the *quantity* and the *quality* of the open space. For example, the greater the percentage of required open space, the larger will be the conservation results it produces. However, it is also important to determine whether all or a large part of the open space requirement can be met with wetlands, floodplains, and steep slopes that limit the usability of the open space for active recreation. Ordinance standards should ideally require that the minimum open space provision be fully met without including any land that is steeper than 25 percent or seasonally wet. It is also relevant to look at whether the ordinance allows the open space requirement to be fulfilled with land that has other limitations for general use, such as power line easements and golf courses (only 50 percent of which should be included in calculations for minimum open space provision because of their limitations for general recreational use or wildlife habitat).

Other zoning aspects to be examined in an audit would include:

- *Minimum Tract Size.* Ordinances prohibiting flexible subdivision design on parcels under 20 acres unintentionally prevent their most effective conservation tool from being applied on those properties. To the extent the ordinance allows (or requires) conservation design on properties of more than five acres, the higher its grades on our scorecard. Even small properties can contribute significantly to community conservation goals, such as when they contain a critical habitat or a valued historic resource, or when they would help connect a wildlife corridor or trail network.

- *Geographical Applicability.* The range of districts where flexible, land-conserving designs are permitted or required, and the percentage of the municipality where such design techniques are welcome, is another zoning variable with important ramifications. Municipalities that restrict these flexible design techniques to only a few residential zoning districts are missing opportunities for conservation and recreation elsewhere in their community. Some officials perceive this approach as applicable only in rural areas because they visualize it as a tool for conserving large areas of open space. Others sometimes view this approach as being dependent on public water and sewerage and therefore restrict it to their higher-density zones. In fact, this technique can work extremely well in all residential districts. However, the percentage and the kinds of land that can be conserved may vary widely. In serviced areas the conservation land percentage would probably be lower (perhaps 25 to 40 percent) and might consist largely of village greens, playing fields, and trail corridors. In unserviced areas the open space ratio might rise to 60 or 70 percent and be composed mostly of resource lands such as fields and forests. The variations in open space percentages can be seen clearly in Table 4-2 in Chapter 4. Techniques for providing adequate water supply and sewage disposal to houses on small lots in unserviced areas, where central facilities for the development are not practicable, are also illustrated in Figure 4-12.

- *Buffering Requirements.* The depth of the required perimeter buffer is another variable that is frequently misunderstood and misapplied. Greater depth does not necessarily provide better screening, except on wooded sites. Concerns about project visibility are often excessive (especially when multifamily construction is not a factor) and are generally much better addressed through planting standards specifying species, size, and spacing of evergreen shrubs and trees in fairly narrow "buffers." Perimeter buffer strips consume much of the required open space in nearly useless ribbons of land and rob site designers of the flexibility that is typically needed to produce the best plan for the site.

SUBSTANTIVE PROVISIONS OF SUBDIVISION ORDINANCES

In subdivision ordinances the auditor would look for substantive provisions relating to the qualities of conservation land that the required open space may or must include and would also examine the design requirements (if any) addressing the relationship of that open space to:

- resources on adjoining parcels (environmental, agricultural, historic, etc.),
- neighborhoods and house lots within the development itself,
- roads bordering the subdivision (particularly with respect to public viewsheds), and
- existing uses on adjoining properties (such as established residential uses or public parkland).

The *quality* and the *configuration* of the open space that is conserved are equally as important as the quantity of the land that is required to be protected. Yet these characteristics are often overlooked or treated only in a cursory and inadequate manner in codes that contain otherwise acceptable provisions regarding the percentage of conservation land that flexibly designed developments must contain.

- *Quality of the Open Space.* Effective codes would, for example, contain fairly detailed provisions relating to the kinds of conservation lands that must be included in the open space in addition to the inherently unbuildable wet, floodprone, or steep areas. These elements of the natural and cultural landscapes should be listed, described, and prioritized in a set of standards or criteria specifically written to guide the delineation and design of conservation areas within new subdivisions so that the most critical resource areas are included. Some municipalities might value woodland habitat above farmland, while others might prioritize fields, pastures, and meadow above forests. Still others might rank historic and cultural resources at the top of their list. Although this kind of provision is one of the most important features of subdivision ordinances seeking to promote community land conservation objectives, it is frequently the one that is most lacking. These extremely important points are covered in greater detail on pages 55–64.
- *Configuration of the Open Space.* Effective codes would also ensure that conservation lands be located or configured so they would ul-

timately become part of a community-wide network of interconnected open spaces, as described on pages 24–26 and 74 77. They should also be used to buffer existing protected areas, such as any public parks, forests, or game lands, as well as preserves or eased lands protected by private conservation organizations such as land trusts.

Procedural Elements of Zoning Ordinances

Under the heading of zoning procedures that should be examined in an audit, the most important procedural aspect involves the way that conservation subdivisions are treated in the submission process. Whether they are permitted *by-right,* or whether they are allowed only as *conditional uses* or *special exceptions,* makes a tremendous difference in how often developers are likely to make use of this option. This is where many otherwise fine ordinances suddenly become ineffective. It is a huge waste of time and effort to write very thoughtful ordinance provisions that would help produce well-designed developments with substantial open space to protect a wide range of natural and cultural features but then to inadvertently include other provisions making this design option unattractive to applicants. Most developers tend to avoid procedures that increase the length of the review period, that subject their proposals to the additional scrutiny of widely advertised public hearings, and that establish a process involving greater uncertainty with respect to the outcome of their applications. Understandably, they much prefer an application route that is familiar, clear, straightforward, relatively brief and inconspicuous, and more or less predictable in the results it produces. For all the above reasons, developers generally shy away from conditional use or special exception procedures.

Communities wishing to exercise effective control over applications for flexible layouts should include provisions pertaining to by-right proposals setting out clear and detailed standards relating to the quantity, quality, and configuration of conservation lands (so-called "greenspace design standards") and give developers maximum flexibility with respect to lot dimensions and street layout. Developers typically know much more about how to build houses and streets than do lay members of municipal boards. Conversely, developers can be expected to know much less about how to delineate conservation areas—which elements to include and how these areas should be laid out to maximize resource protection and facilitate interconnectedness at the neighborhood or community level.

Procedural Elements of Subdivision Ordinances

Procedural elements in the subdivision ordinance that are critical to the success of conservation design include provisions enabling local officials to review proposed layouts while they are still at the concept stage, before substantial engineering costs have been incurred to produce highly detailed (and oddly named) "preliminary" plans. Whether Sketch Plans are just strongly encouraged, or their key elements are formally required to be submitted during a Conceptual Preliminary Plan stage (as recommended in the model ordinance provisions in this book), it is essential that the first layout presented to local officials not be a typical hard-lined, heavily engineered, and expensive "preliminary" plan, which developers are understandably reluctant to modify to any great extent.

Another important aspect of the subdivision submission process that is frequently missing or inadequately prepared is a detailed resource inventory of the proposed development site. Called an Existing Resources and Site Analysis Map, this element provides municipal officials and site designers with information that is absolutely critical for their full understanding of the site (see pages 54–55). It is arguably the most significant document in the entire process because it provides the data base necessary for making informed and intelligent decisions. Details of such plans are described in the model ordinance provisions in Appendix 3 of this book, but they should include a number of locally significant or noteworthy

site features commonly overlooked in most ordinances, such as vegetative patterns (meadows, fields, hedgerows, woodlands, etc.), the location of various forest types, the extent of mature woodlands or individual trees of substantial age and girth, the location of historic or
cultural elements, and the depth of the public viewshed as seen from
surrounding roads or highways.

The presence or absence of procedures requiring site walks by reviewing officials or by their staff or consultants is another aspect that
a community auditor should note because of the greater difficulty of
understanding sites simply by reviewing two-dimensional plans only
in a meeting room or office. Another procedural element that is generally missing is a description of the design process site designers
should follow. Typically, plans are laid out with street alignments done
first, followed by lot lines, with natural features and cultural elements
rarely considered (except insofar as they might pose insurmountable
obstacles, such as wet, floodprone, or steep areas). However, recognizing how difficult it is to design a subdivision really well when these
features are not seriously evaluated and considered from the outset, a
growing number of communities are beginning to require subdivision applicants to demonstrate that they have designed their conservation areas first, followed by house locations, street alignments, and
lot lines.

NONREGULATORY APPROACHES

As applied to the build-out mapping process, the probable success
rate of nonregulatory approaches in conserving land should be as-
sessed realistically. These approaches include:

- donations of easements and fee-title interests to land,
- purchase of development rights or fee-title interest (generally with
  public money from county bond issues or other buy-back programs, but occasionally with foundation grants), and

- voluntary restrictions on development density by landowners
  (called "limited development").

Although the potential for such techniques is certainly higher in
some communities than others, these approaches cannot be expected
to affect more than a very small percentage of land in any given municipality. It would therefore be fair to select a single farm and perhaps a smaller parcel suitable for use as a neighborhood park or recreation area as illustrations of the scale of acreage that might reasonably
be expected to remain undeveloped on the build-out map as a result
of such efforts. (This is not to diminish their importance but rather
to maintain a realistic perspective for the purposes of showing likely
future development patterns.)

Build-Out Maps

One of the most understandable, inexpensive, and effective tools for
showing local officials and residents the ultimate consequences of
continuing to follow current land-use codes is the build-out map, the
third major community audit technique. In a nutshell, such maps realistically plot the potential locations of new streets and houses that
could be constructed on the vacant and buildable land remaining
within the municipality (see Figs. 2-1 and 2-2).

Sometimes called the "coming attractions" map, this document illustrates the "Law of Unintended Consequences" that is frequently
evident in local land-use regulations. Although no community consciously adopts zoning and subdivision ordinances with the expressed
goal of steadily and deliberately converting all of its natural areas and
open spaces into a continuous coverage of contiguous subdivisions,
each consisting of nothing but house lots and streets, that is precisely
the typical result of well-meaning but misguided ordinance requirements.

This build-out mapping process begins by examining the existing
pattern of developed and undeveloped properties in relation to the

community's natural features systems to determine which areas are most vulnerable to change based on the presence or absence of physical constraints to development.

This technique may be applied to particular sections of the municipality or even to large undeveloped properties, but the most dramatic and telling effect is produced when the potential for creating an unending pattern of contiguous subdivisions and road-frontage developments is revealed, running across the full length and breadth of the municipality.

To preserve credibility, it is crucial that development not be projected into areas where natural or regulatory obstacles would prevent it. Future build-out patterns must reflect reduced density where features such as rough or steep terrain, thin or damp soils, or other factors would limit actual development potential. For example, in rural districts where one-acre house lots are permitted, but where developers would normally find it impossible to lay out more than 15 lots on 30 typical acres, the build-out map should reflect the latter density. (This is sometimes referred to as "natural zoning.")

Carefully executed, such mapping is virtually impossible to argue against. It is an objective and graphic illustration of what could easily happen as land is subdivided according to existing regulations. Perhaps the most significant aspect of this technique is its success in demonstrating to local residents and officials that current zoning and subdivision requirements constitute much of the problem by causing or enabling development patterns to resemble vast checkerboards of lawns and cul-de-sacs with little or no meaningful open space conserved in the process. When performed at the borough or township level (areas generally encompassing from 20 to 50 square miles), the mapping scale that has most often been used is 1 inch = 1,000 feet. If performed for specific parcels only, a useful scale is 200 feet to the inch unless the site is quite small. For sites under 20 acres, a 100-foot scale might be more appropriate. Good results can be obtained by using readily available mapping data for contours and slopes (from

the U.S. Geological Survey), 100-year floodplains (from maps published by the Federal Emergency Management Agency), and wetlands (from the National Wetlands Inventory published by the U.S. Fish and Wildlife Service of the Department of the Interior). In the absence of wetland maps, those areas identified as having soils rated as "very poorly drained" (in the county soil survey published by the USDA Natural Resources Conservation Service) provide a fairly accurate approximation for broad illustrative purposes.

Eight Self-Diagnostic Questions for Community Leaders

Each of the following questions has been framed to help municipal officials examine a different aspect of their community's abilities to manage growth in a way that fosters land conservation. For many people, simply posing these questions will help them obtain a clearer understanding of some of the critical activities their township or county must undertake if they are to increase the effectiveness of their land conservation efforts. These questions, which have been posed by Michael Clarke, former president of the Natural Lands Trust, for use in the Trust's Growing Greener program, are intended to help local leaders discover and identify areas that their community should work on.

1. *The Community Resource Inventory.* Have we as a community adequately inventoried our resources, and do our residents and officials have a sufficient understanding and appreciation of them?
2. *The Community Audit.* Are we as a community monitoring and assessing our likely future under its current growth management practices, and are we taking steps to change what we do not like?
3. *Policies for Conservation and Development.* Have we as a community established appropriate and realistic policies for land conservation and development, and do these policies produce a clear vision of lands to be conserved?

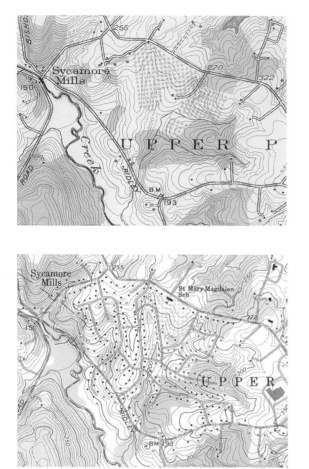

Figure 2-2. Another matching pair of graphics, taken from an actual "build-out map," showing existing conditions (mostly undeveloped land) contrasted with the potential development pattern of "checkerboard suburbia" created through conventional zoning and subdivision regulations.

4. *The Regulatory Framework.* Do our zoning and subdivision regulations reflect and encourage our Comprehensive Plan policies for land conservation and development?

5. *Designing Conservation Subdivisions.* Do we as a community—particularly our local officials, but also our interested residents—know how to work cooperatively and effectively with subdivision applicants?

6. *Working Relationships with Landowners.* Do we as a community have a good understanding of working relationships with our major landowners?

7. *Stewardship of Conservation Lands.* Do we as a community have in place the arrangements required for successfully owning, managing, and using lands set aside for conservation purposes?

8. *Ongoing Education and Communications.* How are we officials maintaining our knowledge of the state of the art in managing growth to conserve land?

Simply asking these questions is likely to stimulate considerable thought about subjects that are typically not in the forefront of issues

Figure 2-1. A matching pair of maps (from USGS quadrangle sheets) showing the same area of Delaware County, Pennsylvania, 40 years apart, illustrating the conversion of rural land into a fairly continuous pattern of conventional subdivisions. A build-out analysis would have enabled people in this community to visualize their future before it happened, and it would have provided them with a variety of alternatives from which to choose for managing growth and preserving local open space. It might also have prompted them to improve their land-use ordinances to conserve their resources through more sensible and sustainable development patterns.

on the minds of many local officials, who are generally too occupied dealing with day-to-day affairs to keep one eye on the horizon. Part of the usefulness of these questions is that they enable people to see important areas that are generally not focused on by anyone in the community. They can help residents and officials take stock of where they are heading as a town, township, or county and to propose a mid-course correction, if necessary. It is my observation that many communities are essentially drifting, without a clear sense of direction. As the saying goes, "If you don't care where you end up, any road will take you there."

However, it is the rare community that cares little about its ulti-mate future situation. The usual problem is that, before such a list of questions is posed, most people living in areas with moderate to high growth rates are unaware that their communities are drifting steadily in the direction of haphazard suburbanization produced by conventional zoning and subdivision codes.

Each year this suburbanization process permanently forecloses more and more opportunities to conserve special areas and natural lands and to create interconnected networks of open space throughout the community. That is why this list, or one similar to it, should be considered and discussed by members of local planning commissions and governing bodies at least once each year.

Chapter 3

Comprehensive Plan Update

This chapter and the two that follow describe the three major elements in a municipal strategy for managing growth to conserve land: the Comprehensive Plan, the zoning ordinance, and the subdivision ordinance. All of these documents can be modified and revised to function as key operating components of a local growth management system focused on land conservation, with the long-range goal being the protection of an interconnected network of protected lands running throughout the community.

Understanding the Importance of Comprehensive Plans

Because municipal Comprehensive Plans in most states are not regulatory documents, with which zoning and subdivision ordinances must be consistent, many people mistakenly discount the critical role such a document can play in the local land-use planning process. For that reason people frequently focus relatively little attention on producing plans with thorough inventories of their community's natural features and cultural resources. They also generally finish writing their plans without carefully examining how those special places could be protected through improved zoning and subdivision ordinances. Because such land-use codes are potentially the municipality's best available tools for implementing its Comprehensive Plan, the plan should always critically review existing local regulations with respect to their effectiveness in truly protecting the community's varied resources.

Furthermore, the Comprehensive Plan should also include specific recommendations for adopting clear standards in local zoning and subdivision and land development ordinances that will address land conservation issues as squarely as these ordinances already address development issues. All too often, local land-use ordinances do not protect any lands beyond those that are wet, steep, or floodprone, as if these three severely constrained kinds of areas are the only elements of the community that are worthy of conservation. In those communities with this kind of limited approach to land conservation, the fate of all the land that is not preserved through public acquisition or through private easement is ultimately to be subdivided, cleared, graded, and built on.

Because it provides the formal rationale and basis for all local land-use ordinances, the Comprehensive Plan is an extremely important link in the whole municipal regulatory process. For this reason it is essential that the Comprehensive Plan adequately document the full range of a community's special features and land resources and that it provide well thought out recommendations as to how current codes should be updated to protect those features and resources. It should also articulate a compelling vision for the future, focusing in particular on the overall pattern of conservation and development that the community hopes to achieve. Such visions typically include generalized maps showing the most suitable locations for new development and the places that should ideally be designed around to create a permanently protected network of interconnected open spaces.

Five Parts of the Plan on Which to Focus

For those interested in protecting the special features of their community, Comprehensive Plans present at least five opportunities for including information or policy statements pertinent to those resources. They are the following:

1. *The Background Information Section.* This broad, introductory section describes the most salient aspects of the municipality, usually in fairly generalized land-use terms. Such aspects typically include local history, natural features, population characteristics, community services or facilities, and the transportation network. This section conveys a general impression of the types of sensitive areas and other special places that exist within the community, their geographic distribution and extent, and their approximate locations.

2. *Resource Inventory.* The ideal inventory is one that is broad enough to include the full range of natural and cultural resources existing in the community while containing sufficient detail to support recommendations regarding appropriate land-use activities and intensities. Although a thorough study of this kind could be quite expensive, municipalities can begin this process by tapping into a considerable body of information from sources that they may access at little or no cost. When outside financial resources are available, municipalities can hire consultants to produce very detailed inventories. This part of the Comprehensive Plan is discussed below in greater detail.

3. *Goals, Objectives and Policies.* This section offers a chance to relate the community's resources to its vision of what it would like to eventually become, after much or all of its permitted development occurs. Communities typically seek to achieve their broad goals through more specifically defined objectives, which are in turn implemented through supporting policies. This sec-

tion should also be viewed as the place to begin resolving potential internal conflicts among competing goals, such as those for resource conservation and economic development. For example, a policy promoting flexibility in the siting standards for new construction, or requiring that new development be carefully designed around a site's special features, would help to reduce future problems by enabling people to achieve both of those broad goals for conservation and development simultaneously.

4. *Other Plan Elements.* The goals, objectives, and policies for resource protection and open space conservation should also be addressed in other elements of the Comprehensive Plan, such as those dealing with housing provision, economic development, sewage disposal, traffic circulation, and other community services and facilities. The purpose is to ensure that each of these elements is written in a context that includes all the others so they will be properly coordinated with the community's resource protection and open space goals.

5. *Plan Implementation.* One of the final and most critical parts of the Comprehensive Plan is the section detailing how its policies will be implemented. In addition to encouraging private conservation efforts and facilitating conservation through various nonregulatory approaches (such as by purchasing land or development rights), the plan should identify and prioritize specific new measures for inclusion in its local land-use ordinances, such as those encouraging or requiring conservation subdivision design and those broadening the layout and density options for landowners or developers to include a wider range of subdivisions laid out with substantial open space. Lastly, the plan should be formally adopted by the municipality as a blueprint to guide future conservation and development decisions.

The Community Resource Inventory: Varying Degrees of Completeness

Although every municipal Comprehensive Plan should contain at least a basic resource inventory, it is likely that some communities will not yet have completed such a document by the time they first consider implementing the conservation measures described in this book. However, there are some short-term alternatives available to municipalities whose Comprehensive Plan does not yet include a proper resource inventory. Such communities should in the meantime include specific language in their existing plan requiring that, in all future development proposals, "the community's special resources shall be protected through the conservation subdivision design process, in which applicants shall prepare detailed site inventory maps (Existing Resources and Site Analysis Maps) that pinpoint the exact locations of environmental, cultural, historic, and scenic features on their properties."

The plan should add that when these features are linear or are part of larger systems (such as stream valleys, ridgelines, blocks of mature woodland, areas of wildlife habitat, or prime farmland), the conservation areas within any proposed subdivision should be laid out so that they can eventually be joined together to form an interconnected network of protected open space with similar lands on the next parcel to be subdivided. The plan might also mention that the preparation of a community-wide inventory is a long-range goal but that such a map would in any event be superseded by the more detailed analyses provided by individual subdivision applicants (much in the same way that site-specific information concerning soil conditions, wetlands, and floodplain boundaries supersedes the official area-wide published maps covering those resources).

The Community Resource Inventory: Nine Elements to Be Included

If the Comprehensive Plan in your community does not yet contain a very detailed inventory of its natural, cultural, and historic resources, consult a good how-to book that focuses on this kind of document. One recent example of such a book is *Where We Live: A Citizen's Guide to Conducting a Community Environmental Inventory,* published by Island Press (Harker and Natter 1995).

The following list provides a basic description of the principal resources recommended for inclusion in the community inventory and sources of readily available published information where such data may be easily obtained.

1. *Wetlands and Their Buffers.* Lands that are seasonally or permanently wet constitute one of the most basic resources in any community. These should be one of the first kinds of resources to be identified, together with dry, upland buffer areas around them. These buffers perform a number of significant functions, such as filtering stormwater runoff, providing critical habitat at the land–water interface, and offering opportunities for wildlife travel corridors. They also provide opportunities for informal walking trails for use by residents of the immediate neighborhood.

    A good general idea of wetland location can be determined by consulting the medium-intensity soil survey maps published by the USDA Natural Resources Conservation Service (formerly the Soil Conservation Service). Soils that are classified as "very poorly drained" fulfill most people's definition of wetland, as they comprise soils in which water is ponded at the surface for at least three months of the year. Other soil types that are sensitive due to their seasonally high water table are called "hydric," where water is typically within 6 or 12 inches of the surface during the late winter and spring. These soils also do not meet minimum standards for septic system installation and should generally be avoided for construction if other more suitable places are available on the property for development. However, these soils will support homes without basements when wastewater is treated off-lot. Another good source of wetlands data is the National Wetlands Inventory maps published by the U.S. Fish and Wildlife Service in the Department of the Interior.

2. *Floodways and Floodplains.* The maps published by the Federal Emergency Management Agency (FEMA) constitute the most accurate and readily available data on the location of floodways and floodplains in most communities. Floodways are the areas where floodwater is expected to move at relatively high velocities, such as along the edges of rivers and creeks, or where floodwater is channelized. Floodplains are those areas expected to be inundated with two or more feet of water at least once during the time period that is specified (typically 100 years).

3. *Moderate and Steep Slopes.* Most communities will find it helpful in achieving their resource conservation objectives to identify two different categories of slopes. Due to their high potential for erosion and consequent sedimentation of watercourses and water bodies, slopes with gradients over 25 percent should be avoided for clearing, regrading, or construction. Slopes of between 15 and 25 percent require special site planning and should also be avoided whenever practicable. Although slope maps are not published, they can be easily prepared by a surveyor, engineer, planner, or landscape architect working from readily available topographic sheets printed by the U.S. Geological Survey.

4. *Groundwater Resources and Their Recharge Areas.* The term *aquifer* refers to underground water reserves occupying billions of tiny

spaces between sand grains and other soil particles, including gravel. They are "recharged" with surface water seeping downward through coarse sandy or gravelly deposits and at low points in the landscape where wetlands frequently occur.

5. *Woodlands.* In areas where the majority of original forest has long been cleared away for commercial agriculture, woodlands may be described as remnants, often located in lower-lying areas with relatively damp soils or on the steeper slopes. Despite— and perhaps because of—their small areal extent, these woodlands play a particularly pivotal role for wildlife in such areas. In other more densely wooded areas, key distinctions will involve those woodlands that comprise the largest, oldest, and healthiest stands of mature native trees, as differentiated from younger second-growth woodlands, conifer plantations, or forests overgrown with invasive vines such as japanese honeysuckle, rosa multiflora, greenbriar, oriental bittersweet, and wild grape. In recent years concern has risen among conservation biologists and others who point out that decreases in the number of some species of "neo-tropical" songbirds (that summer in this country and migrate to Central and South America every fall) have been caused in part by both the reduction and the fragmentation of our temperate woodland habitat.

The best sources for defining the extent of woodlands, hedgerows, or tree lines are vertical aerial photographs that are commonly available through county offices of the USDA Natural Resource Conservation Service. These may be ordered as enlargements at working scales (such as 1 inch = 100 feet) and are indispensable in accurately locating not only tree stands but even individual trees (in meadows or fields, or alongside roads). Aerial photos can also be helpful in locating the relative positions of coniferous and deciduous trees, even when the latter are in leaf, due to the darker coloration of conifers as registered on black-and-white film.

6. *Productive Farmland.* Maps showing the location of soils rated as being "prime" or "of statewide significance" can be obtained from the county conservation districts. Because these maps are typically reproduced on aerial photographs in the county soil survey, it is relatively easy to isolate the instances of these soil types that occur on unwooded parcels where farming actually occurs or where it could take place without the need for massive tree clearing. In certain regions where the vast majority of land is wooded, the fields, meadows, and pastures take on an added significance—at least in local terms—regardless of the productivity of their soils. In such areas, these open fields constitute much of what people generally consider to be "rural character," and they are often highly prized for their scenic value in maintaining a sense of the country landscape. In such cases it is recommended that small fields down to five acres in area should be mapped. At the suggested mapping scale of 1 inch = 1,000 feet, this would be an area about an inch long and one-quarter inch wide.

7. *Significant Wildlife Habitats.* Habitats of threatened or endangered wildlife species should be mapped, at least in their general location, wherever possible. Such information is available from a statewide Natural Diversity Inventory, typically produced by the Department of Natural Resources. Although the exact location of such areas is deliberately not revealed on the published maps (in order to protect the sites from collectors, poachers, and other unauthorized people), the generalized data provide at least a "warning flag" clue to local officials that any development proposed in that area should be laid out with extreme care. Likely wildlife travel corridors linking the areas used as food sources, homes, and breeding grounds should be mapped whenever possible. Anecdotal information from local game wardens and sportsmen can be invaluable in this regard. Also, it is an unfortunate fact that the places where such travel corridors cross

roads are likely to be those with the greatest occurrence of road kills.

8. *Historic, Archaeological, and Cultural Features.* Because published documentation on the location of buildings or other resources with historic, archaeological, or cultural significance is far from complete, landowners and local historians or historical groups should always be consulted after a review of official lists such as the National Register of Historic Places and the historic or archaeological site inventories compiled by state and county offices of historic preservation and cultural resources. In most cases, old buildings, ruins, cellar holes, abandoned roads, stone walls, burial grounds, or other resources will be of local rather than county-wide or regional importance. In areas that witnessed battles, skirmishes, or troop movements during the Revolutionary War or Civil War (or other notable conflicts), it is likely that many such lands will remain entirely unprotected. Earlier sites, such as areas used for burials or encampments by Native Americans or prehistoric peoples, should also be mapped wherever they have been documented. "Windshield surveys" can be a useful source of local information about historic and cultural features. When undertaken, the best results usually occur when teams of two people conduct the surveys, as described in item 9.

9. *Scenic Viewsheds from Public Roads.* Most communities have not conducted scenic viewshed surveys, but many of them could do so quite easily with local volunteer help. At least two people are needed: one to drive and one to annotate a map as they go along. The most helpful type of base map is one that shows existing buildings and the patterns of field and forest. When this information is displayed on a topographical sheet with the ground contours indicated, sight-line limits can be fairly accurately estimated. Tips on conducting scenic road inventories appear in Chapter 12 of *Rural by Design* (Arendt et al. 1994), a

comprehensive resource book on rural planning available from the American Planning Association. Although scenic viewshed protection does not provide sufficient grounds for denying subdivision approval in a conventional subdivision, it can play an important supporting role, supplementing other features of secondary importance.

Official Maps of Conservation Lands, Parklands, and Trails

A time-tested technique that enjoyed more prominence during the early decades of planning and zoning is the Official Map. The purpose of this technique, which is explicitly authorized under most states' zoning enabling legislation, is to provide notice to landowners and intending developers that the municipality has identified certain areas or corridors for future acquisition to serve public needs, typically street connections and parkland. Although land can be identified on Official Maps many years before its intended acquisition, municipalities are legally obliged to purchase that land, at fair market value, within twelve months if the landowner specifically notifies the governing body of his or her intent to build, subdivide, or otherwise develop the land. If within those twelve months the municipality fails to initiate a purchase-and-sale agreement, or to begin condemnation proceedings, the designation is deemed null and void.

Community-Wide Map of Potential Conservation Lands

This relatively new approach is loosely related to the Official Map. Unlike its more formal counterpart, the Map of Potential Conservation Lands does not identify land earmarked for public acquisition. However, it is similar in that it identifies those parts of undeveloped properties where the municipality has preliminarily determined the importance of designing new development around certain land and water features in such a way that an interconnected network of conservation land can be protected. Such areas typically include lands along stream valleys but also potentially include blocks of mature woodland, prime farming soil, historic and cultural features, etc. In practice, a number of the information layers from the Community Resource Inventory Map (in the Comprehensive Plan) are superimposed on a parcel map of the municipality. This technique produces an extremely useful working document that shows the pattern of resources in relation to the undeveloped properties—which is where future changes will occur. When these data layers have been computerized on GIS (geographical information systems) maps, combining any number or mixture of layers becomes extremely easy.

Besides informing local officials of the nature and extent of particular kinds of resources on any property proposed for subdivision development, the potential conservation lands map also supplies the contextual view so that all parties will be able to see and appreciate how designing around certain features could help to preserve an interconnected network of open space running across numerous parcels. Figures 3-1 and 3-2 illustrate how two townships have dealt with the challenge of creating community-wide Maps of Potential

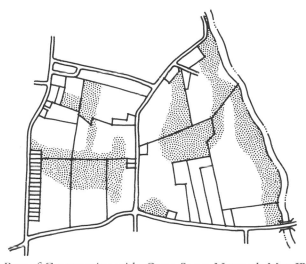

Figure 3-2. Part of Community-wide Open Space Network Map, West Manchester Township, York County, Pennsylvania. West Manchester's Map of Potential Conservation Lands gives clear guidance to landowners and developers as to where new development is encouraged on their properties. Township officials engaged a consultant to draw, on the official tax parcel maps, boundaries of the new conservation lands network as it crossed various properties, showing how areas required to be preserved in each new development could be located so they would ultimately connect with each other. In this formerly agricultural municipality, the hedgerows, woodland remnants, and riparian buffer along the creek were identified as core elements of the conservation network. *Source:* Arendt et al. 1994.

Figure 3-1. Part of Map of Potential Conservation Lands, West Vincent Township, Chester County, Pennsylvania, showing roads, parcel lines, and the following resource areas: wet, floodprone, steep (black); moderate slopes (gray); farmland (vertical hatching); and woodlands (cross-hatched).

Conservation Lands. In the first example, from West Vincent Township in Chester County, Pennsylvania, six layers of resource inventory information have been displayed on a parcel map with computer-driven GIS technology. (Those layers include inherently unbuildable resources such as wetlands, floodplains, and slopes greater than 25 percent—called Primary Conservation Areas—and other land of potential resource value such as woodlands, open agricultural lands of special scenic value, and slopes between 15 and 25 percent—known as Secondary Conservation Areas.) In the second example, West

Manchester Township in York County, Pennsylvania, has utilized its resource inventory to identify a potential open space network in various neighborhoods based on surviving woodlands on a number of adjoining farm parcels where suburban development is very likely to occur over the next 20 years.

For further information on creating such Maps of Potential Conservation Lands in their communities, readers are referred to Design Exercise 1, which provides a more detailed description of the steps involved.

Because this approach does not involve condemnation or public acquisition but instead relies on creative ways of accommodating full legal density on other parts of the properties in question, it does not obligate municipalities to costly future actions and does not diminish the development potential of any parcel. This tool is closely associated with certain zoning and subdivision techniques known as "conservation zoning" and "conservation subdivision design," which are discussed in detail in Chapters 4 and 5, respectively.

After several contiguous parcels are developed according to the Growing Greener design standards contained in the model ordinance language in Appendix 3 of this book, the conservation lands in each one should adjoin those in the next subdivision, thereby protecting an interconnected network of open space. When planned ahead using the kinds of maps shown in Figures 3-1 and 3-2, such greenways can extend across entire townships, linking different neighborhoods with this "new" kind of green infrastructure. The beginnings of such linkages can be seen in Figures 3-3 and 3-4.

Plan Language Regarding Implementation Through Ordinances

Every Comprehensive Plan should contain a fairly detailed section in which the community's existing land-use regulations are frankly and constructively critiqued. In addition to identifying the weaknesses of

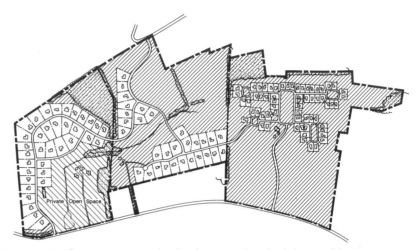

Figure 3-3. The conservation lands (shown in hatched diagonal lines) were deliberately laid out to form part of an interconnected network of open space in these three contiguous subdivisions in Alexandria Township, Hunterdon County, New Jersey. *Source:* Arendt et al. 1994.

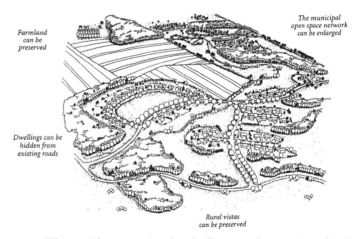

Figure 3-4. This aerial perspective sketch illustrates how various kinds of protected resource lands—croplands, woodland habitat, roadside vistas, and municipal trail networks—will eventually coalesce to form linked open space systems in communities that apply the principles in this book over the medium and long terms. *Source:* Montgomery County Planning Commission, Pennsylvania.

these ordinances in truly protecting the municipality's natural, historic, and cultural resources from being fragmented, cleared, graded, and converted to developed uses, this section of the plan should proactively describe positive, specific improvement that could be made to these codes. Model plan language describing the kinds of ordinance improvements advocated in this book is reproduced in Appendix 2 and interested readers are directed there for further details.

Chapter 4

Conservation Zoning Techniques

Zoning requirements occupy a middle position in the range of local regulatory techniques advocated in this book; they lie between the more general technique called conservation planning and the more site-specific technique known as conservation subdivision design.

Zoning is a tool whose potential for encouraging land conservation has in most communities not been fully appreciated. As commonly applied, zoning has been used primarily to establish limits of maximum permissible building density and to separate uses believed to be inherently incompatible. In many parts of the country, state enabling legislation also specifically authorizes local governments to adopt zoning regulations permitting flexibility to encourage innovative development, or it at least does not prohibit them from doing so.

Unfortunately, most zoning ordinances do not include standards providing sufficient flexibility regarding lot dimensions to allow or seriously encourage design alternatives featuring significant open spaces that would be appealing to existing landowners, potential developers, and future residents. Zoning districts typically establish a single lot size minimum and usually do not require any open space areas to be provided within new developments. Not surprisingly, the resulting subdivision proposals almost always consist of the maximum number of minimum-sized lots, with no conservation areas included in the layouts.

This chapter on conservation zoning describes several practical options offering incentives to encourage open space preservation in new residential developments, and it features several other options containing disincentives designed to actively discourage further subdivisions where conservation areas are not provided.

A Choice of Options for Conservation and Development

At its simplest level, conservation zoning provides landowners and developers with a number of density options geared to a range of open space set aside requirements. To clarify this concept, the five density options described here are illustrated later in this chapter (on pages 35–40) and in the model zoning ordinance article in Appendix 3 as well. For example, in an unserviced, rural zoning district where there is no public water or sewer, the hypothetical base density is 80,000 square feet. However, starting with that density base of 80,000 square feet per dwelling—which under the Growing Greener approach would be geared to a basic 50 percent open space set aside—a choice of density enhancements might be offered across a broader spectrum in exchange for even higher percentages of protected open space. For example, a density of 60,000 square feet per dwelling could be offered when 60 percent open space would be protected, and a 40,000-square-foot density could be granted to secure a 70 percent open space ratio. In addition, other more conventional options could continue to be permitted, although only at lower overall densities. For instance, another option might establish a minimum density of one dwelling for every four acres to accommodate the market for large "estate lots" with no required open space (representing a density disincentive to discourage that kind of layout). And a final option could offer the potential for "country properties"

Table 4-1. Five Options Offered in the Conservation Design Overlay Zoning District (assuming a "base density" of one dwelling per 80,000 square feet adjusted tract acreage, as per the model zoning ordinance provisions in Appendix 3, for this semi-rural area)

	Density (land/dwelling unit)	Conservation Land (minimum percentage)
Current codes	80,000 square feet	none
Option 1	80,000 square feet	50 percent
Option 2	60,000 square feet	60 percent
Option 3	160,000 square feet	none
Option 4	10 acres	none
Option 5	40,000 square feet	70 percent

of at least ten acres, with special incentives described later in this chapter.

For each of the first three density options just described, a different percentage of permanently protected conservation land would be required, as noted in Table 4-1 (as Options 1, 2, and 5).

The reason that a density of 80,000 square feet per dwelling has been used in this book is that case law in Pennsylvania strongly suggests that municipalities may not require lots larger than 80,000 square feet—except where farmland protection is a well-documented policy goal, as typified in many parts of Lancaster County. The above array of *density options* is considered to be lawful because the densest option lies within the two-acre threshold suggested in leading court decisions. The inclusion of low-density options is supportable as long as the municipality offers them among a number of alternatives that must also include higher-density options within the legal range established by commonwealth court decisions.

In the purely illustrative examples presented in this book, the assumed base density is therefore 80,000 square feet per dwelling. Readers from other states should not place any special emphasis on this density number, which probably has no particular relevance to case law where they live.

Far more important than simple numbers is the notion of appropriateness. Requiring 80,000 square feet would be excessive in most areas served by public water, and 60,000 square feet might well be deemed inappropriate where both public water and sewer are available. Just as agricultural densities of 20 and 30 acres per dwelling have been determined to be appropriate in certain Pennsylvania counties where serious farming occurs (such as Lancaster), urban densities of two, three, and four dwellings per acre must be considered to be appropriate in certain situations where the land is fully serviced and is adjacent to existing built-up areas (such as town centers or boroughs). The various overall densities, lot sizes, and minimum percentages of open space shown in Table 4-2 provide examples of how these variables might appear in a municipality that encompasses five very different types of zoning districts, ranging from nearly urban situations to nearly rural ones.

As local officials struggle to determine what overall densities would be appropriate in different parts of their communities, they should review the inventory and analysis of the natural resources contained in their Comprehensive Plans and update the goals and objectives listed in that document. They might also need to refine the wording describing the stated purposes of each of the districts governed in their zoning ordinances so that density requirements will be consistent with the resources on (or under) the ground, the community's goals and objectives, and the purposes for which each particular zoning district has been created.

Although there may be a constitutionally protected right to develop land that is physically suitable for such uses, there does not appear to be a corresponding right to develop properties into a totally land-consumptive pattern that systematically converts every acre of ground into house lots and streets. Simply put, there is no constitutional right to sprawl, and communities may encourage or discourage different development patterns through the use of density incentives and disincentives based on overall base densities appropriate to the general situation in each zoning district.

About the District Types

Table 4-2 provides examples of the kinds of development and conservation patterns that could be achieved in five different kinds of zoning districts. The five district types (shown in vertical columns) exhibit an overall density range of 80,000 square feet per dwelling to 10,000 square feet per dwelling, reflecting substantially different community situations or neighborhood contexts.

The 80,000 square feet overall density (about 1.8 acres per dwelling) approaches the legal limit suggested by a number of judicial precedents in Pennsylvania for suburban-edge and rural areas where there is no explicit, serious commitment to continued large-scale agricultural production—as would be evidenced through landowner support for exclusive agricultural zoning of 20 to 30 acres per dwelling, as many townships in Lancaster County have adopted.

At the other end of the spectrum, the 20,000-square-foot and 10,000-square-foot overall densities would typically be for situations in which the land is fully serviced by public water and sewer and where the existing context is one of neighborhoods built at two, three, or four dwellings per acre (which, in conventional layouts, would translate into lot sizes of 20,000, 15,000, and 10,000 square feet, respectively).

The abstract representation of two semi-rural townships surrounding a more urbanized borough in Figure 4-1 illustrates in a broad, general way the locations of and relationships among possible zoning districts with different development densities and open space requirements in a typical group of contiguous communities in Pennsylvania. It should be emphasized that the choice of densities and the district boundaries must bear a close relationship to the location of public infrastructure (particularly public water and sewer), to topographic and

Table 4-2. District Types Showing the Five Growing Greener Options in Five Different Kinds of Zoning Districts Ranging from Nearly Urban to Nearly Rural (Tract size: 50 acres gross, 36 acres net adjusted tract acreage [ATA])

	District "Type A" Lowest Density 80,000 S.F. Base	District "Type B" Lower Moderate 60,000 S.F. Base	District "Type C" Moderate Density 40,000 S.F. Base	District "Type D" Upper Moderate 20,000 S.F. Base	District "Type E" Upper Density 10,000 S.F. Base
OPTION 1 DENSITY	80,000 sq. ft./dwelling	60,000 sq. ft./dwelling	40,000 sq. ft./dwelling	20,000 sq. ft./dwelling	10,000 sq. ft./dwelling
Number of lots (maximum)	18 lots	24 lots	36 lots	72 lots	144 lots
Lot size maximum	40,000 sq. ft.	30,000 sq. ft.	20,000 sq. ft.	10,000 sq. ft.	6,000 sq. ft.
Lot size minimum	20,000 sq. ft.	15,000 sq. ft.	10,000 sq. ft.	5,000 sq. ft.	4,000 sq. ft.
Lot width (minimum)	100 feet	80 feet	60 feet	40 feet	40 feet
Open space percentage (minimum)	50 percent	50 percent	50 percent	50 percent	40 percent
OPTION 2 DENSITY	60,000 sq. ft./dwelling	40,000 sq. ft./dwelling	28,000 sq. ft./dwelling	14,000 sq. ft./dwelling	8,000 sq. ft./dwelling
Number of lots (maximum)	24 lots	36 lots	54 lots	108 lots	180 lots
Lot size maximum	24,000 sq. ft.	12,000 sq. ft.	11,000 sq. ft.	5,500 sq. ft.	4,000 sq. ft.
Lot size minimum	12,000 sq. ft.	10,000 sq. ft.	6,000 sq. ft.	4,000 sq. ft.	2,500 sq. ft. (attached)
Lot width (minimum)	80 feet	60 feet	50 feet	40 feet	25 feet
Open space percentage (minimum)	60 percent	60 percent	60 percent	60 percent	50 percent
OPTION 3 DENSITY	160,000 sq. ft./dwelling	120,000 sq. ft./dwelling	80,000 sq. ft./dwelling	40,000 sq. ft./dwelling	20,000 sq. ft./dwelling
Number of lots (maximum)	9 lots	13 lots	18 lots	36 lots	72 lots
Lot size maximum	NA	NA	NA	NA	NA
Lot size minimum	40,000 sq. ft.	30,000 sq. ft.	20,000 sq. ft.	10,000 sq. ft.	5,000 sq. ft.
Lot width (minimum)	100 feet	80 feet	60 feet	50 feet	40 feet
Open space percentage (minimum)	0–75 percent	0–75 percent	0–75 percent	0–75 percent	0–75 percent
OPTION 4 DENSITY	10 acres/dwelling	7 acres/dwelling	160,000 sq. ft./dwelling	80,000 sq. ft./dwelling	40,000 sq. ft./dwelling
Number of lots (maximum)	5 lots	7 lots	9 lots	18 lots	36 lots
Lot size maximum	NA	NA	NA	NA	NA
Lot size minimum	60,000 sq. ft.	40,000 sq. ft.	30,000 sq. ft.	20,000 sq. ft.	10,000 sq. ft.
Lot Width (minimum)	130 feet	100 feet	80 feet	60 feet	50 feet
Open space percentage (minimum)	0–90 percent	0–85 percent	0–80 percent	0–75 percent	0–75 percent
OPTION 5 DENSITY	40,000 sq. ft./dwelling	30,000 sq. ft./dwelling	20,000 sq. ft./dwelling	10,000 sq. ft./dwelling	6,000 sq. ft./dwelling
Number of lots (maximum)	36 lots	48 lots	72 lots	144 lots	252 dwelling units
Lot size maximum	12,000 sq. ft.	9,000 sq. ft.	6,000 sq. ft.	3,000 sq. ft.	2,400 sq. ft. (attached)
Lot size minimum	6,000 sq. ft.	5,000 sq. ft.	4,000 sq. ft.	2,500 sq. ft.	2,400 sq. ft. (attached)
Lot Width (minimum)	60 feet	55 feet	50 feet	25 feet	20 feet
Open space percentage (minimum)	70 percent	70 percent	70 percent	70 percent	60 percent

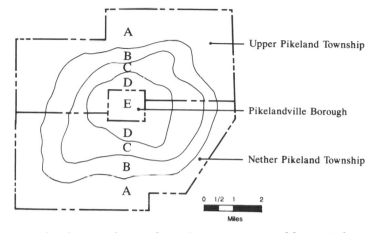

Upper Pikeland Township

Pikelandville Borough

Nether Pikeland Township

0 1/2 1   2
Miles

Figure 4-1. This diagram shows schematic arrangements of five typical zoning districts (A–E) in three adjoining municipalities where densities vary from 800,000 square feet per dwelling (in District A) to 10,000 square feet per dwelling (in District E). The logical pattern is generally concentric, with densities decreasing as distances from central services increase.

environmental features that physically constrain development, and to the various natural resources that the community has identified for different levels of protection. Possible densities, permitted lot size ranges, and minimum open space requirements are listed in Table 4-2. Additional potential variations within District E (the borough) are included in Appendix 3 (pages 190–222), dealing with the design of hamlets, villages, and traditional small-town neighborhoods.

The important point here is that in most municipalities it is appropriate for zoning to provide for a *variety* of districts. In some semi-rural communities it is possible that only three district types might make sense (A, B, and C), unless the municipality also contains an unincorporated village (in which case Districts D and E would probably also be appropriate). On the other hand, in established boroughs and older suburbs located closer to metropolitan centers, the logical range of district types might be C, D, and E (or perhaps only D and

E). However, it is certainly also possible that in many situations individual municipalities might possess such a wide range of neighborhood types that four or even all five district types could be appropriate.

Table 4-2 offers five options to landowners and developers within each of the five district types. Option 1 represents the "basic" option in each district, reflecting the overall "base density" that may be either increased or decreased within specific ranges shown on the table. In District Type A, where the base density is 80,000 square feet per dwelling, for example, the allowable density range would be from 40,000 square feet per dwelling (for village and hamlet designs) to ten acres per dwelling (for "country properties"). Most applicants will probably tend to select the basic density option in their District Type, in this case 80,000 square feet per dwelling, with the provision that lots not exceed 40,000 square feet so that the 50 percent minimum open space requirement can be met.

The five density options offered in each of these five district types are suggestions only. In fact, individual municipalities might decide to offer fewer options in any given district. In Lower Merion Township (Montgomery County, PA) and in West Manchester Township (York County, PA), for example, only one choice is offered to subdivision applicants: an "Option 1" kind of choice that essentially allows them full basic density but only through a conservation design in which at least half the land becomes permanent open space. However, all communities are encouraged to examine the potential advantages of offering the full range of density options and to consider the appropriateness of the full range of district types in their community when updating their codes to incorporate conservation design standards for new subdivisions.

Court precedents in Pennsylvania and many other states strongly suggest that an ordinance's ability to withstand legal challenge is closely related to the appropriateness of the "basic densities" allowed in its various zoning districts. It is also quite likely that broadening the range of development options available to landowners and developers could help ordinances survive court challenges because the options expand an applicant's potential choices and do not represent a single, fixed "density requirement." This is an important legal consideration in Pennsylvania and could well be in other states too. Providing for ranges and choices becomes increasingly important for any district type in which the base density selected by the community could be described as "bcing on the low side." In suburban edge communities with public water and/or sewer, that situation would be reflected by overall densities of 40,000 square feet per dwelling. In unserviced, semi-rural areas, the overall base density of 80,000 square feet per dwelling is sufficiently low that municipalities should very strongly consider offering some range of choice through two or more density options related to open space requirements.

Illustrative Examples of the Various Options in a Rural Zoning District

This section illustrates the physical form that the five basic options could take on a specific 50-acre property in a rural or nearly rural zoning district where the preexisting zoning had traditionally required a standard minimum lot area of 80,000 square feet. The following figures show what the old zoning typically produced and contrast that result with the variety of layouts that could be proposed under each of the five new options. Under three of the options with density equal to or greater than currently permitted under existing ordinances (Options 1, 2, and 5), lots are reduced in size in order to conserve significant percentages of the property. For the last two options involving lower densities (Options 3 and 4), two alternative layouts are possible, showing how applicants could use these flexible standards to produce a pattern of fairly large

estate lots and country properties or to create areas of jointly owned open space that all subdivision residents could enjoy (such as common pastures and bridle trails or other kinds of recreational amenities).

This results-oriented approach is sometimes called "density zoning," in which developers are awarded maximum flexibility with regard to dimensional requirements of their house lots provided they remain within the overall density established for the property. However, the approach illustrated in this book is distinguished from pure density zoning by basic conservation area requirements pertaining to three of the options (1, 2, and 5) regarding the *quantity, quality,* and *configuration* of the undivided open space that is to be protected through these design techniques. The other two options (3 and 4) are justifiable because of their overall reduced densities, which can in some cases offer unique benefits to landowners, developers, and municipalities. These lower-density alternatives also serve to promote valid municipal planning objectives such as preserving woodland habitat, productive farmland, historic buildings in their context, and cultural landscapes.

The figures below illustrate these five options for laying out subdivisions on a typical 50-acre tract at different densities and with different percentages of conservation land, as contrasted with the previous "one-size-fits-all" zoning that essentially required the entire parcel to be cut up into house lots consuming two or more acres of land. It should be remembered that this hypothetical example is located in a semi-rural area of Pennsylvania where there is no public water or sewer and where there is no strong, long-term commitment to agriculture among the remaining farming families (a fact that is reflected in the absence of exclusive agricultural zoning with densities of 20 to 40 acres per dwelling, which in Pennsylvania is popular only in Lancaster and York Counties).

Preexisting Zoning Requirements: Baseline Example

To provide a baseline comparison, Figure 4-2 shows the property as it could have easily been subdivided under the preexisting zoning that mandated minimum lot sizes of 80,000 square feet with no con-

Figure 4-2. CONVENTIONAL LAYOUT AT PREEXISTING DENSITY.

Minimum lot size:	80,000 square feet
Overall density:	One dwelling per 80,000 square feet adjusted tract acreage
Lot yield:	18 lots
Conservation land:	None
Lot size range	
Minimum:	80,000 square feet (1.8 acres)
Typical:	80,000 square feet (1.8 acres)
Maximum:	None

servation areas required as such. Under existing regulations, density is calculated on the basis of the acreage having no severe constraints, such as wetlands, floodways, or slopes over 25 percent. (This net usable land is referred to as "adjusted tract acreage," or ATA.)

It is recommended that local zoning ordinances be amended to eliminate the approach shown in Figure 4-2 as an option. As long as developers are able to attain full density, as-of-right, by dividing entire parcels into only house lots and streets, with no significant conservation lands for permanent protection, many will continue to do so. Density bonuses to encourage developers to submit conservation designs instead have generally been ineffective and self-defeating.

Notes About Lot Sizes in Options 1 Through 5

A range of lot sizes is given for each of the five options. In Options 1, 2, and 5, an "average maximum lot size" is noted in the figure captions and represents the largest lots that could be created (on average) while still attaining the minimum required percentage of conservation land. At the other end of the size range, a minimum lot area is also given and has generally been set at half the maximum average lot size to provide for design flexibility. It should also be noted that several Pennsylvania communities have already eliminated their lot size minima in districts where conservation subdivisions are required. In one such community, conservation design is essentially required on all parcels greater than five acres, where density is strictly limited to one dwelling per 60,000 square feet.

Two of the benefits of establishing a range of lot sizes within each option are that site designers can utilize the most appropriate locations on a parcel for development in the most efficient manner while also increasing the percentage of land that is permanently conserved. This flexibility also allows developers to provide a broader mix of housing product for different markets with different lot size needs. For example, empty-nesters, single-parent households, and couples without children (or with only toddlers) often prefer more compact lots with fewer maintenance demands. Healthy and balanced neighborhoods typically contain a range of house sizes and lot sizes, rather than following a "one-size-fits-all" approach. In all cases, the overall maximum density is controlled so that lot size criteria become irrelevant in the context of limiting the number of homes that can be built.

Option 1: Neutral Density and Basic Conservation

A direct comparison with the same overall density is illustrated in Figure 4-3, showing the conservation benefits and maximum land consumption results obtainable under Option 1. The critical difference is that lots in this layout consume only half of the unconstrained land (32.4 acres), or 16.2 acres. With a "density-neutral" lot yield of 18, lot sizes of 40,000 square feet or less would conserve at least 50 percent of the unconstrained land as open space. The minimum required open space in such a conservation subdivision would be the sum of the constrained land (17.6 acres) plus half the unconstrained land (16.2 acres), or 33.8 acres altogether (about two-thirds of the total property).

Option 2: Enhanced Conservation and Density

Option 2 attains the next step upward both in the percentage of open space conserved and in lot yield (see Fig. 4-4). In that alternative, 24 lots become possible and, in order to conserve 60 percent of the unconstrained land, lot sizes would be capped at about 24,000 square feet, or just over one-half acre. Lots of this size are large enough to accommodate wells, but septic disposal filter beds should generally be located off the lot, such as within the adjacent common open space. (These filter beds may be either individual systems serving only one dwelling, or shared systems serving two or more dwellings. This approach is further described on pages 47–48.)

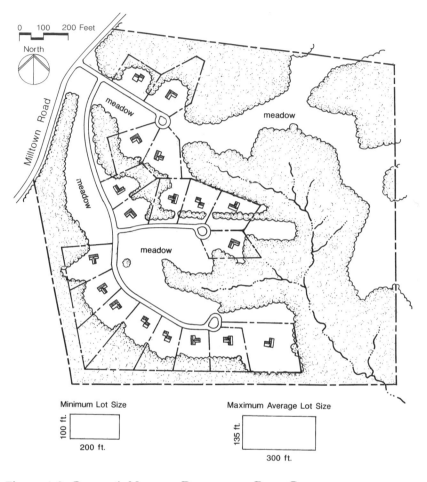

Figure 4-3. OPTION 1: NEUTRAL DENSITY AND BASIC CONSERVATION.

Maximum density:	One dwelling per 80,000 square feet adjusted tract acreage
Lot yield:	18 lots (maximum)
Conservation land:	50 percent (minimum) of adjusted tract acreage
Lot size range	
Minimum:	20,000 square feet (0.46 acres)
Typical:	30,000 square feet (0.68 acres)
Maximum:	40,000 square feet (0.91 acres), on average

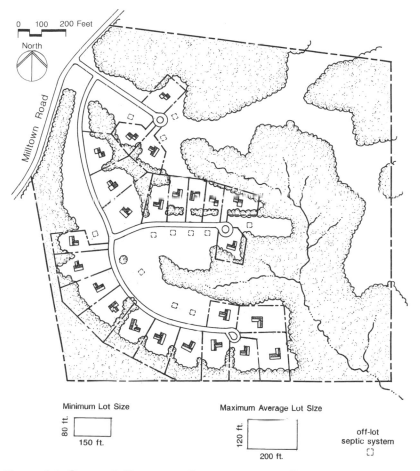

Minimum Lot Size

80 ft.
150 ft.

Maximum Average Lot Size

120 ft.
200 ft.

off-lot
septic system

Figure 4-4. OPTION 2: ENHANCED CONSERVATION AND DENSITY.

Maximum density:	One dwelling per 60,000 square feet adjusted tract acreage
Lot yield:	24 lots (maximum)
Conservation land:	60 percent (minimum) of adjusted tract acreage
Lot size range	
Minimum:	12,000 square feet (0.28 acres)
Typical:	18,000 square feet (0.41 acres)
Maximum:	24,000 square feet (0.55 acres), on average

Option 3: Estate Lots

For those developers looking for opportunities in the upscale or custom market, Options 3 and 4 could offer attractive alternatives. Option 3 is designed for developers who are targeting potential buyers interested in purchasing large homes on exclusive private lots and for whom the attractions of neighborhood amenities and greater neighborhood open space are secondary. To accomplish these objectives, the estate lot option provides for less density (see Fig. 4-5). Because no undivided open space is required to be designated on the plan for conservation purposes, the overall lot yield has been lowered to discourage this approach from general usage.

Option 4: Country Properties

The fourth option is an extension of the third but is geared more closely to the conservation of rural landscapes and for new residents who might be interested in owning and living on small farms (either for commercial use or for hobby purposes), woodlots, or their own private nature sanctuary (see Fig. 4-6). Another use of this option is to allow a historic estate home and its accessory buildings to remain intact while creating a neighborhood of similar "high-end" properties. Potential buyers include the small specialist farmer and those who would enjoy the life of a country gentleman.

Certain incentives could be offered to encourage this low-density option, as described on pages 42–43. For example, density could be calculated on the basis of total tract acreage (not excluding unbuildable land), up to two additional dwellings could be permitted as accessory units (under special size limits and design criteria), and private access roads (or "country lanes") could be permitted to be gravel-surfaced. Lot sizes are flexible so that properties may be sized and shaped to correspond with the terrain and other site features (such as woodland edges). In the example here,

Figure 4-5. OPTION 3: ESTATE LOTS.

Maximum density: One dwelling per 160,000 square feet adjusted tract acreage (3.6 acres)

Lot yield: Nine "estate lots"

Conservation land: None required

Lot size range

    Minimum: 40,000 square feet (0.9 acres)

    Typical: 160,000 square feet (3.6 acres)

    Maximum: None

Note that on this fairly constrained site, approximately the same lot yield could be produced by basing density on 3.6 acres of adjusted tract acreage or by simply requiring five acres in gross, with no deductions for land having inherent physical limitations. Basing Option 3 simply on gross acreage is therefore an alternative approach, but only if the density is set at five acres.

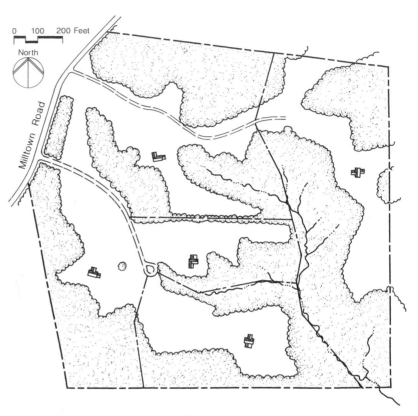

Figure 4-6. OPTION 4: COUNTRY PROPERTIES

Maximum density: One dwelling per ten acres gross

Lot yield: Five "country properties"

Conservation land: None required

Lot size range

    Minimum: 1.5 acres

    Typical: 10 acres

    Maximum: None

the country properties vary in area from about 4 acres to about 14 acres, with one of the lots including land on both sides of the country lane.

Option 5: Village Design with Greenbelt

The highest yield is attainable with Option 5, where 36 lots are achievable based on the 40,000-square-foot density and 32.4 acres of adjusted tract acreage (see Fig. 4-7). However, in order for the 70 percent open space requirement to be met, lots must average not more than 12,000 square feet in area (a little more than one-quarter acre). Lots of this size in unsewered areas are typically served either by central wells and septic disposal facilities or by individual wells and septic disposal systems located within the undivided open space (as described later in this chapter). Because of the considerably more compact nature of development proposed under this option, municipalities may wish to retain greater control over such proposals by classifying them as conditional uses. It may also want to restrict this option to certain locations within the municipality, such as those where planned residential developments (PRDs) are currently permitted (and possibly as an alternative to them, which could result in the elimination of PRDs altogether).

In exchange for the greater density granted under this option, officials may wish to adopt a set of illustrated design standards to guide the design process. This is particularly important if certain kinds of results are among the stated goals of the ordinance—such as "to encourage compact development having many of the same traditional townscape characteristics that typify nineteenth-century villages in the county." Special standards governing the layout and design of Option 5 subdivisions are contained in Article 7 of the model subdivision and land development ordinance provisions in Appendix 3 of this book, including a special set of Illustrated Design Principles.

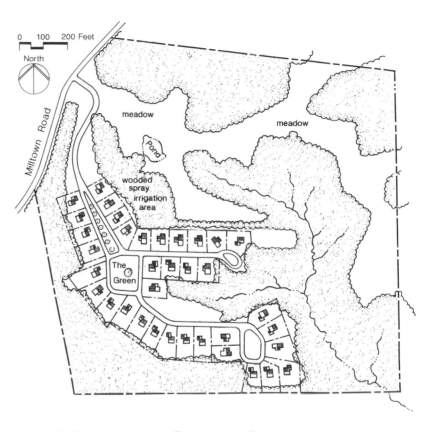

Figure 4-7. OPTION 5: VILLAGE DESIGN WITH GREENBELT.

Maximum density:	One dwelling per 40,000 square feet adjusted tract acreage
Lot yield:	36 lots (maximum)
Conservation land:	70 percent (minimum) of adjusted tract acreage
Lot size range	
Minimum:	6,000 square feet (0.14 acres)
Typical:	9,000 square feet (0.21 acres)
Maximum:	12,000 square feet (0.28 acres), on average

Combining the Options on a Single Property

Applicants could also combine several options on different parts of their property, as illustrated in Figure 4-8. For example, one might combine Options 4 and 5, with the "country properties" located on part of the 70 percent open space required as village greenbelt land.

In Figure 4-8, a 20-acre parcel with no physical constraints is shown as being developed into 16 village lots (typically just under one-quarter acre) and two estate lots of about 6 acres each. The open space in both the village greenbelt and within the estate lots would be permanently protected through conservation easements and would buffer the village on all sides from existing public roads and adjoining parcels. These kinds of layouts with more modest, village-

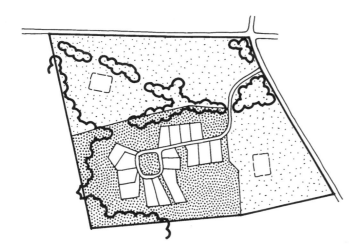

Figure 4-8. COMBINING OPTIONS—OPTION 3 ("ESTATE LOTS") AND OPTION 5 ("VILLAGE WITH GREENBELT").

Maximum density: One dwelling per 40,000 square feet adjusted tract acreage

Lot yield: 16 village lots on eight acres (10,000 square feet each) Two estate lots of six acres each

Conservation land: 70 percent, in four undivided acres of village greenbelt plus ten acres of eased open space on the two estate lots

scale lots and with more formal central open space provide the kind of living environment that many people are seeking these days. This design alternative also allows a broader range of house sizes and types to be provided, better meeting the needs of different families. Combining Options 3 or 4 with Option 5 allows developers to realize additional economic return from that part of the village greenbelt open space that could logically become estate lots or country properties, while still providing a reasonable amount of common open space for the enjoyment of village residents.

For other developers who wish to work within only a single option, the permitted range of lot sizes could be used to create lots of different dimensions to appeal to different markets, provided that the minimum percentage of undivided conservation land is still protected. The basic idea is that as long as the overall density and open space criteria are respected, applicants would be encouraged to be as creative as they would like to be, with a minimum of restrictions pertaining to actual lot size, lot width, setbacks, etc.

How Densities Are Determined

It is recommended that communities establish clear standards and procedures in their zoning ordinance clarifying how maximum density is to be determined. In this regard, it is suggested that such provisions include language offering applicants two methods of estimating the legally permitted density on their parcels. The methods advocated in the model ordinance language in this book offer subdivision applicants two ways to determine their maximum permitted density: (1) on the basis of mathematical percentages and formulas contained in the ordinance, or (2) on the basis of a "Yield Plan."

To produce results that are both realistic and fair, in terms of reflecting the amount of development that would normally have occurred on the property under the preexisting zoning, both methods would employ some use of "net-outs" to exclude a reasonable percentage of certain kinds of inherently unbuildable or severely constrained land.

To follow either of these two approaches for determining density, applicants generally must first prepare a Map of Limiting Conditions on their properties. (This map simply extracts the inherently unbuildable soils, slopes, and floodplain areas from the Existing Resources/Site Analysis Map that applicants are routinely required to prepare as a baseline inventory document under the recommended procedures in the model Subdivision Ordinance language contained in Appendix 3 of this book.) For soils data, the medium-intensity maps contained in the county soil survey published by the USDA Natural Resources Conservation Service may be used. The soils that are classified as "very poorly drained" and "poorly drained" should be shown separately. The first category generally corresponds to wetland soils where water ponds at the surface for three or more months of the year; the second category includes soils that generally are not suitable for septic systems due to the presence of a seasonal high water table not far below the surface. In addition to these soils data, the 100-year floodplain and floodway should both be delineated, and two categories of slopes should be shown (15–25 percent and greater than 25 percent), based on topographical information from the U.S. Geological Survey or from a field survey by a licensed surveyor or engineer.

First Method: Applying Density Factors

The first broad alternative method for determining building density relies on formulas that assign certain density factors (DFs) to different kinds of land, depending on the degree of environmental constraint inherent in specific physical characteristics such as soil depth, slope, wetness, frequency of flooding, and velocity of floodwaters (see Table 4-3). Other kinds of land that could or should not be included within building lots because they are needed for other purposes (such as streets, utility lines, etc.) are also weighted. After these land areas

Table 4-3. Density Factors for Calculating Adjusted Tract Acreage

Density	Factor	Description of Constraint
DF 1	0.00	Street rights-of-way
		Floodways within 100-year floodplain
DF 2	0.05	Wetlands and soils classified as "very poorly drained"
		Soils with bedrock at the surface, rock outcrops, boulder fields (>5,000 square feet)
		Utility easements for high-tension electrical transmission lines (>69 kilovolts)
DF 3	0.25	Steep slopes over 25 percent
DF 4	0.33	Soils classified as "poorly drained" (in unsewered areas)
		Soils with bedrock within 42 inches of the surface (in unsewered areas)
DF 5	0.50	100-year floodplains (excluding floodways or wetlands within floodplains)
		Soils having bedrock within 36 inches of the surface
DF 6	0.75	Soils classified as "poorly drained" (in sewered areas)
		Soils with bedrock within 42 inches of the surface (in sewered areas)
		Slopes of 15–25 percent
DF 7	1.00	Unconstrained land

have been calculated and the appropriate percentages deducted from the gross site acreage, the remaining unconstrained land is known as the "adjusted tract acreage" (ATA).

The above factors are similar to those upheld in a landmark decision by Pennsylvania's Commonwealth Court in 1992 (*Reimer v. Upper Mt. Bethel Twp.,* 615 Atlantic Reporter 2nd, 938–946). In that case the court expressed strong support for such approaches to determining density, which are rationally based on objective and measurable criteria pertaining to the inherent suitability of land for development, as contrasted with "blanket" densities applied to all properties within a zoning district regardless of the presence or absence of physical constraints.

These density factors are then multiplied against the acreage that the applicant's surveyor or engineer determines is covered by each type of constraining feature or characteristic. For example, on the 50-acre property illustrated in Figures 4-2 through 4-7, where street rights-of-way are estimated as consuming 5 percent of the site (2.5 acres), the following site constraints exist:

- five acres are wet but not floodprone;
- three acres are both wet and floodprone;
- seven acres are within the regulatory 100-year floodplain (including three acres of wetland, leaving four acres of dry, nonwetland floodplain);
- one acre has slopes steeper than 25 percent;
- two acres have slopes between 15 and 25 percent;
- two acres have shallow bedrock conditions (within 42 inches of the surface); and
- five acres are classified as "poorly drained" not in the floodplain (in this case with a seasonal water table within only 20 inches of the surface for three or more months per year).

Table 4-4 illustrates how the site constraints noted above on this 50-acre property would relate to the density factors described in Table 4-3.

Table 4-4. Applying Density Factors to Different Land Types within a Typical 50-Acre Tract

Total Area Covered by Feature or Constraint	Density Factor		Adjusted Acreage
2.5 acres of street rights-of-way	x 0.00	=	0.00 acres
5 acres of wetland (outside floodplain)	x 0.05	=	0.25 acres
3 acres of wetland (inside floodplain)	x 0.05	=	0.15 acres
1 acre with slopes steeper than 25 percent	x 0.25	=	0.25 acres
4 acres of dry floodplain (not wetland)	x 0.50	=	2.00 acres
5 acres of "poorly drained" soil (unsewered)	x 0.33	=	1.65 acres
2 acres with slopes between 15 and 25 percent	x 0.75	=	1.50 acres
2 acres with bedrock within 42 inches	x 0.75	=	1.50 acres
25.5 acres of unconstrained land	x 1.00	=	25.50 acres
ADJUSTED TRACT ACREAGE (ATA)		=	32.80 acres

Table 4-5. Lot Yields Under the Five Options

Option 1	80,000 square feet/d.u.*	or 0.54 d.u./acre x 32.55 acres = 17.58 or 18 lots
Option 2	60,000 square feet/d.u.	or 0.73 d.u./acre x 32.55 acres = 23.76 or 24 lots
Option 3	160,000 square feet/d.u.	or 0.27 d.u./acre x 32.55 acres = 8.79 or 9 lots
Option 4	10 acres/d.u.	or 0.10 d.u./acre x 50.00 acres = 5.00 or 5 lots
Option 5	40,000 square feet/d.u.	or 1.09 d.u./acre x 32.55 acres = 35.48 or 36 lots

*d.u. = dwelling unit

For development proposals under Options 1, 2, 3, and 5, the ATA of 32.8 acres would then be multiplied by the permissible density in the zoning district, according to whatever option the applicant elects to pursue. Under the five options described earlier in this chapter, the total lot yields would be as shown in Table 4-5.

INCENTIVES TO ENCOURAGE THE LOW-DENSITY OPTION (OPTION 4)

In order to encourage potential applicants to select Option 4, some communities have offered two incentives. The first allows the homes in these country property subdivisions to be accessed through private gravel driveways or through public streets designed and constructed to special township standards for country lanes (essentially the standard street specifications except for the asphalt driving surface and relaxed standards for street geometry). This reduced standard tacitly recognizes the greatly reduced traffic volumes generated by these low-density developments and the desirability of maintaining rural character while adhering to basic safety standards.

The second incentive is to permit the principal residence to be supplemented by one or two "accessory dwelling units" on each ten-acre lot, these units are limited in size and designed according to certain architectural criteria (to resemble traditional structures on country estates, such as carriage houses, gate houses, etc.). Such structures would not be permitted to be subdivided on separate parcels but would be required, through easements, to remain as part of the entire land parcel or country property.

Second Method: The Yield Plan

The "Yield Plan" alternative involves producing an inexpensive, conceptual design with a conventional lot and street layout in which all the land is allocated to house lots and streets. On that Yield Plan, each lot must contain at least the minimum area of buildable, unconstrained land that is required for all lots in the zoning district where the property is located. That minimum area of unconstrained land, which must be specified in the code, might be one-half to three-quarters of the standard minimum lot size that has traditionally been required in the zoning district. For Yield Plan purposes, the term *unconstrained land* should include all land that is entirely free of the constraints or characteristics described in density factors DF1, DF2, and DF3 in Table 4-3 (land that is wet, steep, or within floodways or street rights-of-way).

Although Yield Plans are conceptual in nature and are not intended to involve significant engineering costs, they must be realistic and must not show potential house sites or streets in areas that would not ordinarily be legally permitted in a conventional layout. For example, on sites not served by public sewerage, density would be determined by evaluating the number of homes that could be supported by individual septic systems on conventional lots. Based on its reading of the applicant's Map of Limiting Conditions and observations made during an on-site visit of the property, the Planning Commission would select a small percentage (say 10 percent) of the lots on the Yield Plan for deep-hole testing in areas it considers to be marginal. If the sample lots pass the percolation test, the applicant's other lots would also be deemed suitable for septic systems for the purpose of calculating total lot yield. However, if any of the sample lots fail, several others (of the township's choosing) would also be tested until all the lots in a given sample pass.

An example of a "Yield Plan" is shown in Figure 5-3, in the next chapter, in which a simple four-step process for designing conservation subdivisions is described.

Dimensional Standards for House Lots in Conservation Subdivisions

One of the more difficult concepts for many laypersons (and some developers) to understand concerns lot size. Conservation subdivisions become possible only by reducing the overall density *or* by reducing lot sizes. In other words, by building fewer homes, or by building the same number of homes on a smaller portion of the site (50 percent or less), the above options offer both of these broad choices.

Where there is a market for low-density "country properties," this form of upscale subdivision (known as "limited development" because applicants voluntarily limit their lot count) can be a good tool to help accomplish community conservation objectives. Limited development designs can benefit from flexible layout standards so that house sites can be located in a way that minimizes their impacts on natural and cultural features. The market for such developments is typically strongest in areas with attractive and well-preserved landscape features, particularly in certain suburban communities where land values are quite high and in outlying areas where there is potential for high-end seasonal homes.

In the majority of situations, however, subdivisions with extremely large lots and reduced density are likely to occur infrequently, if at all. Fortunately, the other options involving more compact house lots and substantial open space offer a huge and mostly untapped opportunity to conserve land through the development process.

The concept of allowing, encouraging, or sometimes even requiring lot sizes to be half (or less than half) the previously established area or width is quite a revolutionary idea in many communities, where the necessity of requiring current minimum lot sizes has never been seriously questioned. Those who contemplate suggesting such an idea must be well prepared to respond positively and convincingly to a number of potential questions or objections.

Municipal officials seeking to promote land conservation through reduced lot sizes must deal with the concerns of not only their constituents but also the developers in their community. These concerns typically focus on three principal perceived problems: (1) the *value* of smaller lots and the houses likely to be built on them, (2) the *appearance* of homes on smaller lots, and (3) the need to provide *sufficient land to accommodate individual septic disposal systems,* in unsewered areas. These concerns are addressed below.

Lot Size and Value

One of the greatest difficulties facing advocates of reduced lot area and width as a means of conserving open space is the preconception in many people's minds that smaller lots are undesirable because they are likely to support homes that are smaller and less expensive than the housing product that has generally been built in the community. This way of thinking is understandable because, in conventional subdivisions with no open space, lot value is strongly influenced by lot size. All other things being equal, two-acre lots generally sell for more than one-acre lots, which in turn command higher prices than half-acre lots, and so on.

However, this situation changes dramatically when subdivisions are designed to offer counterbalancing amenities such as open space providing attractive views and a variety of passive and active recreational opportunities. The high value of smaller lots alongside golf courses and lakefronts demonstrates that lot dimension is by no means the only determinant of lot price, nor is it necessarily the principal one. The same kind of value boost occurs on house lots that abut permanently preserved open space such as public parks (at the municipal, county, state, and national levels) or conservation areas owned by land trusts and conservancies. In fact, experience has shown that smaller lots by no means necessarily result in smaller homes or homes of any lesser value than those typically built on standard lots in conventional subdivisions.

Developers who recognize the value of such lots generally also recognize that such neighborhoods would support homes of similar size and value to those existing elsewhere in the community. One of the clearest examples of this principle is the Plumsock subdivision in Willistown Township, Chester County, Pennsylvania, where the developer created a neighborhood of half-acre lots, leaving two-thirds of the parcel as permanent open space. On these lots he built very large, expensive homes (in the $650,000–$750,000 price range) comparable to those in nearby subdivisions where lot sizes ranged from two to four acres, as is the norm in that community. Market acceptance was extremely good, with brisk sales throughout the project development period. Other subdivisions with more moderately priced homes (around $200,000) could be cited as well, such as Garnet Oaks in Bethel Township, Delaware County, Pennsylvania, where a nature preserve, trails, and a well-equipped children's play area have been provided by the developer to compensate for the smaller lots (12,000 square feet in a half-acre zone). In that development, lots nearest the open space tended to sell first, even though they carried a premium price reflecting that proximity (see Fig. 4-9). (Readers should adjust these dollar figures downward if land values in their areas are substantially lower than those in the Philadelphia metropolitan region.)

Recognizing that open space conservation and not lot sizes per se is the really important feature that municipal policy and regulations should seek to influence in new subdivisions, some Pennsylvania communities such as Lower Merion Township in Montgomery

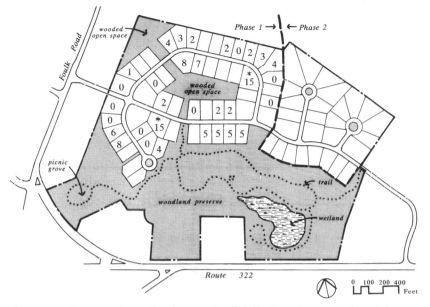

Figure 4-9. Lot premiums (in thousands of dollars) at Garnet Oaks subdivision in Bethel Township, Delaware County, Pennsylvania. The first lots sold tended to be those adjoining the open space, despite the premiums added because of that proximity.

County and Lower Allen Township in Cumberland County have eliminated minimum lot size criteria in the district where conservation subdivisions are required (for all tracts greater than five acres). The experience in these communities is that some developers are building larger and even more expensive homes on the smaller lots than they had previously been constructing on standard subdivision lots prior to the ordinance change. The lesson is that, in the context of conservation subdivisions, real estate values are strongly influenced by the presence of open space, which compensates for reduced lot dimensions.

Further information about the economic advantages enjoyed by lot owners living near open space within or next to their neighborhoods can be found in Chapter 6.

Appearance and Community Character

Another concern frequently expressed by local officials and residents, when lot size reductions are proposed, is that homes on smaller lots and not very attractive and are thus likely to disrupt the community character. In many cases, such comments stem from the difficulty that most people have in visualizing various sizes and widths, especially if there are not many examples of conservation subdivisions in their township or general area. If there are no local examples of conservation subdivisions to visit and view, one alternative would be to seek out examples of larger homes on small lots in nineteenth-century villages and towns or in subdivisions designed and built during the first three decades of this century, which were typically located adjacent to older, established towns and boroughs. Another alternative would be to visit a golf course community to see house lots that are narrower and shallower than one would typically find in a conventional subdivision of recent vintage.

To put these visual concerns in perspective, Chapter 7 includes a wide variety of photographs of conservation subdivisions where lot sizes range from 5,000 square feet to 20,000 square feet. These images are based on illustrative examples from the companion video and scripted slide show that were produced as supporting elements of the state's Growing Greener educational program for municipal officials. When most people see actual examples of homes on smaller lots set in the context of permanently preserved open space, their preconceived ideas about the importance of requiring larger lots tend to fade away. One of the Philadelphia region's largest production builders (Realen Homes) has produced attractive designs for traditional 2,800-square-foot houses with side-loaded garages on lots only 100 feet wide.

Some developers in the same area, who were themselves concerned about the marketability of lots that are not as large and wide as usual, have become very creative in designing fairly commodious homes (with as much as 4,000 square feet of floor space in some up-

Figure 4-10. This drawing of a new house type produced by Realen Homes in Montgomery County, Pennsylvania, shows how fairly large homes with 2,800 square feet can be designed to fit on 100-foot-wide lots, even when they have side-loaded garages (which the market prefers because they are more attractive than models with garage doors facing the street). Land-conserving designs such as these must become better known because many developers assume they need lots at least 120 feet wide to accommodate such homes with side-loading garages.

scale communities) on lots that are only three-quarters of an acre. And by positioning these homes off center with side-yard setbacks of 35 and 5 feet (instead of two fairly useless 20-foot side yards), they have been able to create a housing product that has very pleasing "curb appeal," which realtors have advised is important (see Fig. 4-10). This particular technique works well when all the homes are built by the same developer, but it can also succeed with multiple builders. In such cases, builders should be required to construct all garages and driveways on the same side of the lot so these elements (which require the 35-foot setback) always face a sidewall located just five feet from the common lot boundary. Of course, this type of co-ordination is not necessary when garages are front-loaded or when homes are of a more average size.

Accommodating Wells and Septic Disposal Systems

One of the most frequently perceived obstacles to conservation de-sign in areas without public water or sewer involves the disposal of wastewater. These concerns are addressed in the following sections.

LOCATING LOTS (AND ON-LOT UTILITIES) ON THE MOST APPROPRIATE SOILS

In areas where the minimum lot size has traditionally been 1.5 to 2 acres for the purpose of ensuring that each lot has sufficient suitable land for wells and septic systems, the design flexibility advocated in this book provides for better results. As shown in Figure 4-11, larger lots provide absolutely no guarantee that the best soils available on the development parcel will be included within all the house lots. In fact, large-lot requirements frequently compel developers to create lots that contain only marginal soils, when all the better soils are consumed by other large "land-hog" lots. By reducing lot sizes from 80,000 square feet to 40,000 square feet, or from 60,000 square feet to 30,000 square feet, all of the smaller lots can be provided with the deepest, driest soils the development site can offer. Lots of these sizes

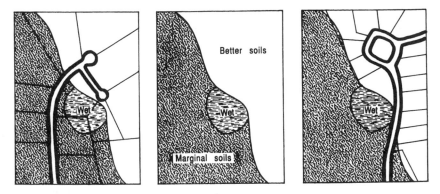

Figure 4-11. Reducing lot sizes can sometimes help subdivision designers lo-cate all homes on the better soils. On the left, six of the thirteen two-acre lots would have septic systems on marginal soils, barely meeting minimum legal requirements, because these lots contain nothing better. By decreasing lots to one acre, all thirteen can be laid out to contain deeper, drier soils (with all wetlands in the conservation area). Sometimes such arrangements require a limited number of "flag lots" connected to the street by driveway access strips, and these specialized lot forms should be allowed when lot width require-ments can be met.

also allow wells and septic systems to be located a full 200 feet apart, twice the distance that county health departments and state environmental agencies typically require, adding a secondary safety advantage.

LOCATING INDIVIDUAL WELLS OR SEPTIC SYSTEMS OFF-LOT

For many years planners widely accepted the premise that in districts with one-acre densities and no public water or sewer, lot size reductions much below one acre (to enable open space set asides) were not physically possible. This premise was based on the generally accepted need—with many common soil types—for roughly an acre of ground on which to locate wells at least 100 feet away from septic disposal fields and from their eventual replacement areas.

However, in recent years a practical approach has evolved to make it possible for individual wells and/or individual septic systems to serve homes on much smaller lots. The conceptual breakthrough is to locate individual wells and/or individual septic disposal fields *off-lot,* within the undivided common open space (see Fig. 4-12). Ownership and maintenance responsibilities would continue to lie with the owner of the lot being served, and the well and/or the septic disposal field would be located on land specifically designated for that purpose on the Final Plan. (As a general commonsense precaution, homeowner associations would typically be required to arrange for all septic tanks in their developments to be routinely pumped once every three years or so. Such pumping prevents excessive sludge accumulation and sewage solid overflow into the drain fields, occurrences which would clog these systems and necessitate expensive repairs. This is a highly recommended practice for homes in all subdivisions, not just those on smaller conservation lots.) These individual drain fields would normally be located under conservation meadows, village greens, and different kinds of active and passive recreation areas, except those involving paving or other kinds of impervious surfaces.

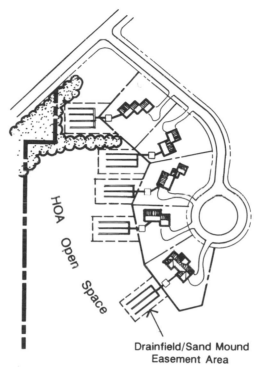

Figure 4-12. This sketch shows how individual septic system disposal areas can be located on adjacent conservation lands where the better soils are found. Existing regulations requiring disposal fields to be situated within house lots should be changed; instead they should require that disposal areas serving one or more homes be located on land designated for that purpose on the final approved subdivision plan, over which the owner(s) of the lot(s) being served have specific easement rights to construct, maintain, rebuild, or replace their disposal areas.

HOA Open Space

Drainfield/Sand Mound Easement Area

A further advantage of locating wells and/or septics off-lot is that they can be situated on those areas of the property that are best suited for this kind of use. Favorable soils for wells and septic disposal fields are often not well distributed on development parcels. While every lot must pass a percolation test before a building permit may be issued, soil conditions can vary widely. For example, percolation tests on certain lots can be quite marginal and just barely pass the state's minimum requirements, while tests on other lots might score very highly. Conservation subdivision layouts provide site designers with the flexibility needed to locate septic disposal areas on those parts of the property having the most appropriate soils and slopes. These areas are often the first to be identified and designed around as an integral part of the undivided open space.

In most cases, developers much prefer individual systems over community systems for two basic reasons. One is the high initial cost for central systems that must be completed and be fully operational before the first house or lot may be sold. The second is approval time, which is much faster with individual systems than it is for centralized systems requiring special engineering design work and approval by local and state environmental officials—frequently a very lengthy procedure. A third and probably less significant factor considered by applicants is that township officials, nervous about complications following the possible failure of community systems serving entire neighborhoods, generally prefer individual systems.

SHARED OR COMMUNITY SYSTEMS

A growing body of municipal experience in Pennsylvania regarding shared septic systems serving all the homes in one or more subdivisions is beginning to demonstrate that many of the potential problems that worry township officials can be avoided or greatly mitigated by proper planning and maintenance. In Upper Uwchlan Township, Chester County, Pennsylvania, for example, knowledge was gained the hard way, through a number of experiences that other townships with hindsight can now benefit from. The lessons learned by Upper Uwchlan are reflected in new standards and procedures adopted by the supervisors in that community. Through these experiences the township discovered that it must take a proactive role in specifying the kind of operating system that will be installed. To simplify routine maintenance and parts replacement, Upper Uwchlan requires that all new systems use one of several time-tested designs. The township also ensures that these systems are properly maintained by trained personnel who perform those services under contract. Upper Uwchlan has demonstrated that it can manage the administrative side of operating these so-called community systems at no cost to the general public. The time that township managers or other staff

spend on each project is fully reimbursed through user fees that the municipality collects and deposits in special township accounts for each subdivision served in that manner.

MUNICIPAL SEWAGE FACILITY PLANS

Municipal sewage facility plans should be adopted (or updated) to set out the official strategy for dealing with wastewater treatment and disposal. These plans should incorporate the strategies described above for flexible subdivision design. With respect to shared or community systems, it is recommended that these plans incorporate a preferred list of alternative systems so that the type that discharges treated effluent directly into water bodies or watercourses is listed only as a final alternative, ranked last in preference. There are several reasons for this general recommendation. One is that such systems do nothing to replenish local aquifers and therefore gradually deplete local groundwater supplies, causing reduced base stream flows (eventually manifested in headwater streams drying up during the summer). Another reason is that such systems introduce enormous quantities of nutrients into streams, rivers, and lakes. Those nutrients indirectly lead to reduced oxygen levels for fish populations by stimulating the growth of aquatic plants, which consume much of the water's available oxygen.

Density Bonuses to Further Certain Public Objectives

In addition to the basic density incentives built into the five options to encourage conservation set asides or lower densities, communities might want to consider offering specially targeted density bonuses to further the following three kinds of public objectives. (Wording relating to these incentives is included in Section 108 of Appendix 3, which contains model zoning ordinance provisions.)

Encouraging Public Usage

The first of these objectives concerns public usage of all or part of the conservation land preserved in new developments. This public usage can be accommodated in a number of ways. One is to grant access easements permitting residents of the municipality to use certain areas of the conservation land, typically trails along stream corridors or other potential linkages into a community-wide network of open space. Another is to donate title to parts of the conservation land to the municipality for use as a public recreation facility, such as a ball field. Because recent decisions by the U.S. Supreme Court have cast a cloud over "exaction" provisions in local ordinances and state laws, which had been used by government officials to exact land donations from developers for recreational purposes without monetary compensation, this book advocates that density incentives generally be employed to encourage developers to donate easements or fee title to lands desired by the community for public recreational use.

Endowing Management Costs

A second objective that could be furthered through similar incentives is the establishment of a special endowment fund by the developer to help pay for continuing maintenance of the conservation land (including payment of taxes and liability insurance premiums). In developments without structural facilities to maintain (such as swimming pools or clubhouses), these operating costs would typically include mowing grassy areas and meadows, maintaining trails and footbridges, controlling erosion, and keeping the woodlands clear of invasive plants, trees, and especially woody vines. Conservation farmland can often be managed by local farmers whose lease payments typically generate a modest income stream, but provisions should be made for the day when those fields or pastures might no longer be of interest to such people (or when such people no longer exist in the neighborhood). Because these areas might then revert to woods,

trails, and forest, management practices should be factored into long-term cost projections.

Although conservation area management costs are generally borne by homeowner associations, they might alternatively become the responsibility of the municipality (for public ball fields, as discussed above) or of a local conservation organization such as a land trust. Although homeowner associations can and typically do raise funds to pay for operating costs via dues paid by their members, and local governments can raise funds through property taxes, land conservation organizations have no similar authority and depend strictly on donations. Endowment funds generated in this manner would qualify as donations because the decision to use this bonus option remains a voluntary act by developers. Also, this procedure is not a form of exaction because the applicant is fully compensated for the endowment gift through the value of the additional lots. Assuming a 5 percent rate of return, an endowment equal to 20 times the annual operating costs would be sufficient in most years to cover expenses. To the extent that such a sum could be generated by an extra several house lots, this is a technique some communities might want to consider offering to developers through a special zoning provision (such as contained in the model ordinance language in Appendix 3).

Encouraging Housing Affordability

A third possible objective is to encourage the provision of housing that would be more affordable to a broader range of local residents, such as retirees or young couples. By allowing a developer to spread land costs over a larger number of house lots, the sales prices can be lowered slightly on each one. Looked at another way, when a developer is permitted 15 lots instead of 10, the land costs for these additional 5 lots is zero, which means that new homes on them can be deeply discounted and sold for a price that basically reflects the actual construction cost, plus associated profits.

Standards for Ownership, Protection, and Management of Conservation Lands

Another key feature of conservation zoning is the provision of comprehensive standards describing ownership options and management responsibilities for the conservation land. Establishing standards for these aspects of conservation lands is just as logical and essential as setting standards for development areas, such as area/bulk requirements and street specifications. (Criteria governing the location and layout of conservation lands are provided in Chapter 5.)

Ownership of Conservation Lands

The land that is protected from further development within conservation subdivisions may be owned by any one or more of the following entities: homeowner associations, municipalities, land trusts, and individual owners of "conservancy lots" (or "country properties"). It is also possible that more than one of these entities will hold ownership of different parts of the protected land within any given conservation subdivision, as illustrated in Figure 4-13.

Obvious examples include the owners of country properties whose land areas may be included as part of the total required open space in subdivisions where Option 4 designs (as illustrated in Chapter 3) are proposed. Another example is the greenway trail or ball field area that may be donated to the municipality by the developer at the former's request, with the remaining conservation land belonging typically to the homeowner association (HOA). In fact, in most cases, conservation lands belong solely to the neighborhood HOA. And the vast majority of such associations have long track records of smooth and successful operation, although some of them have experienced a variety of problems.

There are three key ways to avoid difficulties when establishing homeowner associations:

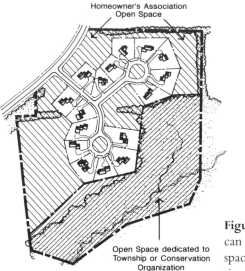

Figure 4-13. Various public entities can own different parts of the open space within conservation subdivisions, as illustrated here.

- First, *membership must be automatic* for all purchasers of house lots or homes. This is accomplished by making membership a condition of sale, and the membership document is only one of many that purchasers must sign at the closing or settlement.
- Second, the association bylaws (which should be reviewed by the municipal solicitor before Final Plan approval is granted) must *authorize the homeowner association to place liens* on the real property of members who fail to pay their dues. The lien clouds the title, preventing the owner from selling until he or she pays all back dues, with interest. (Very few homeowners would withhold dues payment and risk becoming known as a deadbeat or freeloader in their own neighborhood—but this is always a wise preventive measure.)
- Third, it is advisable to *minimize regular maintenance costs* so that dues may remain low. Except in large-scale developments, fancy physical improvements that cost a lot to operate (such as swimming pools, hot tubs, and buildings of any sort) should be very carefully

considered to ensure that their ongoing maintenance will not be a burden for the number of residents involved. In smaller developments, open space maintenance might consist of mowing several greens every week, mowing a meadow once or twice a year, and pruning branches and clearing trees that occasionally fall across a woodland trail. At this level, annual homeowner association dues can be as low as $75 or $100 per family.

Ensuring Permanent Protection of Conservation Lands

The most effective and common method used to protect land set aside for conservation purposes, in this and other contexts, is the conservation easement. This is a legally enforceable agreement permitting the easement holder (or other coholders) to take action to prevent alterations to the designated land and to require that incursions be removed and the land be restored to its preexisting state, if altered in a manner not allowed by the easement. Such easements are permanent and restrictive in nature and are generally written to prohibit all but certain types of activities to occur on them (such as specific types of farming, nature conservation, and passive recreation). In developments containing different kinds of open space, including active recreation facilities, those uses can also be permitted, but the easement document should be accompanied by a map identifying those parts of the property that are subject to different levels of restriction.

Easements run with the title and are recorded in the county register of deeds office. They may be altered only with the express written permission of the easement holder and any other cosigners. Easements are typically granted to land conservation organizations, such as land trusts or conservancies. They may also be granted to units of government at the municipal, county, or state levels. When held by a governmental body, it is advisable that easements also be cosigned by an independent conservation organization to act as a check or balance in the event that future office holders seek to alter long-

standing conservation policies for short-term reasons, or simple expediency.

Granting a conservation easement can sometimes provide financial advantages in terms of federal taxation, but only when the conservation restriction serves a legitimate public purpose and when the building density has been voluntarily lowered by the owner to such a degree that the land's economic value has been reduced. The tax benefits take the form of deductions from federal income taxes over a six-year period and reduced inheritance taxes (based on the land asset value reduction resulting from the easement).

Organizations holding easements typically visit the land at least once yearly to inspect it and to prepare a brief report (with photographic documentation of any infractions). To cover such monitoring costs, a growing number of conservation organizations request an endowment from the developer, in an amount sufficient to produce annual interest income equal to the organization's out-of-pocket expenses. Techniques for generating such endowments were discussed earlier in this chapter.

As mentioned below in the following section, it is highly recommended that the protected conservation land within subdivisions be delineated *outside* individual house lots, and that its boundaries be clearly marked. These steps should help reduce potential problems related to monitoring and enforcing conservation easements on such areas and would enable those lands to be managed according to a set of uniform standards (rather than being neglected or mismanaged). *Covenants, deed restrictions, and wording on the final recorded plan do not adequately protect land from future changes in use or from further subdivision and are thus not recommended protection techniques.* (Illustrating this point clearly is a recent controversy in the Borough of Malvern, in Chester County, Pennsylvania, where borough officials offered to sell an acre of conservation land to a developer for $10,000 to help settle a lawsuit out of court, despite the fact that the borough had received the land as a gift 16 years previously and had signed a covenant promising that the land would never be developed. As the covenant vested all rights on this property with the borough, officials did not violate any law when they acceded to the developer's request, they simply violated the public trust.)

Management of Conservation Lands

Conservation zoning ordinances should include standards to guide applicants in the preparation of management plans for the conservation lands in their subdivisions. Such plans establish management objectives, outline procedures, and define responsibilities for maintaining the conservation areas. Typically, grassy commons require fertilization, irrigation, and mowing; meadows are mown after wildflower seeds have been set; and woodlands frequently require annual pruning not only to keep trails clear but also to check the growth of invasive tree species (such as Norway maple) and exotic vines (Oriental bittersweet, Japanese honeysuckle, multiflora rose, etc.), especially along their outer edges.

After several years of reviewing proposals for conservation subdivisions (which their local zoning requires for all residential developments encompassing more than five acres), officials in Lower Merion Township, Montgomery County, Pennsylvania, engaged the Natural Lands Trust to prepare a model Maintenance and Operations Plan on which developers may base their proposals for ongoing land stewardship activities. Such an approach, clarifying what the municipality wants while helping applicants to satisfy township requirements, is helpful to all parties involved.

Chapter 5

Conservation Subdivisions: Application Documents, Design Process, and Conservation Land Design Standards

This chapter describes the application procedures and illustrates the design process through which conservation subdivisions are recommended to be laid out. It also discusses a set of greenway standards to ensure that the conservation land within such subdivisions includes those elements the community values most highly, in a manner that will enable these resource areas to become part of a community-wide network of protected lands.

These application procedures, design processes, and greenway standards should all be incorporated into the municipality's Subdivision Ordinance. That document forms the third and final "leg" of the regulatory stool that local officials need to have in place if they are to implement the conservation approach to development design advocated in this book. (The other two "legs" are the Comprehensive Plan and the Zoning Ordinance, described in Chapters 3 and 4, respectively.)

In the course of looking at this chapter, readers will observe the special four-step approach that was used to lay out the various conservation subdivision options illustrated in the preceding chapter. This is the methodology that is reflected in the model ordinance language contained in Appendix 3, and it is the process that participants in Design Exercise 2 are encouraged to use as they design their own subdivisions around the central organizing principle of land conservation.

Basic Required Application Documents

Conservation subdivision design begins very logically with two kinds of maps or plans that applicants must submit at the beginning of the application process. These two maps or plans are described below (other key documents required later in the process are described further on in this chapter):

- A *context map* of the subject property in its surrounding neighborhood, showing various kinds of major resource areas or features that cross parcel lines or that are located on adjoining lands.
- A *detailed site resources map* of the proposed development site identifying all the special or noteworthy elements of the natural and cultural landscape, including all features of environmental, historic, or scenic value. This map differs from those typically required in subdivision ordinances because of its dual emphasis on constrained lands (wet, floodprone, steep lands—which most ordinances require to be delineated) and lands without such constraints but having other more positive characteristics that make them stand out in one way or another (which most ordinances neglect to consider).

Site Context Map

The Site Context Map varies in scale according to the size of the parcel to be subdivided. For properties of less than 100 acres, this context map should be drawn at the scale of 1 inch = 200 feet and should extend outward 1,000 feet from the parcel in question. In the case of larger properties, the scale drops to 1 inch = 400 feet but the map extends farther, up to 2,000 feet away. In both cases the infor-

mation to be provided is the same, and it enables planning commission members to understand the site in relation to what is occurring on its surrounding properties. This is most important when linear elements, such as stream valleys, floodplains, ridgelines, wildlife migration routes, historic road tracks or traces, trails, or utility easements, are involved. Blocks of active farmland (particularly prime soils) and woodland (especially mature tree stands) are also important to discern at the neighborhood level to help guide decisions regarding the most appropriate areas to conserve on the proposed development site. Most of the data required on the site context map are readily available from published sources.

Existing Resources / Site Analysis Map

The second map required in the conservation subdivision design process is essentially an elaboration of a standard document commonly submitted when conventional developments are being proposed. However, the Existing Resources/Site Analysis Map provides more information than is typically presented for subdivisions that produce only house lots and streets. Because one of the two main purposes of conservation subdivisions is to conserve the most noteworthy features on the property, a fairly complete (but not necessarily costly) site inventory is needed. Obviously, informed decisions cannot be made when site designers and municipal reviewers are dealing with incomplete data. As with the neighborhood context map, most of the information needed to compile the site analysis map is readily available from existing published sources and therefore should not be economically burdensome for applicants to produce. In a very real sense, *this map is perhaps the single most important document in the subdivision design process because it provides the information base on which every major design decision turns.* (The information that is typically required on these inventory plans can be seen later in this chapter in Figures 5-5 and 5-6.)

LANDOWNER INVOLVEMENT IN SITE ANALYSIS MAP

Many of the special features of interest to site designers will be known to the landowner, who should always be consulted. Landowners typically possess a wealth of information about their properties and can bring a personal familiarity to the design process based on a deep knowledge that comes from their being on the land during every season over a number of years. They will often know exactly where the largest trees are located, where wildlife can be seen at different times of the day and the year, where the seasonally damp areas (such as springtime "seeps" and vernal pools) can be found, and where the most favorable soil conditions are likely to be encountered (based on farming experience or places that burrowing animals prefer to inhabit). The landowner may well also know the locations of meadows or woodlands where particular wildflowers grow, and where any historic features (such as stone walls, cellar holes, or abandoned roads) exist. In short, landowners are likely to be very helpful in identifying those "places of the heart" that give each property its special character or significance. When such elements are incorporated into the design of local conservation areas, the very qualities that attract people to the community will be carefully protected for all later generations to quietly enjoy.

Elements of Existing Resources/Site Analysis Maps: Significance and Sources

The following sections describe the significance of each of the elements or resources that should be identified and shown on Existing Resources/Site Analysis Maps, and they provide information as to where these data can be readily obtained, usually at little cost to the applicant. The various resource areas are grouped into two categories. The first, "Primary Conservation Areas," includes inherently unbuildable lands that are unfit for development. Other resources fall into the category of "Secondary Conservation Areas," which comprises noteworthy elements of the property that are not wet, floodprone, or steep but that should still be considered for conservation purposes. If a community-wide Natural Resources Inventory has been completed as part of the municipality's Comprehensive Plan, that would be the best place to start. The elements to be identified and shown on the Existing Resources/Site Analysis Map include the following:

- wetlands and floodplains
- slopes
- soils
- significant wildlife habitats
- woodlands
- farmland
- historic, archaeological, and cultural features
- views into and out from the site
- groundwater recharge areas

Wetlands

All wetlands should be identified, together with dry, upland buffer areas around them. To the extent that land in such buffer areas would be buildable under federal, state, or local regulations, full density credit would be granted for applicants to use in other locations on their sites. As noted in several other parts of this book, these buffers perform a number of significant functions, such as filtering stormwater runoff, providing critical habitat at the land–water interface, and offering opportunities for wildlife travel corridors and informal walking trails for the immediate neighborhood.

Although the general location of wetland soils can be estimated from the medium-intensity soil survey maps described earlier, or from the National Wetlands Inventory maps published by the U.S.

Fish and Wildlife Service of the Department of the Interior, an on-site delineation by a wetlands specialist will be necessary at some point in the process to provide greater detail. If the applicant simply wants to sketch a rough layout first, to get an approximate idea of the site's potential for conservation subdivision design, these materials will probably be sufficient. However, if he or she wishes to submit a concept plan on which more detailed layouts will be closely based, on-site investigations by appropriate specialists are advisable. Since these studies will eventually be required, they might as well be done as early in the design process as possible to improve the accuracy of every planning step along the way.

Floodplains

Although some municipalities currently allow new structures to be built in floodplain areas provided they are elevated on specially engineered piers, this book recommends against continuation of that practice because it is inherently unsafe and is contrary to broadly accepted principles of sound planning. However, in such communities where floodplain building is allowed, a density bonus—in addition to full density credit—should be offered to encourage developers in those areas to locate new structures, whenever practicable, beyond the 100-year floodplain, as shown on maps published by the Federal Emergency Management Agency (FEMA). On unwooded sites, views to the water will remain essentially the same, while on parcels with intervening woodlands, views can be substantially opened by removing lower tree limbs, an accommodation to developers that strikes a better balance than would otherwise be achievable. Unless wetlands are also present, construction could begin fairly close to the edge of these floodplains. A more effective measure would be to amend zoning to require that new buildings be set back outside all floodplains wherever feasible, with appropriate, internally transferable density credits to avoid the "takings" issue.

Slopes

Because sloping terrain is prone to severe erosion if disturbed, slopes over 25 percent should be avoided for clearing, regrading or construction. Slopes of between 15 percent and 25 percent require special site planning and should also be avoided whenever practicable. Erosion and the overland flow of soil sediments into streams, rivers, ponds, and lakes are detrimental to water quality and aquatic life. Because of the difficulty of logging on steeply sloping land, these areas are frequently also prime locations for mature woodlands and a diverse array of woodland plants and wildflowers. Although slope maps are not published, they can be easily prepared by an engineer, planner, or landscape architect working from readily available topographic sheets printed by the U.S. Geological Survey.

Soils

When on-site sewage disposal is proposed, the most suitable soils for filtering effluent (whether from individual or community filter beds, or from "spray irrigation" or "constructed wetland" systems) are one of the most significant resources around which development should be organized. These locations should be identified and targeted for such purposes, including "reserve areas" for use if primary areas eventually become saturated. The most favorable soils for septic disposal are found where the seasonal high water table or the impervious layer is four or more feet from the surface and possess a medium texture, neither too fine and silty (impeding drainage) nor too coarse and gravelly (providing little filtration).

Other typical limiting conditions involve steepness or stoniness. "Medium-intensity" soil survey maps are available from local county agents of the USDA Natural Resource Conservation Service (NRCS), formerly the Soil Conservation Service (SCS). These maps, which appear in most county soil surveys, are usually quite accurate down to about two acres, meaning that areas smaller than this can differ from the mapped category by being either less favorable or more suitable for the intended purpose than the map portrays. This level of mapping is generally quite adequate for identifying, in a broad-brush manner, the Potential Development Areas shown on the drawings later in this chapter. For purposes of identifying soils that would be suitable for subsurface sewage disposal, the accuracy of the NRCS maps can be either greater or lesser than the two-acre standard, depending on the internal consistency of individual soil types, which can vary from region to region. When dealing with soil types that are highly variable over short distances (such as the shallow-to-bedrock soils of the Pocono Plateau, for example), special site-specific "high-intensity" soil surveys, accurate down to one-tenth of an acre, are strongly recommended at this stage in the design. (As this kind of detailed information eventually will be needed during the review process, when individual house sites and lot lines are proposed, such a requirement would not add to total project costs.)

Another instance in which on-site testing would be desirable is when the soil types occurring on a property are borderline in their suitability for sewage treatment. For example, in areas where septic system regulations require a minimum depth of 24 inches of *natural* soil above the impervious layer or the seasonal high water table, NRCS soil survey categories that include soils ranging from 18 to 36 inches in this vertical dimension will not be sufficiently detailed for the site designer, who will need the results of some on-site testing before he or she can do a good job of identifying viable house sites and lot boundaries. (This is true even when the septic systems are proposed to be situated within the undivided open space, because the locations of the best soils for such facilities play a role in determining where homes can or should be sited.)

Even when sewage will be discharged off site, the medium-intensity maps in county soil surveys are a valuable resource, as they will show locations where basements can be built without flooding and where wetlands can be expected. While they are not a substitute for a detailed wetlands analysis, these NRCS maps will show approxi-mate locations of wetlands through their "very poorly drained" classification (which means that the land is occupied by standing water for at least several months every year). The next wettest soil class, "poorly drained," is a similarly good indicator of the presence of hydric soils where seasonal water tables close to the surface make cellars impractical and road construction more costly.

Significant Wildlife Habitats

Habitats of threatened or endangered wildlife species form part of the Primary Conservation Area of any site and should be designed around and buffered. Wildlife travel corridors and overwintering areas that are known or believed to exist by wildlife professionals (such as local game wardens) should be protected by inclusion in the conservation areas designated within the development. Locations that have been officially documented by the state's Natural Diversity Inventory or on any county-level inventories should be identified on the development plan and buffered with additional open space, if feasible, for added protection.

One of the greater challenges facing wildlife managers today involves minimizing the continued fragmentation of natural areas caused by new development, which at best often safeguards only isolated "islands" of habitat without maintaining essential land and water connections needed on a regular basis by native animals. The importance of creating continuous greenways along water bodies and watercourses lies primarily in their habitat conservation benefits (in addition to water quality protection and recreational trail opportunities). When isolated wildlife populations dwindle below a certain number (because their habitat has been fragmented and diminished to the point that it is unable to provide adequate food, water, and shelter), there is great danger that they will fall below their "minimum viable population" level and will disappear entirely from the locality.

Other habitats, such as vernal pools, belong in Secondary Conservation Areas to whatever extent is feasible so that most of them will be safeguarded as well, reinforcing the "web of life" in the area's natural ecosystem. In both cases, of course, full density credit is allowed for all otherwise buildable land designated for conservation uses.

Woodlands and Vegetation Patterns

Woodlands occurring on wetland soils or on steep slopes are addressed above and should be designated as Primary Conservation Areas on the Existing Resources/Site Analysis Map. Those located on higher, flatter terrain that is easily buildable sometimes contain areas of mature timber stands worth protecting. To the maximum extent practicable, such areas should become Secondary Conservation Areas to be designed around.

In largely agrarian areas where the remaining forested land is a patchwork of remnant woods, efforts should be taken to conserve as much of the woodlands as possible, along with hedgerows. Although their wildlife habitat value has been much diminished from what it once was, these patchy woodlands can still provide breeding and feeding opportunities for many species of birds and small mammals. In areas where woodlands constitute the primary land cover, Secondary Conservation Areas might include the most mature stands or places where unusual species or special habitats occur.

Because of rising costs of woodland clearing and stump disposal—estimated to be $10,000 per acre by one Pennsylvania developer—and a growing preference among many home buyers for wooded house lots offering greater privacy and requiring less maintenance, the goal of minimizing woodland clearing is likely to be abetted by market forces in the future.

The best sources for defining the extent of woodlands, hedgerows, or tree lines are the vertical aerial photographs that are commonly available through county offices of the USDA Natural Resource Conservation Service. These may be ordered as enlargements at working scales (such as 1 inch = 100 feet) and are indispensable in accurately locating not only tree stands but even individual trees (in meadows or fields, or alongside roads). Such photos also provide data on the location of coniferous and deciduous tree stands. On sites that are predominantly wooded, there is no substitute for requiring that applicants' engineers conduct tree surveys showing locations of trees over a certain diameter (say 12 inches), by species. Although such a requirement would have been unreasonable in most situations ten years ago, technological advances—such as the development of global positioning systems (GPS)—enable engineers and surveyors to pinpoint tree locations very easily by clicking on each tree over a certain girth.

This kind of detail enables site designers to take maximum advantage of these landscape elements, which can add immense value and enjoyment to new neighborhoods. Even a simple line of trees between abandoned fields is a feature worth designing around for its value in privacy screening, the welcome shade it casts in summer, and the limited habitat it provides.

In open-field situations where the original vegetation patterns have long since disappeared, two resources can help site designers. The first and simplest are the aerial photos mentioned above, particularly those taken in late winter or early spring, showing dark areas indicating seasonally saturated soils. These wet "stains" indicate the presence of former streams or drainages that may have been diverted or dried up after the installation of tiles or subsurface drains by the farmer or his precedessors. These areas are the logical locations for siting revegetated greenway corridors running through the development, with possible connections to similar open spaces crossing neighboring properties slated for future housing. Tree and shrub species particularly appropriate for such areas include red maple, sycamore, sweet gum, willows, larch, hemlock, ironwood, red-osier dogwood, and winter-

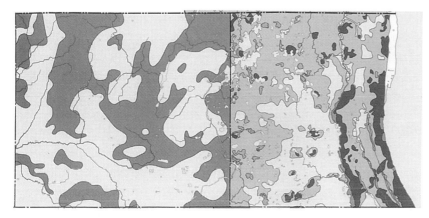

Figure 5-1. The presettlement vegetation pattern in an area lying north and northwest of Chicago has been mapped as part of the publication *Chicago Wilderness: An Atlas of Biodiversity.* It shows oak woodlands, savannah, prairie, wetlands, and dune complexes. Where the land has not yet been developed it has typically been cleared for agriculture or grown into woodland. Although relatively little remains of the presettlement vegetation, prairies and savannahs can be restored as part of management plans for conservation land in subdivisions based on the Growing Greener concept.

berry. An example of a subdivision "parkway" linear open space element based on such photo analysis can be seen in Figure 704D-39 in the Illustrated Design Principles in Appendix 3.

A second source for such information is maps of "presettlement vegetation patterns" such as those published at the township level by the state of Michigan. These kinds of maps, which are also available for parts of other midwestern states such as Illinois and Minnesota, provide valuable information regarding the original location of forests, savannahs, grasslands, and so on, and can therefore be enormously helpful for those interested in ecological restoration (see Fig. 5-1). (See the case example descriptions of conservation subdivisions in Chapter 7, particularly those for The Fields of St. Croix and Prairie Crossing.)

Farmland

In solidly agricultural areas where there is broad agreement between landowners and local governing officials that farmland should be protected in the most effective manner—through extremely low density zoning ("effective agricultural zoning"), urban growth boundaries, and the transfer of development rights—the design approach to subdivisions advocated in this book will have limited applicability. (For example, conservation subdivision design could still be useful in buffering developments located along the outer edge of urban growth areas where house lots would otherwise directly abut working farmland. This approach also has great applicability within urban growth areas where neighborhood parks and open space are desired aspects of the new high-density subdivisions.)

In other areas where court decisions have set density limitations at a much more suburban level (such as several acres per dwelling), the prospect for preserving a viable agricultural land base over the long term is much slimmer. In such areas the most that can probably be anticipated is that a certain percentage of farmland will remain in production through a variety of techniques such as the purchase of development rights (PDRs), the transfer of development rights (TDRs), and conservation subdivision design. Of these three, the latter appears to offer the most practical alternative, given constraints on public funding for PDRs and the numerous institutional and market problems associated with TDRs conducted on a municipal level.

According to many state environmental agencies, commercial agriculture frequently contributes to water quality problems in the groundwater and surface waters of many farming counties. However, farmers could be made more aware of a variety of technical ways in which they could operate their farms for high crop yields in an environmentally sensitive manner. Spreading manure in appropriate amounts and at the right time and allowing untilled filter strips to grow along streambanks and drainage channels are two such examples.

In areas where there is a distinctly less clear and strong commitment to preserve farmland than there is in jurisdictions that have already adopted strict agricultural zoning, a "toolbox" approach relying more heavily on the techniques described in this book probably offers local officials their most effective method. In such areas, where properties typically contain both fields and upland woods, environmental organizations generally advocate conserving the wooded areas as the first priority. This is because the latter provide a much richer and more diverse habitat for wildlife and because most of the original forest in such areas has already been cleared away for commercial agriculture, creating hot, dry, well-drained monocultural fields in place of shady woodlands, wetlands, and natural meadows supporting a wider variety of wildlife.

Former fields can be converted easily to wildlife meadows where many species of native grasses, wildflowers, and shrubs can provide cover, food, and habitat for birds and small mammals (as has been done at the Gwynedd Wildlife Preserve of the Natural Lands Trust in Upper and Lower Gwynedd Townships, Montgomery County, Pennsylvania). In metropolitan fringe areas, it is also possible to retain some of this land in specialized high-value crops, such as vegetables, fruit, and nursery stock. Such arrangements seem to work best on larger sites when overall building densities are relatively low, in the range of one acre or more per dwelling. One example is the highly successful Farmview development in Bucks County, Pennsylvania, where Realen Homes built on half-acre lots (half the size usually required under existing one-acre zoning), leaving nearly 150 of its 300 tillable acres in crops (and donating that conservation area to a local land trust). This was the fastest selling development in its price range in the county, largely because people are buying permanent views of open space when they purchase lots in this subdivision. Several other developers have since copied Realen's example, boosting the amount of farmland protected through conservation subdivision design to about 500 acres within a recent five-year pe-

riod. Because land trusts can offer relatively attractive terms (low rents just to cover property taxes, and long leases), they are often in a better position than most rural landowners to set conditions regarding the use of pesticides, manure, and so on, and to be more selective about whom they lease to.

Historic, Archaeological, and Cultural Features

Landowners and local historians or historical groups should always be consulted after a review of official lists such as the National Register of Historic Places, the corresponding "State Register," and inventories compiled by county historic preservation staff. In most cases old buildings, ruins, cellar holes, earthworks, stone walls, burial grounds, and other resources will be of local rather than county-wide or regional importance. Nevertheless, as with small tree groups or nesting areas of relatively common waterfowl, it is worthwhile to steer roads, houses, and lawns to other parts of the development site to avoid impacting them when other, more suitable, locations exist for these new uses.

Because even outstanding structures listed on the National Register are not protected from demolition (unless federal funds would be involved, or unless they are also governed by a strict local historic district ordinance), these resources possess none of the legal status accorded to environmentally sensitive wetlands or floodplains, and therefore should be considered as part of the Secondary Conservation Areas. In places possessing features such as stone walls marking old field patterns and sites of battles or skirmishes during past wars, such areas would be classified in the same way—placed within the open space so that they may remain intact and also be buffered wherever appropriate.

As no building density value is lost through this approach, it makes good sense even from a business point of view. On a wooded tract in Spotsylvania County, Virginia, one developer located his lot lines and houses to avoid disturbing or too closely encroaching on an old mill site and lengthy earthen trenches used during the Civil War. Similar steps are being taken in Currituck County, North Carolina, where the owner of a development parcel bordering Currituck Sound has expressed interest in utilizing these creative design techniques to avoid impacting a significant Woodland Era Native American site, while also increasing the number of new homes that would face onto the water across a waterside conservation area.

Views Into and Out from the Site

This aspect of site design is often one of the most important from the perspectives of both the developer and the general public, who tend to see properties from different vantage points. Developers usually wish to maximize attractive views outward from potential house sites, while the public typically desires that new development be as visually inconspicuous as possible. Although these two objectives can easily conflict, it is often possible for development to be sited or buffered in such a way that everybody's principal interests are accommodated.

From a developer's point of view, it is desirable to maximize the number of homes with attractive views. This can often be achieved in creative ways that are less disruptive than the results produced through conventional platting. In areas with visually prominent ridges on which homes may be perched, Secondary Conservation Areas might include the ridgetops, requiring that new development be located sufficiently below the crest that the horizon will continue to be defined by the ridgeline rather than by rooftops. For situations in which this is not feasible because of steeply sloping hillsides or parcel configurations, houses should be designed with a low profile, and sufficient woodlands should be retained (or planted) around and behind them to soften their visual impact. Large clear-cuts to open up panoramic views should also be prohibited, and cutting should be limited to "view tunnels" from principal rooms and thinning of lower limbs to create "view holes" through the foliage.

In lakefront or riparian locations offering views of water bodies or wetlands, the design procedures recommended in this book would generally allow a greater number of such lots, with views through a wooded greenway where lower limbs may be removed so that the water (or wetlands) would be visible from living room windows. In addition to these "view lots," a very large proportion of the remaining lots in a well-designed conservation subdivision will abut or face onto other types of open space, such as commons, greens, ponds, meadows, and woodlands. Given the alternative of a conventional development—in which one-third of the lots have immediate views of the water and the other two-thirds have immediate views of their neighbors' picture windows or back yards—and a conservation subdivision—in which the vast majority of lots enjoy views of water, meadows, greens, woods, or other natural features—the choice seems clear. The large *total* number of view lots in a conservation subdivision, including those with water views filtered through greenway buffers and views from interior lots bordering other kinds of open space, makes conservation subdivisions more desirable and marketable than developments consisting of a fringe of waterfront lots and many "back lots" having no views of anything except other house lots.

This design approach benefits not only developers and realtors but also future residents and the general public. Greenway buffers provide the best of both worlds, helping to screen new waterfront development while not obstructing important views. One of the best examples of this is Woodlake in Midlothian, Virginia, 18 miles southwest of Richmond. Home sales have been brisk in both waterfront and interior locations in this award-winning development, in which a 75-foot-deep greenway runs along the edge of the water, between Woodlake's most expensive homes and the Swift Creek Reservoir, providing a delightful walking or bicycling experience for those who live adjacent to the greenway as well as residents of interior lots (where single-family homes sell for as little as $80,000). The water is clearly visible through the wooded buffer from all abutting homes, while habitat and water quality are protected to a much higher degree than would have been the case with conventional development.

The highly successful Woodlake example demonstrates that providing water views and greenway buffers are not mutually exclusive, and it suggests a new planning principle for waterside development: each site should be laid out with greenway buffers, *as if the adjacent water body were a reservoir supplying drinking water to the community.*

As pointed out earlier, views of farmland preserved within conservation subdivisions can also add value to new house lots; and to the extent that home sites are located away from existing public roads, at the far edges of fields as seen from those thoroughfares, some rural character can be maintained with each new development. See Figure 5-13 later in this chapter for an illustration of how the foreground meadow design approach can help to minimize the visual impact of new development on properties with open land fronting onto public roads.

Groundwater Resources and Their Recharge Areas

Aquifers are underground water reserves occupying billions of tiny spaces between sand grains and other soil particles, including gravel. These reserves are replenished when precipitation and surface water seep downward through well-drained deposits of sand or gravel or at low points in the landscape such as wetlands. Present groundwater levels in some low-lying farming areas are several feet lower than they were before drainage ditches and tiles were installed to make formerly wet ground suitable for commercial agriculture. These areas are buildable today for structures without basements and where sewage is disposed of through public sewers or with central sewerage linked with a private disposal facility (such as spray irrigation) located on higher, drier ground on other parts of the site (or on a neighboring property). Since stormwater detention ponds often dip into areas of high groundwater, runoff entering them can recharge the underlying aquifer with dissolved pollutants (typically excess nutrients from agricultural or lawn fertilizers), requiring special buffering along drainage swales to remove as much of these substances as possible.

Although many aquifer recharge areas consist of soils that are not inherently unbuildable (such as excessively drained sands and gravels and certain of the less severe hydric soils), they should be avoided for construction when other parts of the property are available and are less constrained by environmental factors. As with all other kinds of buildable land that are placed into natural open space in a creative development plan, full density credit should generally be allowed for these soils (when their buildability is not in question, and typically when wastewater is proposed to be treated in a central location or off site).

When it is not feasible to rearrange the development pattern within a site to minimize such impacts, density transfers to neighboring properties (under a "landowner compact" agreement between two or more adjoining landowners, or under a TDR plan involving nonadjacent parcels) should be thoroughly explored. Sometimes these strategies can be combined, each playing a partial role in the process of creative development and land conservation. (Landowner compacts are described in Appendix 2, which provides model language for comprehensive plans. See also Arendt et al. 1994.)

Techniques to augment aquifer recharge through conservation design are further detailed in Chapter 6.

Integrating the Information Layers and Ranking Site Features for Conservation Priority

Once all the pertinent resources have been identified, located, and evaluated in terms of their significance, they must be drawn onto overlay sheets (typically tracing paper) and viewed together. Because ten sheets of even the lightest tracing paper would be too dense to show all the underlying information, even if they were placed on a light table (or taped to a large window on a sunny day), it is recommended that several types of features be drawn onto the same sheet— preferably features that do not coincide in terms of their location on the site. (If clear acetate sheets are available for this purpose, they would be the easiest materials to use.) A composite map can eventually be prepared by looking at all the information layers together, to see the overall pattern of potential conservation areas.

All *buildable* land will consist of those areas *not* limited by the basic constraints posed by the Primary Conservation Areas (wetlands, floodplains, and steep slopes), and these will emerge clearly as the appropriate sheets are placed together.

After integrating these most basic and critical information layers, which typically constitute only a small fraction of any site, the remaining land is examined with regard to the other layers. This residual land to be considered for conservation will therefore consist of one or more of the other resource types, which must be prioritized to select those that are the most critical, significant, or irreplaceable. Those that meet such tests are placed into Secondary Conservation Areas, which typically consume no more than half the buildable land on the site, leaving the other half for homes, yards, and streets.

Ranking Site Features for Conservation Priority

As a rule of thumb, the first four features listed above—wetlands, floodplains, slopes, and soils—take first priority for inclusion in the designated open space, as they represent highly sensitive environmental resources that are generally considered to be unbuildable in a legal sense, in a practical sense, or for reasons of common sense. They should be placed in Primary Conservation Areas, the first type of open space to be drawn on any site plan.

Within the second broad category of open space, called Sec-

ondary Conservation Areas, resources vary more widely in importance, vulnerability, or fragility. Within each type of resource there are examples of greater and lesser significance, whether one is looking at woodlands (from large or mature stands or unusual species, to woods that are young, diseased, already thinned out, or degraded by invasive vines, for example); farmland (soils rated from "prime" to "of local significance"); or sites of historic, archaeological, or cultural interest (from inclusion on a federal list of buildings deemed to be eligible for nomination to the National Register, to a typical pristine example of local vernacular building traditions, to a much altered older house missing many original features).

Those features ranking among the top of their category (such as *mature* woodland or *prime* farmland) should always be included in the open space protected as Secondary Conservation Areas. When decisions must be made regarding the sacrifice of one resource to preserve another (such as developing fields to save woodlands, or vice versa), they should be based on broad community-wide or county-wide considerations. For example, if one resource type is scarcer or more unusual than another, or if it contributes to biodiversity or water quality in a more compelling way, that could provide the basis for deciding which is to be spared.

In short, priorities for conserving or developing certain kinds of resources should be based on an understanding of what is more special, unique, irreplaceable, environmentally valuable, historic, scenic, and so on, compared with other similar features or compared to different kinds of resources altogether. Although this process will always contain some subjectivity, a ratings approach can help to reduce inconsistent and arbitrary choices. Within each category it is often fairly obvious which features are the most worthy of preservation. The harder decisions usually involve comparisons between different categories, such as whether a small isolated woodland or a historic house should be designed around when it is impossible to save both.

It is the general recommendation of this book that natural areas typically take precedence over human artifacts, except in situations where the latter are clearly exceptional. The reason is that buildings can often be reconstructed or moved and can certainly be photographed and documented with measured drawings. On the other hand, it is more difficult to re-create a wetland or a mature forest because of the interrelationships among plants, animals, soil, and water that each natural site comprises. There is also a growing body of evidence that it may be nearly impossible, without intensive management, to regenerate a mature deciduous woodland in certain parts of the country, such as in southeastern Pennsylvania, for example, due to invasive vines and alien species of shrubs and trees (such as Oriental bittersweet, rosa multiflora, Japanese honeysuckle, wild grape, Tartarian honeysuckle, Norway maple, etc.) that seed themselves and infest newly afforesting areas. Of course, in certain areas with numerous and significant historic locations, such as pastures and ridges that once witnessed major conflicts in the Revolutionary War or Civil War, battle-related resources could take precedence for conservation over other types of buildable land, such as prime farmland or mature woodlands.

There will generally be special reasons in each municipality or county for favoring one resource type over another. In areas where forests cover most of the land and fields are relatively uncommon (such as through much of New England and the southern states), the most favored approach might be to locate new development among the less significant parts of the wooded uplands (without mature tree stands) and to leave farmland intact. In much of the southeastern and south-central parts of Pennsylvania, the reverse landscape pattern exists, providing a logical rationale for a policy preference that is exactly opposite the one just described. Taken in its own context, each policy should make sense for the area in which it is applied.

Special Procedural Steps Recommended for Conservation Subdivisions

For all subdivisions, but particularly those involving conservation-sensitive designs, the best results are likely to be achieved when an open and cooperative working relationship is fostered between the municipality and the applicant. Friction and conflict can be minimized through clearly stated standards and procedures in the zoning and subdivision ordinances, which can help to avoid misunderstandings about the community's expectations. The process can also be smoothed by expanding opportunities for contact and communication between applicants and the planning commission from the very beginning. Several special steps that are recommended to be incorporated into the Subdivision Ordinance are described below (with model language provided in Appendix 3).

- *Preapplication Meeting:* A preapplication meeting is encouraged between the applicant, the site designer, and the planning commission (and/or its planning consultant) to introduce the applicant to the zoning and subdivision standards and procedures, to discuss the applicant's overall objectives, and to schedule site visits, meetings, and plan submissions.
- *Site Visit:* After completing the Existing Resources/Site Analysis Map, applicants should arrange a time for planning commission members to walk the property with them, their engineer, and site designer with copies of that document in hand. The purpose of the site visit is to familiarize all parties with the property's existing conditions and special features, to identify potential site design issues, and to provide an informal opportunity to discuss site design concepts. This would be an appropriate time for the location of conservation areas (both primary and secondary) to be discussed so that a general agreement about the overall layout might be achieved from the start.

- *Sketch Plan:* Applicants should always be strongly encouraged, if not required, to submit a Sketch Plan showing at least the general location of proposed development areas and conservation areas. In some states, the enabling legislation does not allow local governments to require Sketch Plans in addition to the Preliminary Plan and the Final Plan. In such states this step should remain voluntary, as a separate procedure. Sketch Plans cost little to prepare because they involve virtually no engineering input except for a general knowledge of soil and slope conditions (which are pertinent for septic systems and street alignments). In their most basic form they may consist of simple "bubble maps" drawn on clear overlay sheets placed on top of the Existing Resources/Site Analysis Map, and for this reason they are sometimes referred to as "Sketch Plan Overlays." However they are produced, Sketch Plans provide an excellent opportunity for mutual communication at a very critical stage of the subdivision process, before large sums are expended to meet the substantial engineering requirements for detailed designs. Most applicants are understandably reluctant to modify their proposals after they have been heavily engineered because those documents represent a sizable investment of funds.

- *Conceptual Preliminary Plan:* This book recommends that municipalities return to the original intent of Preliminary Plans, as first envisioned in most states' enabling laws. Although many communities have since blurred the distinction between the "preliminary" and the "final" plan, the first document had originally been intended by legislatures to be fairly conceptual in nature and not costly to produce. On the other hand, the purpose of the Final Plan was to supply the highly detailed drawings on which construction decisions would be based.

Because developers sometimes choose to exercise their legal right not to submit Sketch Plans, this book's model ordinance language for preliminary plans defines them as essentially conceptual in nature, requiring them to provide approximate dimensions and to show approximate locations rather than very precise ones. These Conceptual Preliminary Plans are essentially the same documents as the optional Sketch Plan and they serve a similar purpose: to permit discussion on the overall concept prior to preparing expensive engineering drawings that are really not needed by municipal officials until later stages. When preparing Conceptual Preliminary Plans, applicants should be strongly encouraged to follow the special four-step design approach for laying out conservation subdivisions, as described and illustrated in the next section (and detailed in the model ordinance language in Appendix 3).

The Conceptual Preliminary Plan is followed by submission of a Detailed Final Plan in the next 90-day period. Extensions to these two periods can usually be negotiated between the applicant and the municipality fairly easily when there is an indication of good faith on both sides.

The Four-Step Approach to Designing Conservation Subdivisions

The design process for conservation subdivisions is firmly based on the detailed site information provided through the Existing Resources/Site Analysis Map, together with off-site data shown on the Context Map regarding potential linkages to resource areas on adjoining properties and the surrounding neighborhood in general. The primary purpose of this design approach is to provide landowners and developers with their full legal density in a way that conserves not only the most special features of the proposed development site, but that also helps to protect an interconnected network of conservation lands extending across the community. *The heart of this design process can be summarized as four sequential steps beginning with the all-important identification of the conservation land that should potentially be*

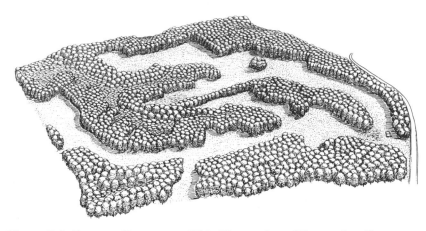

Figure 5-2. EXISTING RESOURCES: This 50-acre site will be used to illustrate how a basic conservation subdivision can be designed using the four-step approach. This is the same site that was employed in Chapter 4 to show how five different potential development-and-conservation options could be implemented under the model zoning provisions in Appendix 3 of this book.

Figure 5-3. YIELD PLAN.

protected. Those steps, which are illustrated in Figures 5-5 through 5-10, are: (1) identifying conservation areas, (2) locating house sites, (3) aligning streets and trails, and (4) drawing in the lot lines.

"Yield Plan" to Determine Density

As an alternative to deducting certain percentages of various kinds of constrained land—in order to determine the *net* developable acreage on any given tract—ordinances can establish procedures for preparing a simple "Yield Plan," as illustrated in Figure 5-3.

Under this approach, applicants submit a lightly engineered sketch showing the maximum number of lots they could reasonably expect to achieve through a conventional layout, given the presence of fundamental building constraints such as wetlands, floodplains, and steep slopes (over 25 percent). In unsewered areas, the planning commission would then require that a 10 percent sample of lots, of its choosing, be tested for on-site septic suitability. If all these lots pass, the number of lots shown on the Yield Plan is approved; but if any lots fail they are deleted and another 10 percent sample is required. Again, local officials would select those lots to be evaluated, focusing on those that appear to be the most marginal or dubious.

Figure 5-3 is a Yield Plan and Figure 5-4 illustrates what the property would look like if that Yield Plan were implemented.

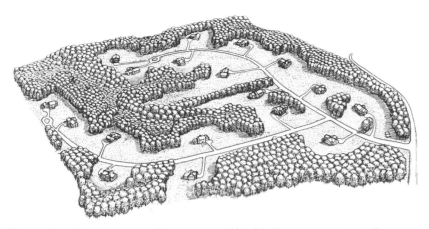

Figure 5-4. CONVENTIONAL SUBDIVISION: This bird's-eye perspective illustrates how the property would appear if the Yield Plan were built.

Step 1: Identifying Conservation Areas

Step 1, involving the delineation of lands to be conserved, is divided into two parts. Part 1 is to locate the inherently unbuildable parts of the property that are wet, floodprone, or steep (Primary Conservation Areas). Part 2 involves selecting a certain proportion (usually at least half) of the remaining relatively unconstrained land and designating that as a Secondary Conservation Area. The choice as to which elements of the site are to be so considered should be guided by clearly ranked criteria for determining conservation areas, which are discussed later in this chapter. In general, the features that are selected for inclusion in Secondary Conservation Areas are those which are the most sensitive environmentally, the most significant historically or culturally, or the most scenic.

This property's Primary Conservation Areas are fairly straightforward, consisting of well-defined wetlands and floodplains, often bordered by steeply sloping ground (see Figure 5-5). Some of these unbuildable areas also include Secondary Conservation Area elements, such as mature woods in the bottomland hardwood forest and on the

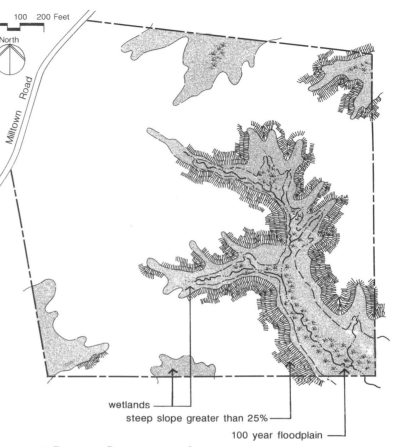

wetlands ─┐
steep slope greater than 25% ─┐
100 year floodplain ─┘

Figure 5-5. PRIMARY CONSERVATION AREAS.

steep slopes that were passed over by timber harvesters because of their limited accessibility.

Secondary Conservation Areas also include the upland woodlands, the "Great Oak," two wildflower meadows, a couple of serpentine rock outcroppings, a family cemetery, the cellar hole of the original farmstead, and a stone wall and hedgerow running across the middle of the property (see Fig. 5-6). The rural character of the site, as seen from the township road, is also defined by the open views into

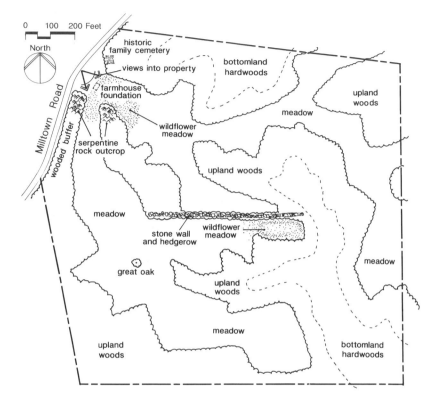

Figure 5-6. Secondary Conservation Areas.

the upper meadow and by the wooded buffer just to the south of that opening. Typically, very few of these elements would be preserved with a conventional layout, as illustrated in the Yield Plan showing the baseline density under the preexisting zoning ordinance (see Fig. 5-3).

Coincidentally, this is the general approach used by designers of highly successful golf course developments, with the basic distinction that here the subdivider preserves natural areas such as fields, meadows, and woodlands and creates informal open spaces such as neigh-

borhood commons. *Expressed in simple terms, designers of conservation subdivisions substitute greenways for fairways and provide community greens in place of putting greens.* Whether one is interested in building homes around a facility for a single sport, or arranging them in a parklike setting full of natural features that all can enjoy (including wildlife), the only practical way is to begin by defining the open space first.

When the first sketch is attempted, the site designer should not be reluctant to "greenline" more land than he or she thinks will eventually be designated as open space. This will ensure that no potentially desirable area is prematurely left out, excluding it from consideration in the design process.

This exercise will quickly identify the likely core areas of future development on the property. One should then work outward from those cores, careful to recommend for development only those other areas that appear to be least important to conserve when looking at the site as a whole (including its relationship to resources existing on neighboring parcels).

Step 2: Locating the House Sites

As with golf course developments, the next design step is to identify potential house site locations. Since it is well known that most people prefer (and are often willing to pay extra) to see open space from their windows, it makes economic sense to create as many view lots as possible and to provide usable open space within convenient walking distance from all the other houses.

One obvious way to maximize the number of view lots is to minimize their width and maximize the livability of the homes built on them through creative modifications (such as designing houses with a windowless side wall virtually abutting one side lot line, and another sidewall containing windows facing onto a wider side yard— and toward the "blind" side of the next house).

Another way to increase the number of houses with views is to design several flag-shaped lots with long narrow strips of land connecting them with the street. These lots are especially useful in odd corners of a neighborhood, such as at the end of a cul-de-sac or along a sharp curve in the street. Although they are essentially variations on wedge-shaped lots common in such situations, they often provide more usable yard space than do wedge-lots since their shape in the area where the house is situated tends to be more rectangular.

Although flag lots are most appropriate in relatively low-density subdivisions where the overall density is one acre or more per dwelling, these "flag lots" can also be useful at higher densities and should generally be permitted in all developments, with certain restrictions. To curb potential abuses, they should be limited to no more than 15 or 20 percent of the total number of lots (for instance), and when the "flag" portion is less than 10,000 square feet the planning commission should be authorized to require adequate visual screening between adjoining lots (particularly those that share a front–back boundary).

Although it is rarely possible to design layouts so that every house has a view over major open space, it is often feasible to give most houses a view of at least a minor open space, such as a small neighborhood common or village green, or several acres of trees and grass around a small pond doubling as a stormwater retention facility, attractively landscaped with native species such as red-twig dogwood shrubs.

Once the Primary and Secondary Conservation Areas have been delineated, the remaining lands that stand out as the most logical places to situate the house lots and streets are called Potential Development Areas (see Fig. 5-7).

Step 2 involves locating house sites within these Potential Development Areas in a way that maximizes the number of homes enjoying direct views of the conservation land (see Fig. 5-8).

It is clear that identifying house sites before lot lines and streets allows building locations to be carefully selected so that natural, his-

Figure 5-7. POTENTIAL DEVELOPMENT AREAS.

torical, or cultural features worth preserving, including large trees and prominent rock outcrops as well as historic or cultural features such as stone walls, cellar holes, battle trenches, and archaeological remains, can be avoided. Because it is not always possible to draw the Secondary Conservation Areas sufficiently large to include all these features, some of the less significant areas might fall into those parts of the site slated for development. However, the flexibility of this design approach enables the majority of such features—and all of the best ones—to be designed around.

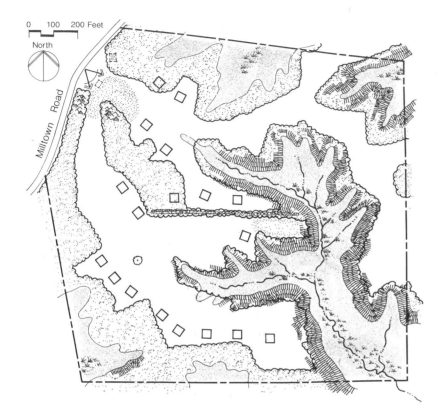

Figure 5-8. Locating House Sites.

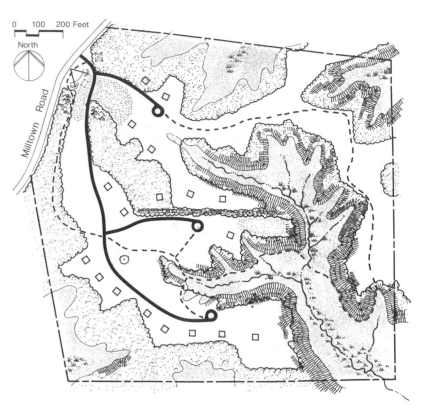

Figure 5-9. Aligning Streets and Trails.

Step 3: Aligning Streets and Trails

After the conservation land has been at least tentatively identified and potential house sites have been sketched in, the third logical step is to determine the best way to access every residence with a street system (see Fig. 5-9). This part of the exercise essentially involves "connecting the dots." Readers should note that the *single-loaded* streets (with houses on one side only) in the conservation design are not longer or more expensive than the *double-loaded* streets serving the same

number of lots in the conventional layout on the Yield Plan illustrated in Figure 5-3.

Areas with relatively level or rolling topography pose few street design challenges from an engineering standpoint, with the major considerations being to avoid crossing wetlands and to minimize the length (and cost) of new access streets. There are further considerations from an environmental perspective, such as avoiding large trees, mature tree stands, or wildlife habitats. Sometimes it is possible to split the travel lanes so that they curve apart forming an elongated, boulevard-style island between them, where a certain large tree or other natural or historic feature may be preserved and given visual prominence. (When the preservation of large trees is involved, it is essential that the entire area under the canopy's outer "drip line" be kept undisturbed from heavy construction equipment, which can easily cause permanent damage to root systems. To achieve this, temporary construction fences should be erected ten feet beyond such drip lines until all construction activity has been finished in the tree's immediate location.) An excellent example of tree and woodland preservation in a new conservation subdivision is "Garnet Oaks" in Bethel Township, Delaware County, Pennsylvania, where the developer's site designer carefully aligned streets to avoid impacting major trees and where all contractors and subcontractors were required to attend a special training seminar on tree conservation practices cosponsored by the Morris Arboretum and Realen Homes.

Step 4: Drawing in the Lot Lines

The fourth and final step is the easiest, once the conservation areas have been delineated, the house sites located, and the road alignments determined (see Fig. 5-10). At this point in the design process, drawing in the lot lines is usually little more than a formality (and one that is unnecessary in condominium developments where all land is jointly owned). Clearly the most significant aspects of a development, from the viewpoint of future residents, are how their houses relate to the open space, to each other, and to the street (see Fig. 5-11). Lot lines are the least important element in the development design process, yet they and the street pattern are typically the first items to be set down on paper.

Maintaining livability on the somewhat smaller lots needed in conservation subdivisions does not pose much of a design problem in zoning districts where the normally required lot is one or two acres. The

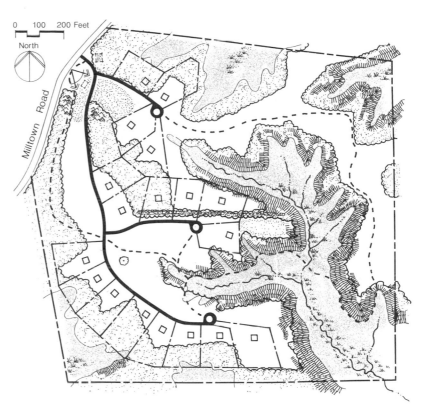

Figure 5-10. Drawing in the Lot Lines.

challenge increases as density rises and lot sizes become more compact. As mentioned above in Step 2, lot lines in high-density, single-family developments can be drawn fairly close to side walls with few or no windows, enabling larger and more usable side yards to be provided on the opposite side of the house. This approach can be taken further by building on one of the side lot lines ("zero-lot line" construction).

The issue of appropriate lot depth is directly related to the presence or absence of open space along rear lot lines. When conserva-

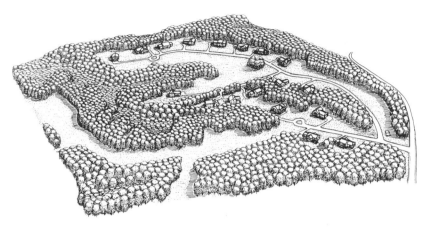

Figure 5-11. Bird's-eye perspective illustrating a conservation subdivision using the four-step design approach.

tion land is located immediately behind them, there is good justification for shortening proposed house lots, as the open space visually extends the perceived depth of back yards.

Therefore, a logical argument can be made to reduce both the width and the depth of lots where houses are located off center (i.e., closer to one side line, thereby maximizing one side yard) and where lots abut conservation areas behind them. In developments with public sewerage or with private central treatment facilities (such as "spray irrigation"), where zoning densities might allow one dwelling per 20,000 square feet of land, 75 percent open space can be achieved by designing house lots of 5,000 square feet. These smaller, village-scale lots are often deemed to be more desirable than conventional half-acre lots by several distinct groups of potential home buyers—such as empty-nesters, young couples, and single parents with a child or two—who want some private outdoor living space but who also wish to minimize their yard maintenance responsibilities. This is especially true when the lots back up to protected open space, which psychologically enlarges the dimensions of the actual lot.

Architects, landscape architects, and site designers have for many years recognized that the most efficient use of a house lot occurs when the house is located "off center and up front." Equal side yards generally produce two functionally useless areas on lots narrower than 80 feet, and front yards are practically useless in any case because they are so much within the public view. Unless homes are located along heavily traveled streets with considerable traffic noise, there is little need for deep front setbacks to provide buffering. Placing homes where front porches or stoops are within conversational distance of sidewalks helps create conditions for friendlier neighborhoods, where passersby can exchange pleasantries with residents sitting on porches on weekend afternoons or summer evenings.

Note on Design Sequence for Village Layouts

The above sequence of steps is generally modified in situations where a more formal, neo-traditional, or village-type layout is desired, as in Option 5 developments. In such cases, Step 2 becomes the location of streets and squares followed by the location of house sites. Whereas the relationship between homes and open space is of the greatest importance in more rural conservation subdivisions, the relationship between buildings, streets, and squares is the dominant design consideration in the neo-traditional approach to site design. Both design approaches place more emphasis on the designation of public open space and on the provision of sidewalks, footpaths, and trails—in an effort to foster a pedestrian-friendly community atmosphere—compared with conventional suburban "cookie-cutter" layouts offering just house lots and streets.

Technical Notes on Street Design

A number of more technical recommendations regarding street design considerations are provided below. Many of these points can be seen by closely examining Figure 5-10 and by consulting Section 704 on illustrated design principles in Appendix 3.

- *Avoiding Long Straight Segments.* From an aesthetic and speed control perspective, it is important to avoid long straight street segments. Curving roads in an informal rural cluster layout or shorter straight segments connected by 90-degree and 135-degree bends in a more formal or traditional townlike arrangement are preferable. (Variations that combine elements of these approaches are also possible, such as short curvilinear segments terminating in frequent intersections where the choices are to turn left or right, thereby making it more difficult for motorists to travel at excessive speeds.)

- *Providing "Terminal Vistas."* Whenever possible, street systems should be designed so that their curvature or alignment produces *terminal vistas of open space elements,* such as village greens, water features, meadows, or playing fields. (In Figure 5-10, street vistas are terminated by meadows and woodlands generally, but also specifically by a large free-standing oak tree.) This technique will maximize the visual impact of such areas so that residents and visitors will correctly perceive the conservation emphasis that has guided the development design and will recognize the subdivision as contributing positively to the community's open space goals. The objects of these vistas are often in the direct line of sight at "T" intersections but can also be provided on land along the *outside* edge of street curves.

- *Introducing "Reverse Curves."* The use of S-shaped "reverse curves" in street design is advised because of their grace and beauty. However, this serpentine alignment should be employed in conjunction with relatively long horizontal curve radii (at least 250 feet) and on streets where traffic speed will not generally exceed 30 mph. The common prohibition against reverse curves in municipal street standards is a carryover from the highway design manuals on which many such ordinances were based. While reverse curves without

intervening straight sections (or tangents) can be unsafe for high-speed traffic, a completely different situation exists for local access streets in residential subdivisions.

- *"Single-Loading" Certain Street Segments.* Another design approach that has proven to be of value in both land conservation and real estate marketing is the use of "single-loaded streets." This is a technical term describing streets having houses on only one side. When lots are trimmed down in width, developers can easily reserve certain street lengths for single-loading—such as alongside conservation areas or around village greens or commons—without increasing their average house lot to street length ratios. In Figure 5-10, almost the entire street length is single-loaded (or in some places without house lots on either side), yet its overall length is appreciably shorter than the street system required to access conventional large lots (see Fig. 5-3).

  Single-loading provides all subdivision residents with welcome views of their conservation land as they drive, bike, jog, or walk through their neighborhood on a daily basis, increasing everyone's quality of life and property values. Sales records in subdivisions featuring single-loaded streets show that homes located there sell faster and for premium prices compared with similar houses elsewhere in the development. Not surprisingly, when all the streets in a subdivision are double-loaded (as is often the case in many unimaginatively designed "cluster" developments), conservation areas are essentially hidden behind continuous rows of house lots and the streetscape takes on a very ordinary appearance, much like those found in conventional "checkerboard" subdivisions.

- *"T" Intersections.* In order to keep traffic speeds as low as possible, residential streets that interconnect with other streets should do so through T-shaped intersections where vehicles cannot proceed forward in a straight line but must instead come to a full stop and turn to the left or right. This concept is shown in Section 704 of

Appendix 3 on illustrated design principles, particularly Figures 704D-24, 704D-27, and 704D-37. These terminating T's should occur every one to three blocks, except on designated major collector streets (for which boulevard design as shown in Figure 704D-68 is recommended).

- *Street and Trail Connections.* Streets serving new developments should, whenever possible, be designed to *connect with other parts of the neighborhood and with adjoining properties* that are potentially developable in the future. Although many developers strongly resist such connections, preferring to market their houses as being in self-contained neighborhoods, the lack of connecting streets between developments ultimately frustrates normal travel between neighborhoods, forcing everyone back out onto the community's principal road system to travel to homes in adjacent subdivisions. One way of addressing this need is to provide cul-de-sacs with "stub-street" extensions to the adjoining properties, to facilitate future connections. In circumstances where cul-de-sacs are unavoidable (typically for topographic reasons, as in the demonstration site illustrated in this chapter), they should always be provided with pedestrian and bike linkages to other nearby streets or to a neighborhood trail system. Where space permits, they should also be designed with a central island where existing trees have been preserved or where native species trees, shrubs, and wildflowers can be planted. Where additional off-street parking is needed, these cul-de-sacs can also function as well-treed "parking courts."

Preserving Rural Character Through "Foreground Meadows"

One interesting way to employ single-loaded streets in open-field situations is to use them in creating foreground meadows bordering the public road that serves the development. Upon entering a conservation subdivision laid out in this manner, one's first view would be of a wildflower meadow (or horse pasture), with homes located at the

Figure 5-12. View across a protected meadow toward a group of new homes built at the edge of the woods. This view, from a township road, typifies the pattern of conservation and development represented by the examples illustrated in Figure 5-13.

far end of this open space, facing this landscape feature (see Figs. 5-12 and 5-13). If such a meadow or pasture were bordered instead by a double-loaded street curving around behind it, the view from the public road, the subdivision street, and the meadow would be of house backs, typically dominated by sliding glass doors, pressure-treated decks, and asymmetrical arrangements of windows (perhaps further graced by swing sets and toolsheds as well). Not only do most new houses look far better from the front, where builders spend extra money creating "curb appeal," residents also prefer the back yard privacy provided by not turning their rear walls toward the public road in this far too typical manner.

Design of Conservation Lands

Another key feature of the conservation subdivision ordinance is the provision of comprehensive standards governing the location and layout of lands to be conserved through the subdivision process. (Guidance on ownership options and management responsibilities is also critically im-

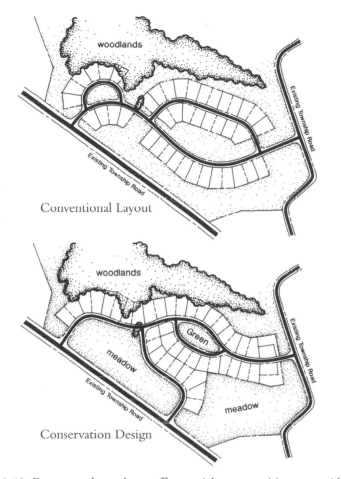

Figure 5-13. Foreground meadows offer special opportunities to provide attractive buffers between new homes and existing thoroughfares bordering the subdivision. In the above two examples, where a typical "suburban cluster" approach on the left is contrasted with a "conservation design" with the same number of house lots, it is worth noting that the preferred approach on the right does not require any additional street length, nor does it utilize lots that are narrower. Another unusual feature, not central to the concept of foreground meadows, is the use of two flag lots, on the extreme right, paired with two frontage lots, so that all four homes would face the existing township road across a smaller grassy expanse. This provides a slightly more formal and attractive secondary entrance to the subdivision, compared with side yards.

portant and is covered in Chapter 4.) Establishing standards for what to include in conservation lands and how they should be configured is just as logical and essential as setting standards for development areas, such as area bulk requirements and street specifications.

Location of Conservation Lands

Ideally the lands delineated for conservation purposes within individual subdivision proposals will correspond at least generally with a community-wide Map of Potential Conservation Lands, adopted by reference as part of the Comprehensive Plan, as described in Chapter 3. As mentioned in that earlier chapter, the principal value of such a map is to help the community protect an interconnected network of open spaces, such as along stream valleys, wildlife corridors, ridgelines, and blocks of woodlands or prime farmland. In this way the conservation lands in each new subdivision would constitute "building blocks" in the community's overall greenway strategy. New subdivisions designed under any of the five options described in Chapter 4 should, at minimum, contain Primary Conservation Areas comprising all land having severe environmental constraints, such as wetlands, floodplains, and steep slopes. In addition, for subdivisions following Options 1, 2, and 5, some 50 to 70 percent of the remaining land should also be designated as Secondary Conservation Areas. These areas would typically include significant aspects of the property such as mature woodlands, wildlife habitat and travel corridors, prime farmland, historic or cultural features, and scenic viewsheds from public roads.

Layout of Conservation Lands

The three basic principles of designing conservation areas are described and illustrated as follows (see Fig. 5-14):

• *Conservation areas should include the most sensitive resource areas of a*

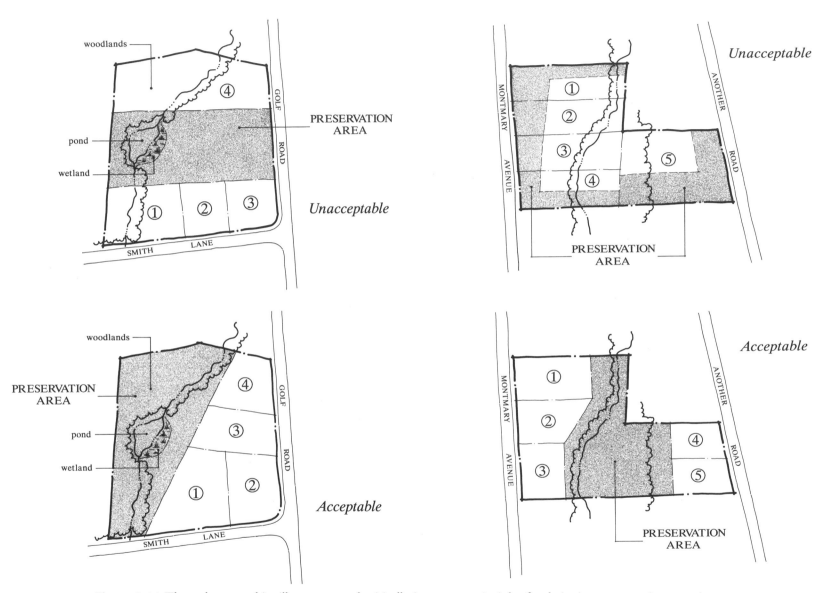

Figure 5-14. These three graphics illustrate several critically important principles for designing conservation areas in new subdivisions so that the development impact on their ecological and habitat values would be minimized. Preservation areas should include the most sensitive resource areas of the property (left); be designed as one large block of land with logical straight forward boundaries (right); be designed as part of a larger continuous and integrated open space system (facing page).

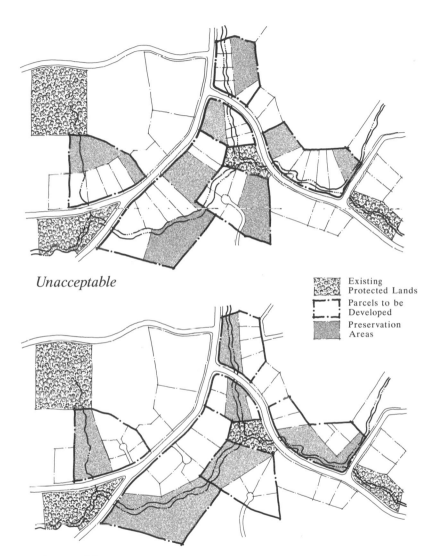

Unacceptable

Existing
Protected Lands

Parcels to be
Developed

Preservation
Areas

Acceptable

property. In addition, they should include locally significant features of the property, such as hedgerows, hillocks, and scenic viewpoints.

- *Fragmentation of conservation land should be minimized so that these resource areas are not divided into numerous small parcels located in various parts of the development.* To the greatest extent practicable, this land should be designated as a single block with logical, straightforward boundaries. Long, thin strips of conservation land should be avoided unless necessary to connect other significant areas or when they are designed to protect linear resources such as streams or trails.

- *Conservation areas should be designed as part of larger continuous and integrated open space systems.* Whenever possible, they should connect with existing or potential conservation areas on adjoining parcels.

Another very important principle is that conservation land should not be permitted to be divided into individual back yard areas unless it is located in a "limited development" with a gross density of five or more acres per dwelling.

Prioritizing Site Resource Areas for Conservation

For a more complete discussion of how to prioritize resource areas for conservation, readers should refer back to pages 62–64.

In southeastern Pennsylvania where the Natural Lands Trust is active, it is recommended that preference generally be given to natural areas over human-made items in the landscape, and that within the natural world, buildable woodlands be afforded greater protection than buildable farmland when one must decide which to favor. In addition to their greater wildlife habitat value and stormwater filtering capacity, woodlands typically do not pollute watercourses and water bodies, as do farm fields with their greater nutrient loads, pesticides, and erosion sedimentation problems. This recommendation should not be interpreted as favoring natural areas such as woodlands in every situation, for there may be occasions on specific sites where cropland conservation and/or historic preservation could assume relatively greater importance than woodland habitat protection.

Readers are also referred to the model regulatory language for subdivision ordinances in Article 6 of Appendix 3 for more detailed provisions regarding the following kinds of resource areas:

- groundwater resources
- stream valleys, swales, springs, and other lowland areas
- woodlands
- upland rural–agricultural areas
- sloping terrain
- significant natural areas and features
- historic structures and sites
- historic road and view corridors
- trails

Chapter 6

Benefits of Conservation Planning and Design

Readers might wonder why they should bother learning how to recast their zoning and subdivision ordinances to provide more choices for landowners and developers, and to set conservation design standards for new subdivisions, when more commonly practiced approaches seem to be working adequately, at least at a casual glance.

There are several reasons that the approaches described and illustrated in this book offer significant advantages to all parties concerned, and they are detailed here under three headings:

- Environmental and ecological benefits
- Social and recreational benefits
- Economic benefits

Environmental and Ecological Benefits

In addition to preventing intrusions into inherently unbuildable locations such as wetlands and floodplains, conservation subdivision design also protects terrestrial habitats and upland buffers alongside wetlands, water bodies, and watercourses, areas that would ordinarily be cleared, graded, and covered with houses, lawns, and driveways in a conventional development.

There are at least four environmental and ecological benefits to employing conservation subdivision design instead of conventional layouts. These include wildlife management, water quality protection, greater aquifer recharge, and environmentally sensitive sewage treatment and disposal.

Wildlife Management

Conservation biologists tell us that riparian woodlands along rivers, creeks, and streams offer our "best hope for creating a system of interconnecting corridors" for a variety of wildlife at all levels of the food chain, from aquatic organisms and fish to amphibians and small terrestrial mammals (such as raccoons, muskrats, and otters) that link the aquatic system to the adjoining upland.

Natural areas preserved in conservation subdivisions therefore provide important terrestrial habitat for wildlife to dwell in and travel through. The greenways that are one of the hallmarks of conservation subdivision design provide cover and naturally sheltered corridors for various species to move through as they travel from their nests and burrows to their feeding places or hunting grounds.

In addition, conservation subdivisions can include areas managed as wildlife or wildflower meadows. Cut once a year, at the end of the summer after flowers have bloomed and seeds have been set—and after the young from ground-nesting species have fledged and departed—such areas require the barest minimum of maintenance in terms of mowing, irrigation, and fertilization. In return, they provide food and cover for birds, insects, and small mammals.

Greater Water Quality Protection Through Improved Buffers

Besides shedding less stormwater than conventional developments, conservation subdivisions provide larger areas of natural vegetation that act as buffers to help filter stormwater flowing into lakes, ponds, rivers, and streams, trapping pollutants and excessive nutrients dissolved or suspended in storm runoff. Leaf litter and ground cover can also slow stormwater velocity, thereby reducing soil erosion and stream sedimentation. Reducing runoff velocity allows stormwater to be absorbed into the soil and taken up by the vegetation. Buffers also offer important infiltration and "recharge" benefits because they help maintain adequate flows of filtered water to underground aquifers (on which local wells and headwater streams depend). Tree canopies provide shade that is especially important in maintaining cooler water temperatures needed by certain aquatic species during the hot summer months.

The minimum effective greenway width for water quality buffering depends on factors such as the permeability of the soils, the steepness of the slopes, and the amount and type of plant material growing there, in addition to the volume and character of the pollutants likely to be found in the runoff. To filter runoff from residential developments in which a moderate amount of lawn fertilizer is used, wooded buffers 100 feet deep on slopes not exceeding 8 percent should be adequate.

For development design purposes, it should be noted that full density credit is allowed for all otherwise buildable land located within the recommended greenway buffer.

Where these buffer areas are not currently wooded, they should be planted with a variety of native species trees and shrubs and allowed to revegetate naturally through a general "no-cut" policy (except for creating informal walking trails; removing invasive alien plants, vines, and trees; and selective pruning of lower limbs to allow water views from the developed areas).

Provision of such buffers should significantly reduce the size and number of stormwater detention basins needed on the development site. This lowers infrastructure costs and frees land for other uses. Since 30 to 50 percent of stormwater runoff in cluster developments comes from roofs, detention basins could be further reduced by directing roof runoff to lawns and into "French drains" in back yards or open space areas.

Greater Aquifer Recharge Through Improved Stormwater Management

Conservation design offers a more effective and less costly approach to stormwater management compared with conventional development. The two basic reasons for the superiority of conservation design is its lesser disturbance of the subdivision parcel as a whole (leaving a greater percentage of woodlands and meadows in their natural state), and its ability to provide more opportunities for filtering runoff and replenishing underlying groundwater supplies.

Even when a conventional subdivision is engineered to meet all typical code requirements, it produces a net negative "water balance" after development. This means that less rainfall is able to percolate into the ground, denying local aquifers their normal and necessary recharge. Good conservation design aims for surface drainage, wherever possible, rather than piped systems because the former allows runoff to percolate into the soil. It is not enough simply to detain stormwater flow in basins or ponds to prevent streambank scouring, erosion, sedimentation, and downstream flooding.

Aquifer replenishment is essential for maintaining stream flow during dry summer months, which is in turn necessary for the health of aquatic habitats. Although the groundwater impact of individual developments is usually not terribly significant, the cumulative effect of hundreds of acres of native woodland and meadows being evenly graded and covered with streets, driveways, patios, rooftops, and lawns (which themselves have a surprisingly high runoff coefficient) can be very considerable over the long run. Many people do not realize that manicured lawns function almost as "green asphalt," shedding most of the water that falls on them. In contrast, natural forest soils with similar overall slopes can store up to 50 times more precipitation than neatly graded turf.

By reducing the overall area of impervious surfaces and suburban lawns that would otherwise be created, conservation design reduces the total *volume* of stormwater runoff that is generated. By minimizing conventional site grading, it offers multiple opportunities for the reduced runoff to infiltrate the ground closer to where the precipitation falls and therefore reduces the size and cost of heavily engineered structures (such as basins and ponds). By reducing site disturbance, natural drainage patterns can be respected and preserved, thereby preventing runoff concentration that would lead to bank scouring, erosion, and streambed sedimentation. Conservation design is very conducive to the new concepts of "headwater streets" (which are scaled to actual traffic and parking needs) and to nonstructural solutions such as grassy swales (instead of curb-and-gutter) and "rain gardens."

Rain gardens, as pioneered in Prince George's County, Maryland, are low-lying areas landscaped with moisture-tolerant grasses, wildflowers, shrubs, and trees that are planted in areas where stormwater runoff is intercepted, filtered, and absorbed into the earth (see Fig. 6-1). They are also recommended for large pear-shaped islands in the middle of cul-de-sac turnarounds. Plants and soils remove pollutants from this runoff, which naturally filters down through specific layers of soil, sand, and organic mulch. Over the next several days following a storm, this moisture irrigates the garden's grasses, trees, and flowers. Tree and shrub species that both thrive in sunny mid-Atlantic locations and tolerate "wet feet" include red maple (*Acer rubrum*), American sycamore (*Platanus occidentalis*), willow oak (*Quercus phellos*), shadbush (*Amelanchier*), sweet pepperbush (*Clethra alnifolia*), winterberry (*Ilex verticillata*), and red-osier dogwood (*Cornus sericea*). Among the recommended species for flowers and grasses are daylilies, yellow flag (*Iris pseudacorus*), larger blue iris (*Iris versicolor*), Marsh marigold (*Caltha palustris*), swamp mallow (*Hibiscus*

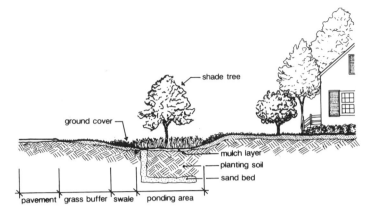

Figure 6-1. This cross-sectional view of a "rain garden" shows its various component elements and its relationship to roads, swales, lawns, and houses. Such features help manage stormwater more effectively, replenishing local aquifers while at the same time adding beauty and interest to the landscape.

moscheutos), sedges (*Carex* sp.), rushes (*Juncus* sp.), tufted hairgrass (*Deschamnpsia cespitosa*), and cardinal flower (*Lobelia cardinalis*). The above species are known to be hardy and will generally flourish in rain gardens with minimal maintenance (typically only weeding is required). They have been specifically selected to provide welcome color in various seasons (other shrub species being the showiest in the winter landscape). See also Figure 704D-29 in Appendix 3.

When development is proposed on open field areas where the site appears to be virtually flat and featureless, important clues can often be gleaned from aerial photographs taken in the early spring, which typically show areas of lighter and darker soils. The darker areas usually indicate moister locations where former wetlands were drained many years ago by farmers who installed subsurface tiles for this purpose. The most logical place to locate rain gardens is therefore in these areas. By deliberately crushing or otherwise disrupting the tile drains, developers can help to reestablish the original wetland vege-

tation, combining this effort with the design of linear "greenway" parks and neighborhood footpath systems to achieve a double benefit.

When sidewalks are provided, they should be located on the far side of drainage swales and pitched toward those swales which can therefore receive their runoff. In curb-and-gutter situations, sidewalks should be pitched away from the street toward bio-retention filter strips provided along the edge of the right-of-way, with shade trees planted in "tree lawns" between curbs and sidewalks.

The conventional wisdom is that curbs and gutters are unavoidable when house lots are reduced below 10,000 square feet, but the key is not lot size per se but rather overall density. In open field situations, for example, land can be graded so that streets and homes occupy very minor "ridges" created across the property (virtually imperceptible to the eye), so that all stormwater will drain to linear rain gardens running through the common open space located in "greenway" corridors behind the house lots. This approach has been employed very successfully in two developments known well in the planning profession. One is Village Homes, a 240-unit conservation subdivision designed by Michael Corbett in Davis, California, where virtually all the runoff flows into gravel-filled infiltration trenches meandering through conservation areas behind practically everyone's house. The natural stormwater management design saved approximately $800 per household in engineering and construction costs, enabling the landscaping budget to be increased by a like amount. Corbett, who has lived in this development since its inception, also notes that the landscaping in his neighborhoods requires one-third less irrigation than is needed in surrounding developments because the groundwater below Village Homes has been continuously recharged through precipitation captured and retained on the site. Because off-street parking is provided on each house lot, parking lanes are not needed and streets function well at 20 to 25 feet in width despite the relatively modest lot sizes (averaging 4,500 square feet). Those lot sizes enable Village Homes to achieve an overall project density of 3.6 dwellings per acre. However, these village-scale lots are set within a framework of nearly 30 acres of open space (40 percent of the site) in the form of greenways, playing fields, neighborhood commons, allotment gardens, orchards, and a small vineyard.

Another quite different example is Harbortown, a higher-density, neo-traditional development of gridded streets in Memphis, where 800 dwellings, together with a mixed-use community center (featuring shops, an inn, a marina, restaurants, offices, and a school), are being built on a 130-acre site. Justly renowned for its small-town quality of urbane streetscapes with vistas terminating in formal squares, Harbortown's less publicized asset is its "emerald necklace": a crescent-shaped greenway occupying the site's original low-lying areas. These areas have been designed as a linear park connecting many neighborhoods with a footpath system meandering alongside numerous detention ponds and through undisturbed woodlands. Because of "new urbanist" design style, Harbortown's streets are all curbed and its stormwater management system is more conventional than that at Village Homes. However, it demonstrates how certain elements of conservation design can significantly improve the livability and functionality of developments built at densities typical of traditional small town neighborhoods across the country and offers a design example worth emulating in proposed extensions to older towns. See Figures 704D-83 through 704D-85 in Appendix 3.

Environmentally Sensitive Sewage Treatment and Disposal

Conservation subdivisions also offer greater opportunities to implement environmentally sensitive sewage treatment and disposal systems known alternatively as "land treatment," "spray irrigation," and "wastewater reclamation and reuse." These terms describe variations of a well-documented technology that is superior to conventional mechanical systems in many ways because they produce only very small amounts of sludge by-products and because they help to replenish local aquifers (rather than diverting the treated water into rivers, lakes, or oceans where it flows into different systems, often carrying heavy nutrient loads that degrade the receiving waters and aquatic habitats downstream).

With spray irrigation, wastewater is heavily aerated in deep lagoons where it receives a "secondary" level of treatment, similar to that provided by conventional sewage plants. It is then applied to the land surface at rates consistent with the soil's natural absorption capacity. Nutrients in the treated wastewater are taken up by the vegetation, which may range from woodlands and meadows to farm fields and golf courses. This approach has a long and successful track record in Chester County, Pennsylvania, where more than 50 such systems have been in operation for upward of 20 years.

Some of the county's more progressive golf courses, such as the one at Hershey's Mill, East Goshen, Pennsylvania, are irrigated and fertilized with community wastewater treated with this technology. This practice is well accepted by residents and golfers in this upscale development because it is cost-effective, safe, odorless, and environmentally sound. Woodlands are irrigated with treated wastewater in the Kennett at Longwood retirement development near Longwood Gardens in East Marlborough Township, and meadowland in Upper Uwchlan Township is sprayed with similarly treated effluent. And in Buckingham Township, Bucks County, subdivision wastewater is used to irrigate fields of corn. In all these cases the treated wastewater is sprayed within a few hundred feet of homes, without problems or complaints.

Another innovative and cost-effective sewage treatment system that benefits the environment is the approach known as *constructed wetlands,* as exemplified at the Fields of St. Croix in Lake Elmo, Min-

nesota, also included in the case studies. In a typical constructed wetland, wastewater is treated in two cells commonly filled with coarse
gravel where two types of plants are installed. In the first cell, plant
species are selected for their ability to pump oxygen down to their
root zones, creating aerobic conditions that speed treatment, with
bacteria, enzymes, fungi, and protozoa breaking down the pollutants.
In the second cell, nutrient-tolerant plants transport water out of the
system by evapotranspiration and beautify the garden with their colorful floral display. Whereas hard-stemmed plants (cat-tails, horsetails,
rushes, blue flag, and yellow flag iris) are used in the first cell, soft-
stemmed plants (arrow arum, canna lily, taro, pickerel rush, sweet flag
and woolgrass) are favored in the second cell. As the treated effluent
is reduced in volume with this methodology, drain fields can usually
be downsized.

Although the conservation design approach allows for innovative
treatment systems to be implemented, subdivisions may of course
also be served by conventional sewage plants, by individual septic systems, or by a variety of in-ground community septic systems. The key
point here is that *the layout flexibility allowed with conservation subdivisions makes it easier for site designers to locate subsurface septic systems on
those parts of the property that are best suited for such facilities.* In conventional developments built without central sewers, septic systems are
located on each lot, regardless of whether soils are well suited for septic disposal or really very marginal. As long as soils meet the absolute
minimum standards required under law, they may be used for drain
fields, and many such installations eventually fail because soil conditions are borderline in their suitability (see Fig. 4-11). However, in
conservation subdivisions, house lots can be located on the best soils.
If the area of superior soil is not very extensive, the development can
be laid out so that either individual or community septic systems are
located "off-lot" on the best soils within the community open space
(which may also function as a village green, playing field, or wildlife
meadow, as shown in Figure 4-12).

Social and Recreational Benefits

As used in this book, the term *conventional subdivision* refers to residential developments in which all the developable land is divided
into house lots or streets. The only open space is typically undevel-
opable wetlands, steep slopes, and storm water management areas.
There are no nice places to walk, open meadows for wildlife, or playing fields for children. Furthermore, almost all of the land has been
cleared, graded, and converted into lawns or private back yards. As a
result, residents of conventional subdivisions depend upon their cars
even more to bring them social and recreational opportunities. Conservation designs offer social and recreational advantages over conventional layouts in several distinct ways.

Pedestrian-Friendly Neighborhoods

The formal greens and commons typically featured in conservation
subdivisions present opportunities for neighbors to meet casually and
to get to know each other a little better. Whether they are walking
the dog, enjoying a game of catch with their children or grandchil-
dren, or just out on a stroll to see spring flowers, autumnal foliage, or
local wildlife, neighbors have more opportunities to become better
acquainted with one another when they are outside and on foot. This
phenomenon is especially evident at Village Homes in Davis, California (see Fig. 7-11b).

Numerous national surveys have documented that taking short
walks is one of the most frequent and popular forms of recreation enjoyed by Americans. The basic elements of pedestrian-friendly neighborhoods are "inviting places to walk" and "interesting destinations."
Under the first category one might list shady sidewalks and woodland or riparian trails. The second category could include natural
areas such as woodlands, meadows, and viewing points over ponds,
lakes, creeks, and bays, as well as human-made elements such as
greens, commons, and playing fields (see Figs. 7-9c and 7-9d).

Another advantage of conservation subdivisions is that their more compact yards typically require less maintenance, allowing people more free time to spend enjoying the greens, trails, and other features in these well-designed "natural neighborhoods."

Community Activities

Community activities occur in a surprising number of conservation subdivisions, from annual picnics to summer sports events and races, to garden tours and winter skating parties. This is not to suggest that such development forms always produce a great deal of social activity, but they do seem to foster more neighborly interaction and a stronger sense of community pride than often exists in conventional developments, especially when the site designers have provided attractive footpath systems connecting the homes with interesting places to visit.

Community-Wide Greenways and Trails

Conservation subdivisions also make it easier for municipalities to implement community-wide greenway network plans, as illustrated in Figures 3-1 through 3-4 in Chapter 3 dealing with Comprehensive Plans. To achieve such "greener visions," local officials generally depend in part (sometimes to a very great degree) on land designated for permanent conservation purposes in new subdivisions. Therefore, the role of developers in this process of protecting linked open space systems is absolutely critical in many communities lacking sufficient resources to purchase these lands outright or even to purchase their development rights.

Conservation subdivision design offers a practical method of safeguarding essential links in future greenway systems, especially those along stream valleys or hilltop ridges without incurring public expenditures, disturbing landowner equity, or curtailing developers' rights to build to the maximum permitted density. Developers can also generally be persuaded to dedicate a portion of their subdivision open space to the local government for active or passive public recreation. This may take the form of a "green ribbon" of public trails through the otherwise private homeowner association open space. In Worcester Township, Montgomery County, Pennsylvania, Natural Lands Trust (NLT) staff redesigned a proposed subdivision, which was bordered on two sides by township and state parkland, to include a greenway connection along the course of a brook that flows between the two parks.

In West Hanover Township, Dauphin County, Pennsylvania, NLT prepared designs for two contiguous full-density conservation subdivisions in which one development doubled the size of the preexisting township park and connected it to a proposed township greenway trail located on the far side of the second subdivision. And in Wallace Township, NLT assisted a local landowner with conceptual designs for a conservation subdivision that will expand one of the township's parks while achieving full density.

Some jurisdictions are beginning to look at conservation subdivision design as their principal tool for *buffering existing public parkland* from the incursions of development on adjoining parcels. To achieve this objective, municipal zoning and subdivision ordinances should specify parkland buffers as one of the required design elements of open space systems proposed in new conservation subdivisions. Among many park professionals, this approach is known as the "adjoining lands strategy."

Communities with Multiple Conservation Subdivisions

Remarkable results in land conservation have been achieved through the land-use planning process in a number of communities in which the local political leadership has been receptive to new ideas and willing to initiate amendments to existing codes guiding developers toward more innovative design approaches for their new subdivisions.

In Pennsylvania, the first townships to experience multiple

successes in conservation subdivison design are located in Bucks County, where in the mid-1970s the county planning department developed the concept of "performance zoning." This results-oriented approach demonstrated how superior site design could be achieved by relaxing conventional lot size and setback requirements, dimensional criteria that had traditionally been employed by local officials to limit the number of homes that could be built on any given property. Replacing these indirect density controls (which produced monotonous checkerboard layouts of house lots and streets completely covering the landscape) with smarter model regulations where density is based on a site capacity analysis similar to the "net-out" criteria described on pages 41–43 of this book, county planners were able to persuade officials in many municipalities that this approach would lead to more sensitive layouts and significant conservation of open space.

Some of the first highly successful examples of the "performance approach" to subdivision design occurred in Buckingham Township, where officials actively promoted this idea, but other nearby communities have also enjoyed similarly notable results. Among these is Milford Township, where nearly 200 acres of land in more than a dozen subdivisions have been permanently protected through this process. Milford is also among six communities that have adopted the same basic model zoning and subdivision ordinances after detailed review and adjustment by the multijurisdictional Quakertown Area Planning Committee (QAPC), a progressive step in this home-rule state, recognizing that these neighboring municipalities share common characteristics and similar development pressures and can benefit from following a consistent regulatory strategy. This approach has succeeded at the local political level largely because these model provisions continue to be administered by township and borough officials. Always looking ahead for ways to improve the quality of their land-use regulations, several QAPC communities have recently updated their original performance zoning to include further refinements offered through the Growing Greener program.

Other Pennsylvania communities with multiple conservation subdivisions include Lower Merion Townshop in Montgomery County (which was the first municipality in the commonwealth to require substantial open space areas in new subdivisions), West Manchester in York County (the first to link that kind of requirement to a map of potential conservation lands adopted by the township), and Lower Makefield in Bucks County (which has experienced the fastest rate of land protection using this technique—more than 500 acres of prime farmland during its first five years of use). Through conventional "buy-back" programs (such as purchase of development rights [PDR]), this acreage would have required the expenditure of $3.5 million of taxpayers' money.

Building on community interest generated by a slide lecture illustrating the land conservation opportunities offered by creative subdivision design techniques presented by the Center for Rural Massachusetts in the late 1980s, officials in Westborough, Massachusetts incorporated these principles into their new Open Space and Recreation Plan in 1996. From that document, which contained maps showing the potential for protecting interconnected networks of open space on the remaining undeveloped parcels, it was a short, logical step to update the existing zoning and subdivision regulations to be consistent with those open space goals. Over the last several years, developers have proposed four conservation subdivisions securing critical linkages to the open space network that had been pre-identified on the Action Plan Map in the above-mentioned plan. Although the potential for protecting this network would have been even greater had the community initiated these steps 10 or 20 years earlier, the results that are being achieved are nonetheless very significant, and would never have occurred without these planning efforts.

Model for the Midwest

Exceeding Lower Makefield's achievement, Hamburg Township in Michigan's Livingston County has protected more than 1,000 acres of open space within the last seven years, and this figure continues to rise as more developments are approved. Results such as this demonstrate that through the Growing Greener program, developers can become any community's greatest conservationists. Once again the county planning department was the catalyst for change, inviting this author to present an educational session on conservation design to local officials in 1990. (See Figures 7-9a through 7-9d.)

In taking the lead, the county planning department has stimulated interest in this approach through a number of other channels as well. One of its first projects was to prepare a "build-out" map of four adjoining townships showing future development patterns as they would be likely to unfold according to current sprawl zoning. Second, it produced model zoning amendments enabling community officials to require conservation design in at least certain designated resource overlay districts. This model language is clearly explained in layperson's language in a 70-page design manual featuring a question-and-answer format addressing typical concerns about this more creative design approach. The goals of this effort are summarized in the manual's title: *Protecting the Environment, Agriculture, and the Rural Landscape* (or "PEARL" for short).

Several years later the county planners followed up on that publication with a series of three larger booklets, one of which presents case studies of actual conservation subdivisions, among which several Hamburg examples were featured. Two of that community's leading examples are included in Chapter 7. The county planning department selected Hamburg as the location for its first workshop on creative subdivision design because Hamburg was the county's fastest growing township and also because of its tradition of openness to new ideas. The concepts clearly resonated with the host officials, who adopted an Open Space Community ordinance in 1992. Despite the fact that the open space option is neither mandated nor encouraged by a density differential (such as a bonus or by reducing allowable density for conventional layouts), developer interest in this approach has been very high. In this community the key to generating that interest lay in offering sensibly scaled street design criteria to developers as an alternative to the excessive and outdated standards for public streets adopted by the County Road Commission.

In a political climate where there was support for encouraging open space design but not at the additional community cost associated with density bonuses, and where the newer idea of "density *disincentives*" (reducing lot yield) to actively discourage conventional layouts had not been conceived, Hamburg's decision to offer an attractive option for private streets has been hugely successful among developers, with 33 of the last 34 subdivisions being proposed with conservation design and streets not built to freeway standards.

Although none of the local residents, officials, or developers wanted to see any more wide streets built with 66-foot rights-of-way cleared to the ground to assure highway-style sight distances, the County Road Commission has held firm to its unsupported belief that lessening its standards would increase the county's liability exposure and open it to lawsuits. As an alternative to the road commission's excessively wide standards for pavement and clearing, Hamburg offers private street construction standards as a viable alternative.

Although the township lacks the legal authority to offer more appropriately scaled standards for public streets (because public street construction and maintenance lie exclusively within the county's jurisdiction), the private street alternative has proven to be very popular among the area's leading developers, who see twin financial benefits from their reduced costs and the increased marketability of homes built along streets that are significantly more attractive because of the larger number of trees that can be saved. Wherever possible, the author recommends that public street standards be updated to conform with the very reasonable standards published by the American

Society of Civil Engineers (ASCE) in its seminal volume *Residential Streets*. Unfortunately, local engineering consultants and county road commissions often rely instead on the public street standards promulgated years ago by the American Society of State Highway Transportation Officials (AASHTO). Those standards tend to be based on accommodating higher design speeds—which is a self-fulfilling prophecy as most people tend to drive faster on wider pavements with extremely gradual curves. Because the county had adopted AASHTO standards for public streets, it was logical for Hamburg to use the same group's standards for private streets. Fortunately, their private street standards were in fact appropriately scaled for residential neighborhood situations and were actually not very dissimilar from those recommended by the ASCE for public streets. A happy medium was struck, and it has proven to be a strong incentive for developers to select the open space design option in this community. The principal points of difference are the minimum widths for right-of-way (50 feet with curb-and-gutter vs. 66 feet) and pavement (18–20 feet instead of 30 feet), based partly on design speeds of 20–25 mph instead of 30 mph. Tree clearing throughout the right-of-way is not required for private streets (only to the back of drainage ditches, where the street is not curbed).

Economic Benefits

Conservation subdivision design offers distinct and measurable economic advantages over conventional layouts in at least five different ways, reflecting various stages or periods in the life of a project.

Lower Costs

The first advantage of conservation subdivision design is the opportunity it offers to *reduce infrastructure engineering and construction costs*. To the extent that single-family house lots can be narrowed, or that multiple-unit dwellings can be incorporated, street and utility runs can be shortened. This reduction becomes greater as the development pattern itself becomes more compact and village-like, but it is also measurable even when houses are interspersed with open space to provide good views from the maximum number of homes. Conservation design can also reduce the number of costly or contentious wetland crossings needed by avoiding parts of a site where such conditions exist. And, to the extent that street pavement is reduced, the size and cost of stormwater management facilities can also be lessened. The shorter street and utility systems that often result from more compact layouts can also reduce the public sector's long-term infrastructure maintenance costs.

Subdivisions designed in this conservation-minded manner are also much less expensive to create than another well-known kind of development that features a specialized type of recreation: golf course communities. The costs of transforming fields, meadows, and woodlands into regulation golf courses are extremely high for a number of reasons, chief among them being the typical need to move and shape two or three million cubic yards of soil. Added to this are the extra costs associated with meeting increasingly stringent environmental regulations designed to prevent degradation of the groundwater or downstream surface waters from the fertilizers, herbicides, and pesticides that are usually applied to the turf. Other concerns that applicants must address include erosion, sedimentation, habitat and species protection, thermal pollution (from removal of woodlands that shade ponds and streams), and the impact of heavy irrigation requirements on local water supplies. All of these costs and concerns are substantially lessened by conservation subdivisions that leave 50 to 75 percent of a development site relatively unchanged or intact as natural areas.

Marketing and Sales Advantages

The second advantage occurs during the marketing and sales period, when developers and realtors can capitalize on the amenities that have been preserved or provided within the development. These positive features can form the basis for an *environmentally oriented marketing strategy* highlighting the benefits of living in a community in which upland forest habitat and productive farmland have been preserved, along with riparian or wetland buffers and wildlife meadows. Sales brochures should be prepared to illustrate and describe neighborhood trails through protected greenways paralleling creeks or traversing ridgelines, and formal commons for passive recreation and specific facilities for certain active sports should also be mentioned.

This technique has been used successfully by an increasing number of developers, including Realen Homes, at its Garnet Oaks development in Bethel Township, Delaware County, Pennsylvania. Research conducted by that firm confirmed home buyers' general preference for house lots abutting or facing onto protected land. The majority of the first lots sold in Garnet Oaks were those that adjoined the woodland preserve or the central open space (also wooded). These lots sold quickly, even though most commanded premium prices based on their adjacency to the protected area, which gave them more privacy and more of a rural feeling (see Fig. 4-9).

Recognizing their customers' desire for a rural setting, the developers emphasized the neighborhood open space in their marketing approach and even published a nicely designed interpretive guide to the trail system that their landscape architect had laid out through the woodland preserve. Copies of this guide were given to prospective buyers, who were encouraged to take a stroll along the trail before leaving to visit the next subdivision on their lists. The relatively rapid sales rate in this subdivision is attributed, in part, to the unique parkland experience that these buyers encountered at Garnet Oaks.

Further confirming this information, a national survey of people who shopped for or bought a home during 1994 has revealed that, of 39 features critical to their choice, consumers ranked "lots of natural open space" and plenty of "walking and biking paths" as the sec-

ond- and third-highest rated aspects affecting their decisions. According to the survey director, Brooke Warwick of *American Lives,* these results demonstrate that consumers are becoming more selective and are looking more and more for the kinds of features that encourage informal social interaction among neighborhood residents in relaxed parkland settings. Perhaps significantly, golf courses within developments ranked 29th on the list, just below tennis courts.

The art of marketing the benefits of living near conservation land in new subdivisions typically emphasizes that buyers of smaller lots are actually purchasing much more than their individual lots. In a development with half-acre lots and 40 acres of open space, a smart salesperson would describe the opportunity to buy 40-1/2 acres of land for the same price that one would otherwise spend on a one- or two-acre lot with no attendant open space. With open space ranging from 50 percent to 65 percent in such subdivisions, sales strategies focusing on this kind of amenity strike a responsive chord among many home buyers, particularly when lots are laid out to maximize views of the conservation land. When given a choice, consumers have demonstrated their clear preference for buying homes that look out onto farmland or other open space rather than houses from which the only view is of their neighbor's picture window or back yard.

Value Appreciation

A third advantage is that homes in conservation subdivisions tend to appreciate faster than their counterparts in conventional developments. This fact may be used as part of the marketing approach when selling or reselling homes in such developments. One of the more widely known studies of this type compared two subdivisions in Amherst, Massachusetts, built at about the same time, with very similar houses that originally sold for almost the same price, at the same overall density (two dwellings per acre). The only real difference between the two developments is that homes in the first were located on half-acre lots with little community open space, while those in the second were built on quarter-acre lots with 36 acres of open space, including mature woodlands, trails, a large meadow, a swimming pond and beach, a picnic grove, a baseball diamond, and tennis courts that also serve for basketball use. After twenty years the homes in the second development sold, on average, for $17,000 more than their counterparts in the other subdivision, where lots were actually twice as large. This 13 percent price differential is attributable to the neighborhood open space amenities, all other aspects being nearly equal (Lacy 1991, also quoted in Arendt et al. 1994). Other examples of the positive influence of open space upon residential property values have been documented in *Economic Impacts of Protecting Rivers, Trails, and Greenway Corridors,* a publication available at no charge from the National Park Service.

Reduced Demand for New Public Parkland

From the local government perspective, a fourth advantage of conservation subdivision design is that the natural areas that are preserved and the recreational amenities that are provided in such communities help to reduce the demand for public open space, parkland, playing fields, and other areas for active and passive recreation. Current deficiencies with regard to such public amenities will inevitably grow larger as population continues to rise. To the extent that each new development meets some of its own local needs, pressure on local governments will be lessened in this regard, a factor that may make such designs more attractive to local reviewing bodies.

Smoother Review

The fifth advantage occurs during the review period, which is likely to proceed more smoothly because site designers have anticipated and taken into account many of the concerns that would otherwise become time-consuming and costly issues to resolve. While it might not be possible to avoid all potential problems or conflicts, the potential for confrontation and dispute can certainly be minimized by site planning that is sensitive to the conservation objectives of township or county officials and interested residents.

Chapter 7

Examples of Subdivisions with Substantial Conservation Areas

This chapter presents eleven "case examples" of conservation subdivisions in nine states, from Maine to California, demonstrating a variety of resources that have been protected through sensitive site design. The overall densities of these developments are typical of those found in the suburban–rural fringes in most metropolitan regions around the country and as such should be broadly applicable to many readers' local experiences.

- *Ringfield,* Chadds Ford Township, Pennsylvania
- *The Ponds at Woodward,* Kennett Township, Pennsylvania
- *The Fields of St. Croix,* City of Lake Elmo, Minnesota
- *Prairie Crossing,* Grayslake, Illinois
- *The Preserve at Hunter's Lake,* Ottawa, Wisconsin
- *The Meadows at Dolly Gordon Brook,* York, Maine
- *Farmcolony,* Stanardsville, Virginia
- *Westwood Common,* Beverly Hills, Michigan
- *Hunter's Pointe and Solitude Pointe,* Hamburg Township, Michigan
- *The Ranch at Roaring Fork,* Carbondale, Colorado
- *Village Homes,* Davis, California

Ringfield

Location: Ring Road, Chadds Ford Township (formerly Birmingham Township), Delaware County, Pennsylvania
Development Period: 1977–1986
Site Designer: Richard Chalfant, Wilmington, Delaware
Developer: Richard Chalfant, Wilmington, Delaware

Approximately 55 acres of this 64-acre site have been preserved as open meadows and natural woodlands. An informal network of woodland trails links the various neighborhood areas with three ponds, and consideration is currently being given to supplementing this system with additional trails mown across or around several of the wildflower meadows to offer more diverse walking choices to the residents.

The township's Planned Residential District allowed the developer to achieve full density (at it's two-acre standard) and wisely did not impose any restrictions on lot size, width, or street frontage. This flexibility permitted the site designer wide latitude in fitting the homes into the landscape and the topography to take full advantage of views and sunlight. The homes in Ringfield occupy quarter-acre lots, all of which both face onto and back up to permanent open space. These lots are large enough to suit the owners' needs partly because they abut open space at the rear and partly because no land is wasted on front lawns (see Fig. 7-1a). Homes are situated at modest setbacks from the street with door yard gardens or informal landscaped areas instead of grassy yard space. Of the total, 25 homes are single-family detached, two are semi-detached, and six are townhouses. They range in floorspace from 2,700 to 3,600 square feet. The townhomes, in the center of the property, are fairly commodious at 2,400 square feet each, with three full baths.

With meadowland, dogwood trees, and a pond occupying the public viewshed along Ring Road, the layout of the neighborhood helps to preserve the township's rural character. Also facing Ring Road is the original stone farmhouse, situated on a separate lot.

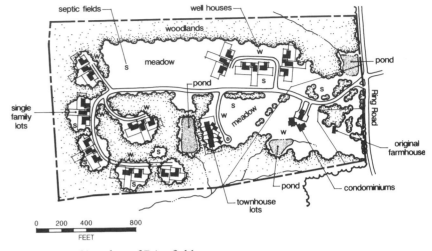

Figure 7-1a. Site plan of Ringfield.

Figure 7-1b. The conservation meadows at Ringfield, which are covered with russet-colored broomsedge (*Andropogon virginicus*) in the autumn, require minimal maintenance, offer habitat variety for local wildlife, and provide convenient areas for subsurface sewage disposal.

Figure 7-1c. As the ponds at Ringfield are located within the common open space, they are accessible to all neighborhood residents and are also protected from woodland clearing, lawn extensions, and other typical suburban encroachments that would diminish their water quality.

Homes are served by six deep wells, each supplying three to nine dwellings with up to 350 gallons of water per day per house. Only minimal treatment is needed to control minor acidity and iron content. The six wells and numerous shared septic drainage fields are all located in the common open space. To ensure longer life and smoother operations, accumulated solids are removed from the septic tanks by the homeowner association once every several years, a practice that should be followed in all subdivisions in which septic tanks are employed. Treated effluent is piped under pressure from these tanks to the drain fields by twin pumps that run sequentially, an approach that extends their lives and provides an emergency pump in the event one should require repair.

In addition to providing wildlife habitat and areas for quiet contemplation, the three excavated ponds are sometimes informally used for ice skating in the winter, but only during extremely cold periods when the ice is very thick. A proposal to install "dry hydrants" in them to provide an on-site source of water for firefighters is under consideration.

The Ponds at Woodward

Location: Kennett Pike, Mendenhall, Kennett Township, Chester County, Pennsylvania
Development Period: 1989–1991
Site Designer: The Brandywine Conservancy, Chadds Ford, Pennsylvania
Developer: The Harlan Corporation, Bryn Mawr, Pennsylvania

This 120-acre property with 57 homes illustrates how landowners who are concerned about the ultimate disposition of their family lands can craft a solution with the assistance of land trust staff, and market their vision to developers who are amenable to blending conservation and development. As a result of this collaborative relationship, two-thirds of the property has been permanently protected, including ten acres of mature woodlands and a working orchard (producing apples and peaches) encompassing more than 50 acres. Moreover, the family's economic return was substantially increased over that which a conventional alternative would have generated.

Under the township's two-acre zoning this land was capable of being subdivided into 57 two-acre house lots, but it was also eligible for the Planned Residential Development (PRD) option under which four times as many dwellings could have been built. The two elderly brothers who owned the orchard asked the Brandywine Conservancy to comment on the concept plans submitted to them by potential developers, who had offered them $800,000 to purchase their property to build a 230-unit PRD. Not impressed by the quality of the site designs submitted to it for review by the developer's engineer, Conservancy staff offered to lay out a more sensitive site plan based on the standard two-acre density but with the flexibility provided by the PRD regulations. Through discussions with the owners, neighbors, and township officials, a number of concerns were identified, including maintaining the orchard, protecting the woodlands, retaining the farmhouse and barns, and buffering the public viewshed as seen from Kennett Pike. These four goals became the conservation areas around which the alternative plan was designed.

Because everyone expected that the new 57-lot conservation design would not generate as high a return for the landowners as would a 230-unit PRD plan, the township offered to contribute $50,000 to the brothers to help them make up the difference. The family's concept plan, featuring 70 percent open space, was then actively marketed to developers, five of whom were interviewed, and their past projects were examined. At the conclusion of these evaluations, the Harlan Corporation of Bryn Mawr was selected. Developers engaged in a small bidding war over this property and thus the brothers received multiple offers, the highest one being about $1.3 million. Although involving only one-quarter the number of lots possible on the PRD plan, the more sensitive design increased the brothers' yield by 62 percent, rendering the township's subsidy unnecessary.

Although the township's standard two-acre zoning did not permit lot size reductions to enable land to be conserved, Conservancy staff utilized the flexibility of the PRD regulations to achieve their design objectives. As there is no law (not even an "economic law") requiring developers to build to the maximum density allowed under any ordinance, this did not pose a problem to the township or to anyone else. In fact, all parties were extremely pleased with this approach. The review process proceeded relatively smoothly, with considerable community support demonstrated for the proposal by neighbors, other residents, and officials. Altogether the development contains 31 detached single-family residences on one-third to one-half acre lots, plus 24 large condominium units attached in groups of three, with each unit occupying roughly 9,000 square feet of land, on average, in this part of the development. It should be noted that these attached units, which were located along a "single-loaded" street segment pro-

viding open space vistas both back and front, sold even faster than the detached houses and at prices three times higher than any condo had previously fetched in that township (see Fig. 7-2a). In addition, the working orchard operates a popular "pick-your-own" business, a Friends' nursery school occupies the original nineteenth-century farmhouse, a stained glass craftsman operates a small gallery and retail shop in an outbuilding, and a cabinet maker practices his trade in the barn.

Although the site is served by public water and natural gas, sewage is treated on site. After leaving an engineered sand filter, the treated effluent is absorbed by three subsurface leaching fields located within conservation areas that now serve as meadows and grassy open space.

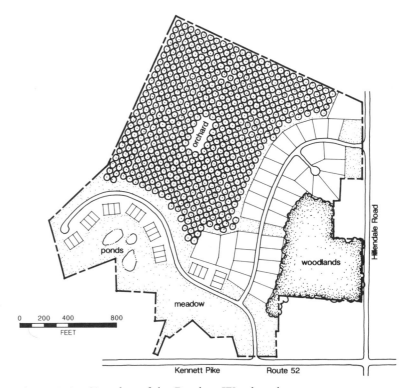

Figure 7-2a. Site plan of the Ponds at Woodward.

Figure 7-2b. This part of the apple orchard is situated directly across the street from a group of homes that overlooks one of the ponds behind them. Such "single-loaded" streets, which offer unobstructed views of the open space to all who drive, walk, bike, or jog along them, improve marketability and sales because they incorporate green vistas into the everyday experience of neighborhood residents and are clearly not "less efficient," as commonly thought by conventional-minded developers.

Figure 7-2c. The rear decks on this row of homes provide relaxing views of peach trees, which exhibit a riot of color every spring.

The Fields of St. Croix

Location: Lake Elmo, Minnesota
Development Period: 1997–2000
Site Designer: Robert Engstrom
Developer: Robert Engstrom Companies, Minneapolis, Minnesota

Located in the St. Croix River valley 20 minutes northeast of downtown St. Paul, The Fields of St. Croix is a premier example of conservation subdivision design, one that received the 1998 Land Use and Community Award from the Minnesota Environmental Initiative. Of the 226 acres on this site, which the developer assembled from three separate farms, more than 60 percent is devoted to permanent open space uses including village greens, playing fields, agriculture, a nursery with native grasses and wildflowers, a restored prairie, wooded hillsides, and two ponds.

The overall design concept preserves long scenic views into the property across open farmland as seen from State Highway 5, which borders the eastern edge of the site. At the same time, the design locates the homes toward the center of the parcel, away from traffic noise and closer to the woods, ponds, and the large prairie restoration area on the western third of the site (see Fig. 7–3a).

The Fields of St. Croix was built under the city's relatively new open space development ordinance, the idea for which was spurred by the submission of a concept plan for this particular site. It was a situation in which the developer needed greater design flexibility to achieve his open space objectives than was permitted under the previous code, and local officials recognized it as an opportunity to update their regulations to allow the kind of superior site design demonstrated by Engstrom's initial concept plan. One of many positive results of this development proposal and the ordinance revision process is that the city's new zoning extends flexible design standards to an area encompassing 4,400 acres (nearly seven square miles) of semi-rural land within its jurisdiction.

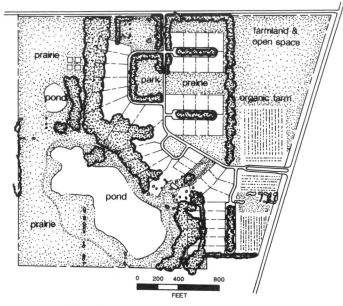

Figure 7-3a. Site plan of the Fields of St. Croix.

Figure 7-3b. Approximately 30 acres of land have been restored to their original prairie vegetation using native grasses and wildflowers propagated at the developer's own private nursery.

Although the site's 226 acres would have yielded approximately 65 house lots under the ordinance's base density of six dwellings per 20 acres, the final approved plan allows 100 homes through bonuses that bring the density up to 9 dwelling units per 20 acres. The ordinance's 50 percent density incentive has successfully encouraged the provision of community greens and trails as well as the preservation of historic structures. In addition to the unusual environmental features noted below, the design includes miles of trails for walking, jogging, or roller-blading, a central park large enough to accommodate natural areas, neighborhood play activities and a tot lot. Sales have been extremely strong, with 80 percent of the 45 home sites in Phase One selling within the first six months. Lots vary in size from 10,800 square feet to 2.3 acres and range in price from $44,500 to $150,000, the most expensive ones being those backing up to the wooded hillside overlooking the two ponds and principal prairie restoration areas.

Of the development's more noteworthy and unusual attributes several stand out as truly exemplary features:

- Thirty acres of land restored to its original prairie habitat with native grasses and wildflowers indigenous to the region, plus ornamental grasses and perennial flowers, many of which were raised by the developer at a special nursery on his property.
- The retention of productive farmland in active use. Although only a small part of the original cropland remains, this acreage has proven ideal for a new kind of "metro-farmer" tilling the land and adapting to changing circumstances in an increasingly suburban location. In a situation in which continued production of traditional low-value crops such as corn and soybeans on a small parcel would not generate sufficient income to be feasible, specialty horticulture, tree and shrub nurseries, and the concept of "community-supported agriculture" (CSA) have provided better uses for the land. At The Fields, Natural Harvest, a CSA organi-

zation, produces organically grown vegetables and flowers for its members, including both residents and other townspeople who pay a yearly subscriber fee. Additional produce is sold to nearby restaurants.

- Wastewater treatment and disposal utilizing state-of-the-art constructed wetlands technology, discharging fully treated effluent into the ground, thereby also recharging the local aquifer. Importantly, this approach removes greater amounts of nitrogen and phosphorus than do either conventional mechanical systems or standard septic systems. Because of their smaller size, ease of replacement, and greater design flexibility, constructed wetland systems are becoming the system of choice in many developments built under the city's new open space ordinance. The system at The Fields was the first one in the state licensed by the Minnesota Pollution Control Authority.

- Stormwater management designed to handle nearly all precipitation on site through retention, evaporation, and infiltration.

- Restoration of a Civil War–era barn as a community center for residents and available occasionally to others, such as local conservation groups.

- Community streetscape and security are enhanced by reduced public street standards permitting land and street widths of 14, 16, and 18 feet.

- Distinctive homes of stylized Craftsman or Prairie architecture are energy-efficient, built according to EPA Energy Star standards.

All of the common open space and the restored barn are owned by the community association. The non-common open space encompasses the tilled fields, but both types of conservation land are permanently protected through easements held by the Minnesota Land Trust.

Prairie Crossing

Location: Grayslake, Lake County, Illinois
Development Period: 1997–present
Site Designer: William J. Johnson, Bainbridge Island, Washington
Developer: Prairie Holdings Corporation, Grayslake, Illinois

Of Prairie Crossing's 667 acres, more than 450 (or about 70 percent) will remain as permanent open space. That land includes 160 acres of restored prairie, 158 acres of active farmland, 13 acres of wetlands, a 22-acre lake, three ponds, and several community greens and neighborhood parks (see Fig. 7-4a). The agricultural portion of this open space includes horse pastures, a boarding stable, homeowner garden plots, and a ten-acre community-supported organic farm from which 100 member families receive a bushel of fresh produce and cut flowers each week during the 20-week growing season for an annual subscription of up to $400.

Prairie Crossing's open space has been designed as the western anchor of the adjoining Liberty Prairie Reserve, a 2,500-acre cooperative land preservation project whose principal players have been the Lake County Forest Preserve District, The Nature Conservancy, and Libertyville Township (which in 1986 approved a $22 million bond issue to protect land in that community), along with individual landowners. Trails are being developed to make the reserve accessible to the public, with a regional trail connecting Prairie Crossing via an underpass.

The residential portion of Prairie Crossing has been sensitively laid out to preserve existing hedgerows and windbreaks and to provide sites for 317 single-family homes on lots ranging from 6,000 to 20,000 square feet. All the lots have been designed to abut and overlook the protected open lands. Four house types bear different relationships to the green space: village lots (60), meadow lots (131), field lots (54), and prairie lots (72). Homes ranging from 1,140 to 3,428 square feet have been designed by three prominent Chicago archi-

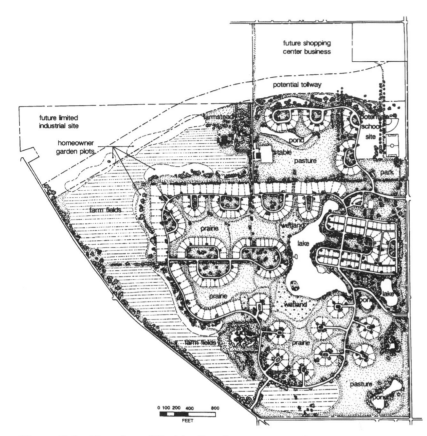

Figure 7-4a. Site plan of Prairie Crossing.

Figure 7-4b. A small pond graces one of Prairie Crossing's several neighborhood parks, through which runs a segment of the community's ten-mile trail network (which also connects it with a regional commuter rail station located close to one edge of the development).

Figure 7-4c. All of this community's 317 homes look out onto various parts of the 450 acres of open space permanently protected as part of the original conservation design—either formal parks or informal fields, prairie, or wildlife habitat. The homes pictured here back up to community open space abutting and buffering the 2,500-acre Liberty Prairie Reserve located on a neighboring parcel.

tects in updated versions of vernacular Midwestern farmhouses. They feature front porches, traditional roof pitches and overhangs, double-hung windows, and clapboards exposed four inches to the weather. Super-insulated and nearly air tight, these homes cut heating and cooling costs roughly in half. All conform to the U.S. Department of Energy's specifications for energy efficiency in its Building America program.

Prairie Crossing reflects the vision of Gaylord Donnelley, the late printer who purchased the property in 1987 for $7,500 per acre from a developer whose high-density proposal for the site had been opposed by the county and neighbors throughout 15 years of lawsuits.

A key part of the site design has been a state-of-the-art system for treating and absorbing stormwater on the site. Runoff is reduced both by building streets 8 to 12 feet narrower than are typical in subdivisions with lots of these sizes and by the use of roadside swales in which native plants absorb and filter some of the precipitation. These swales lead to wetland areas where further biological treatment occurs before the water reaches the lake, whose broad surface serves as a large holding area. This approach is estimated to reduce waterborne pollutants by 85–100 percent and to cut runoff volume by two-thirds. Such a high level of treatment is especially important at Prairie Crossing, where the runoff flows into Almond Marsh, a sedge meadow and 80-acre wetland to which the state has given its highest ecological protection. The high water quality also allows swimming and other nonmotorized recreational uses, as well as the reintroduction of native fish species to the ecosystem.

Homeowners are encouraged to plant their yards with native grasses, wildflowers, and shrubs, and one of the model homes has been landscaped in this way to show prospective and existing residents how this can be done. Several residents have employed this approach extensively on both their front and back yards, where conventional suburban lawn has been replaced by a combination of native trees and shrubs (hackberry, hawthorn, witch hazel, and chinkapin oak) and wildflowers indigenous to the area (purple coneflower, prairie coreopsis, aster, sweet William, and baptisia). This ethic is taken to an even higher level on the restored prairie within the common open space where the plants of the mesic and wet mesic prairies provide a rich wildlife habitat.

Among the built amenities at Prairie Crossing are its community center (an 1890s dairy barn rescued from another site and restored by the developer), a large village green overlooking the lake, a swimming beach, and neighborhood parks with playgrounds, athletic fields, and tennis courts. In addition there are ten miles of trails for walking or riding, providing connections between neighborhoods and the new commuter rail station. The regional trail network will ultimately link to the Des Plaines River Greenway through the Liberty Prairie Reserve.

The open space is maintained according to a special management plan prepared by a restoration ecologist that specifies best management practices for the various kinds of conservation lands. These and other common maintenance costs are paid for by the homeowner association. Also, an innovative endowment fund receives one-half of one percent of the sales price each time a house is sold. These funds will be used to enhance the common natural resource and recreation areas in the future.

The Preserve at Hunter's Lake

Location: Town of Ottawa, Waukesha County, Wisconsin
Development Period: 1994–1998
Site Designer: Teska Associates, Evanston, Illinois
Developer: Siepmann Realty, Waukesha County, Wisconsin

Of the 270 acres on this property, more than 180 (or nearly 70 percent) will remain as permanent conservation land. In addition, the entire three-quarter-mile frontage on Hunter's Lake will remain undisturbed except for the addition of a small boating dock for use by neighborhood residents.

Of the special features of this property, one of the more noteworthy is the way the Ice Age Trail winds through the center, along a heavily wooded path. When the developer first acquired the property, this trail followed a straight line along the site's eastern boundary, taking hikers on a relatively uninteresting route out in the open and exposed to the hot sun. As part of a 1,000-mile trail system administered by the National Park Service, tracing the southernmost extent of the last glacier, the developer saw this trail as an added amenity for The Preserve's residents and offered to reroute it to its present location. Past positive experience with another segment of the same trail, in their Hawksnest subdivision in Delafield Township, convinced the Siepmanns of the benefits such a relocation would bring to all parties. Secondary trails connect this main spine with each part of the neighborhood, as they do at Hawksnest.

One of the aspects of this development that struck the author is that its layout so clearly mirrors the "four-step" conservation design approach described and illustrated on pages 65–74 of this book. Examining the final site plan, one can easily see how the initial design impulse was to identify those parts of the property that should be preserved and "designed around." Of the natural areas on this site, the two most significant are the lake edge and the upland woods (see Fig. 7-5a).

Figure 7-5b. Only two houses in this carefully designed, award-winning subdivision can be seen from the lake itself. A common dock with several canoes belonging to the homeowner association is reached via a neighborhood trail.

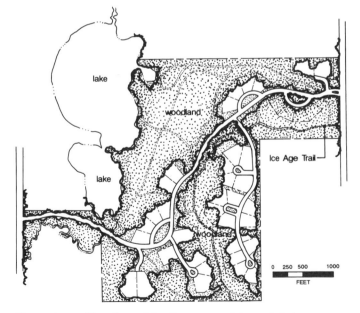

Figure 7-5a. Site plan of the Preserve at Hunter's Lake.

Figure 7-5c. This conservation meadow is overlooked by several houses and is traversed by a footpath that connects with the Ice Age Trail, a long-distance trail administered by the National Park Service. The Preserve is an outstanding example of "the golf course development without the golf course," substituting greenways for fairways, and community greens for putting greens.

Although most of the lake margin is low-lying and unsuitable for construction, most developers would have been tempted to create as many lots as possible along the western edge of the uplands and extend their lot lines right down to the water, effectively blocking access by owners of other lots in the neighborhood. In addition to the wet lake edges that would be classified as Primary Conservation Areas under the four-step design approach, the terrestrial woodland habitat represented by the mature stands of oak, maple, and hickory covering about half of the balance of the property would easily qualify as the most logical Secondary Conservation Area that could be identified on the property. Although most developers would perceive these shady wooded locations as ideal places in which to site new houses, the ecologically more sensitive approach of positioning homes on the open fields and former sheep meadows, from which the original forest cover had been cleared many decades before, was selected by the Siepmanns. With the open land identified as Potential Development Areas, the second, third, and fourth steps (siting houses, connecting them with streets and trails, and drawing lot lines) follow easily in logical progression.

This development is also characterized by an unusual level of respect for the site's historic structures, all of which were in poor to extremely poor physical condition at the time of purchase. From smaller elements such as stone walls and a tiny caretaker's cottage to the original farmhouse and barn, careful, sensitive rehabilitation characterized the developer's efforts. The cottage now serves as a community meeting room with a passive outdoor recreation area behind it in the former back yard, while the farmhouse has been sold on its own lot as a residence. The barn, once considered for demolition, was spared when the engineer's initial street alignment was modified to bypass it. The developer feels that the money spent on its repair was recovered through premiums added to the prices of lots within its viewshed. These lots sold extremely quickly because of the historic ambience the barn gave to that part of the neighborhood.

Street design was another carefully considered element at The Preserve, with woodland clearing minimized by constructing streets with curb-and-gutter design in forested areas. More than half the street length is either single-loaded or entirely open on both sides, adding significantly to the rural character of the development. All but two of the lots along the main spine road are situated back behind a crescent-shaped access drive, sometimes called an "eyebrow." The open spaces within those islands, typically approximately an acre, are managed as meadows or woodlands rather than as clipped grass. Three cul-de-sacs terminate in commodious planting islands, into which the developer moved more than 100 existing trees from the street alignment elsewhere on the property. In one case, a cul-de-sac has been modified to become a "loop lane" with a central median running its full length, lending a particularly attractive touch to the four lots it serves. Another aspect of the street alignment is its reverse curves, where segments curving in opposite directions are joined together without the standard straight-line connecting strip required in most ordinances (an inappropriate carryover from highway design standards on which many local street ordinances are based).

Elements such as those described above, as well as the painstaking care with which existing wetland vegetation was removed, held in on-site nurseries, and reestablished around the new stone bridge constructed across Scuppernong Creek, helped the Siepmanns win the coveted *National Wetlands Award for Land Stewardship and Development* from the U.S. Environmental Protection Agency for its superior land plan at The Preserve.

The Meadows at Dolly Gordon Brook

Location: South Side Road, York, Maine
Development Period: 1996–1999
Site Designer: William Anderson, York, Maine
Developer: Duane Jellison

The Meadows at Dolly Gordon Brook is one of a half-dozen subdivisions approved in the last several years by the York Planning Board, working closely with the York Land Trust to ensure that a significant percentage of the development remains as permanent open space. Equally important, this working relationship between the town and the trust has resulted in a high degree of quality control regarding the nature of the land that is to be protected and minimization of adverse environmental impacts on any part of the subdivision (including lands within the "development envelope"). To date, nearly 350 acres of land have been protected in this manner, making the town somewhat of a model for local officials and land trusts in other communities to emulate. It should be added that the cooperative spirit in York has also included many developers, who have recognized the mutual benefits of designing new residential developments with open space that provides an excellent marketing tool.

Of this 79-acre site, all but 24 acres have been permanently protected by a conservation easement. Of the 55 protected acres seven are in a hayfield along South Side Road, creating a foreground meadow that preserves the neighborhood's rural character and shelters homes from the increasing traffic on this major collector (see Fig. 7-6a). Forty-eight acres of forest land are preserved toward the rear of the property, where two tributaries of the York River flow through wet

Figure 7-6b. Sweeping views across "foreground meadows" from the entrance street leading into the property, a 700-foot length without homes on either side. This approach protects the town's rural character as seen from South Side Road. Note the absence of curbs and the street's modest 18-foot paved width.

woods. The woodland preservation element of this plan is significant because, under the town's zoning ordinance, developers could also have built on the high ground between the two streams had they desired to do so. If a conventional two-acre lot pattern had been followed, the habitat would have been seriously fragmented and substantially cleared of its large trees. Among the developer's economic reasons for choosing smaller three-quarter-acre lots were to conserve large attractive trees that add value to the entire neighborhood and to minimize the $9,000 per acre costs of removing and disposing of tree stumps. In this case the developer chose to work closely with the land trust, which was charged by the planning board with advising on the designation and management of the open space and overseeing the cutting of pedestrian trails, which are planned to eventually link up with a wider neighborhood trail network.

Homes at The Meadows range from $225,000 to $425,000. These

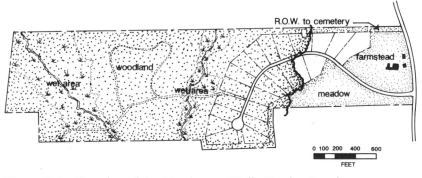

Figure 7-6a. Site plan of the Meadows at Dolly Gordon Brook.

Guidelines for Developers Working with the York Land Trust

When cluster development is proposed and substantial conservation open space is part of the plan, the Planning Board may suggest that the developer consult with the York Land Trust (YLT) about the possibility of granting an easement to YLT on the future Homeowners' Association (HOA) conservation open space. The following are the steps in the process:

1. From the beginning of YLT's involvement in the project, and throughout the process, the Planning Board will be informed in writing about discussions with the developer, progress made in negotiations, and suggestions from the Trust, based on inventory research.
2. The developer will supply YLT with a survey drawing and plan of the proposed development.
3. The developer and YLT will discuss the proposed use of the conservation open space. Will the open space be segregated from construction, roads, and services? Will the open space be impacted, during development and after, by uses other than conservation and agreed-upon passive recreation? Who will locate and supervise the clearing of any proposed pathways? Does the developer understand the environmental concerns and goals of YLT?
4. If YLT and the developer find common ground in this initial discussion, the developer must flag the proposed open space area(s). YLT members will then walk the area(s) with the developer. Parking areas for future monitoring will be identified. An understanding of the conclusions reached in these meetings will be exchanged in writing by the developer and the Trust. The conclusions reached will also be communicated to the Planning Board by both parties in writing.
5. If conservation values commensurate with the goals of YLT are found to exist in the proposed conservation area(s), YLT will conduct a preliminary inventory to further document the value of the land to the Trust. This inventory will be sent to the developer and to the Planning Board. There will be a charge to the developer for this service. This charge will be based on the hourly fees of YLT's environmental consultants.
6. After completing the preliminary inventory, the YLT Board of Directors will discuss the conservation area(s) and the possibility of an easement. The Board will subsequently indicate its findings in writing to the developer and to the York Planning Board. This communication will indicate the Board's consensus on whether or not to proceed, and it could possibly include suggestions that may arise from the preliminary inventory.
7. If the YLT Board decides to proceed as part of the project, it will negotiate the easement document and the HOA bylaws with the developer. If this process is successful, and following receipt of a copy of the easement and the HOA bylaws, the YLT Board will indicate in writing to the Planning Board and to the developer that the easement document and the HOA bylaws are acceptable.
8. The YLT will request a stewardship endowment donation from the developer upon the Trust's acceptance of the easement. This donation is calculated on acreage and future monitoring responsibilities. An exchange of letters will document agreement on the donation.
9. Barring late changes or interim violations, the YLT Board will vote on acceptance of the easement after the final hearing by the Planning Board.
10. Permanent pipes or cement monuments delineating the conservation open space must be placed by the developer within 30 days of project approval by the Planning Board.

spacious, custom-designed residences contain up to 3,500 square feet of floorspace and feature two- and three-car garages.

Wastewater from the 24 homes is handled through individual septic systems located on each lot, but the open meadowland provides alternative locations for a community system should that ever become necessary.

A final feature of note is the street design, which begins with a 700-foot length of roadway without any houses as it gently curves with the topography across the front meadow, adding grace and beauty to the neighborhood.

The designated open space is permanently protected through a conservation easement held by the York Land Trust. The participation of the York Land Trust has nearly become a routine part of the subdivision review process in this coastal Maine community, with the planning board frequently inviting the Trust's active participation from the earliest sketch plan stage onward. This arrangement has been mutually beneficial, with the Trust identifying potential conservation areas and trail linkages from the outset, before any layout patterns have begun to solidify. Trust members make it a point to walk the property with applicants and town officials and to see firsthand the resources and conservation opportunities it presents. Its recommendations are taken very seriously by planning board members and therefore also by developers who are anxious to avoid delays—and who also incur the costs of detailed site inventories to determine the areas that should be "designed around" and protected. When developers reject Trust recommendations to reduce certain negative impacts of their layout on natural areas, the Trust has held to its standards and has declined further involvement, highlighting the importance of careful site review and prompting the planning board to consider tightening its ordinance requirements. The Trust frequently accepts easements on subdivision open space and has adopted a set of guidelines (see the accompanying box) that are given to devel-

opers by the town planning staff from the beginning in situations in which applicants are proposing to create conservation areas for subsequent acceptance by the Trust. The town strongly encourages developers to work with the Trust so that the Trust will ultimately accept an easement on the open space, and this system has worked well.

Farmcolony

Location: Parker Mountain, near Stanardsville, Greene County, Virginia
Development Period: 1974–1976
Site Designer: Michael Redd, North Palm Beach, Florida
Developer: Farm Development Corporation

Nestled at the base of the foothills of the Blue Ridge Mountains in Virginia's Greene County, Farmcolony is another excellent example of the four-step approach to subdivision design. From studying the layout, it is apparent that the site designer consciously identified all the parts of the property he wanted to conserve as open space as his first step and then located the houses to take greatest advantage of the views he thus protected. The street alignment is clearly a secondary consideration, a functional ribbon of asphalt simply connecting the houses to the main road that borders the property. And the lot lines are relatively unimportant and could have easily been drawn closer to the houses themselves.

When asked about his layout approach some 20 years after the fact, Michael Redd said that he simply followed his instincts as a site designer, trying to avoid impacting the property's most attractive features that he and his client recognized as a significant potential selling point for the house lots. Although this project was the first of its kind in the county and broke previously uncharted ground in the development business in this part of the state, lots sold very well from the beginning, proving that if one has a good idea one does not need precedents to ensure success.

Of the property's 289 acres, 120 have been permanently conserved as farmland and about 70 are located in a woodland preserve (see Fig. 7-7a). Most of the farming portion is planted with hay, and the remainder is used as pasturage for cows, calves, sheep, and horses, with a small poultry house supplying residents with fresh eggs. Since its inception, the farming operation has been run by a farm manager hired by the homeowner association. In the early years of the development, the manager was also a local farmer; but for a number of years one of the residents undertook this role, which supplemented his retirement income and provided him with an occupation he enjoyed. He recently retired and the farm is now managed by the homeowner association's board of directors with volunteers helping with the chores. The wooded areas occupy the steeper parts of the site and are threaded with bridle and hiking trails for use by the residents and their neighbors. This land has also been set aside as a bird sanctuary.

Farmcolony was developed in a "density-neutral" manner, meaning that its number of house lots (48) are the same as would result from a conventional plan in this five-acre district, given the terrain and other natural features constraints on the property. As the property is located some 85 miles west of Washington, D.C., few residents

Figure 7-7b. View from the veranda of one of the houses located on a low ridge overlooking the 150 acres of fields and pastures owned in common by the residents and managed jointly for continued livestock and crop production in this award-winning subdivision near Charlottesville, Virginia.

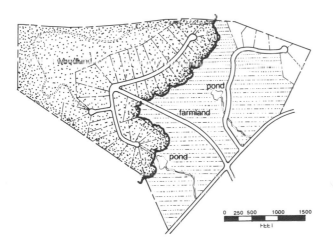

Figure 7-7a. Site plan of Farmcolony.

Figure 7-7c. View across pastures and fields back toward the homes (situated on the far ridge near the horizon line), with the original farmhouse in the middle distance. Surrounded by protected conservation land, this structure functions as a community building, with overnight accommodation available for guests of Farmcolony residents.

are regular commuters. Most work in nearby Charlottesville or are empty-nesters looking for a place where they can enjoy the country setting without having to personally maintain or manage rural acreage. The original farmhouse is owned jointly and serves as overnight accommodation for guests of the residents. It also contains a meeting room, an activity room, and a library.

County officials who were initially skeptical of the Farmcolony approach for protecting farmland came to see it in later years as a far more effective method than their zoning's traditional five-acre minimum lot size, which actually destroys the viability of farmland for future production purposes by dividing the resource land into lots that are too big to mow and too small to plough. As word spread about Farmcolony in neighboring counties and states, local officials from as far away as Calvert County, Maryland, came to similar conclusions about the benefits of conservation design, having also come from an initial perspective favoring huge multi-acre house lots. Farmcolony's largest impact might be in its influence on planning practices in other areas experiencing greater growth pressures, such as Calvert County, which liked the idea so much it adopted zoning standards effectively mandating this kind of "rural clustering" in 1993. Since its inception, that ordinance amendment has helped conserve more than 3,000 acres of land in that county, a track record which has in turn begun to influence planning policy in neighboring counties.

Winner of the Culpeper Soil and Water Conservation District's Conservation Award and Virginia's Clean Water Award, Farmcolony was also the recipient of the Governor's Environmental Excellence Award for 1991.

Westwood Common

Location: Village of Beverly Hills, Michigan
Development Period: 1996–1998
Developer: David Jensen, Beverly Hills, Michigan
Site Designer: Gibbs Planning Group, Birmingham, Michigan

This project differs from others featured in this chapter in its more formal site design and layout, demonstrating that the basic principles of conservation design are fully compatible with those of the "New Urbanism." The central green, which covers approximately half an acre, possesses an interesting trapezoidal shape and is bounded by streets on two sides only. On the other two sides, homes front directly onto this open space, separated only by a paved footpath. As all the houses at Westwood Common have rear garages accessed via back lanes or shared drives, this novel design approach is easy to achieve. When one pauses to think about it, there is no reason that streets must run alongside the fronts of all house lots (see Fig. 7-8a).

Fully 70 percent of the property is dedicated as permanent open space, including about 12 acres through which flows a 1,000-foot section of the Rouge River. Although much of that land is either wet or floodprone, this conservation parcel could have easily been divided

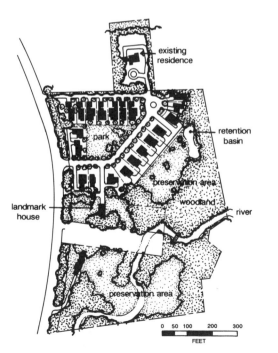

Figure 7-8a. Site plan of Westwood Common.

Figure 7-8b. View from the front porch of one of the 12 houses framing the quarter-acre central common.

Figure 7-8c. Another view of the common showing the direct relationship between the house lots and this formal open space. These house lots have no street frontage whatsoever and are accessed only by foot from the front, with driveways leading to rear service lanes. Ordinances should therefore eliminate the standard requirement for street frontage in conservation subdivisions, and site designers should take note of this creative approach. The developer, who was initially somewhat skeptical of this arrangement, found that his homes possessed greater "curb appeal" when there was neither a curb nor a street right in front of them.

and added to a number of the abutting house lots, denying the rest of the residents any access to or enjoyment of this special part of the property. Plans for this open space include a wooded walking trail network, meadows for informal ball games, and a gazebo overlooking a pond that will have a fountain during the summer and provide for skating in mid-winter, all of which enhance the quality of life at Westwood Common.

The phenomenal market success of Westwood Common is perhaps the most remarkable part of this story. Despite the fact that prevailing prices in all the surrounding neighborhoods were in the $150,000 to $300,000 range, homes at Westwood sold for between $400,000 and $600,000. They are, of course, commodious and very nicely appointed (with 2,600 to 3,800 square feet of floor area), but the real key to their salability lies mostly with the masterful site design produced by the Gibbs Planning Group. Here buyers recognized the opportunity to live in a neighborhood that was full of character and brimming with open space, views of which are framed by the windows of 20 of the 23 homes. Nine of the houses feature walk-out basements as well.

Testimony to the value enhancement of the site design is the fact that a preexisting house fronting onto one of the public roads bordering the property rose in value from $150,000 to $280,000 after it was incorporated into the new neighborhood through minor alterations to reorient the garage and driveway so they both faced in the opposite direction, toward the new internal subdivision street.

Westwood Common also demonstrates that decisions running counter to prevailing trends and conventional wisdom can pay handsome dividends. This development, which outperformed all other subdivisions in the county, achieved this distinction with lots ranging from 5,000 to 7,000 square feet (40 to 58 feet wide, and 100 to 120 feet deep), essentially one-quarter the usual minimum lot size in the district (25,000 square feet). All homes are served by public water and sewer.

The only homes located on larger lots are the three preexisting residences, two of which came with substantial acreage, including a historic sandstone house moved to the property many years ago from Grosse Pointe. However, that home in particular has been incorporated into the streetscape and frames the southern edge of the central green.

Hunter's Pointe and Solitude Pointe

Location: Lee Road and Hamburg Road, Hamburg Township, Livingston County, Michigan

Development Period: 1993–1995

Site Designers: Progressive Engineering and Ore Creek Development Company

Developers: Mickey Stanley and M. Kelly

Of the 33 conservation subdivisions approved and built in Hamburg Township since the Open Space Community ordinance was adopted in 1992, which have together conserved more than 1,000 acres of land, these two developments are perhaps the most successful from a design standpoint. The process for determining density in such subdivisions in this community is through a "parallel plan," not unlike the Yield Plan described on page 43 of this book.

Comprising nearly 55 acres, Hunter's Pointe contains 45 lots averaging 24,000 square feet in area and ranging from 120 to 150 feet in width in a zoning district where one-acre lots had been the norm. Housing prices are as high or higher than those in nearby conventional developments with full-acre lots because of the large percentage of open space and the range of recreational amenities provided. Altogether, 21 acres of upland open space have been permanently conserved, in addition to 8 acres of wetlands—meaning that slightly less than 25 acres was consumed in house lots. Approximately three-quarters of the lots either back out onto or front on protected open space. Close to one-third of the street length is single-loaded, which is to say that it borders open space on one side so that this aspect of the property is brought into view for all who drive, walk, bike, or jog

along it (see Fig. 7-9a). An extensive three-mile network of trails (six feet wide and surfaced with wood chips) links various parts of the neighborhood with each other and with the open space, skirting wooded knolls and edging along the margins of the wetlands and pond. One of these trails leads to an elevated gazebo offering sheltered views across the wetland nature sanctuary for birders and other observers of wildlife. Another trail leads around a pond and connects with open space and trails in a neighboring conservation subdivision, Breckenridge, immediately to the north. Access agreements in the easements specifically permit residents to walk the trails in both developments. A basketball court within one of the conservation areas provides another recreational opportunity for residents.

With 74 acres, Solitude Pointe contains nearly 20 more acres of land than Hunter's Pointe, but it yielded only four more house lots (49), because of greater natural features constraints on the property, including a bog with several rare plant species. Its 30 acres of open space consist of nearly 20 acres of wetlands and 10 acres of high-

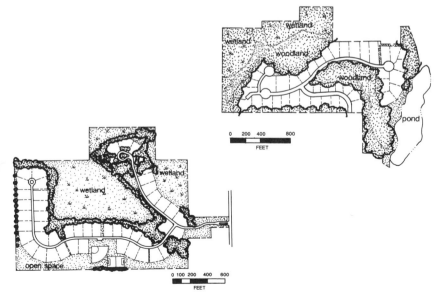

Figure 7-9a. Site plans of Hunter's Pointe and Solitude Pointe.

Figure 7-9b. In the many conservation subdivisions in Hamburg Township, children can literally ride their bikes out their back yard and onto the trails leading down to ponds, playing fields, and other open space areas. The trail in the foreground was recently redressed with new wood chips by a group of neighborhood residents in a "clean-and-green" activity conducted by the homeowner association.

Figure 7-9d. A baseball diamond and a soccer field occupy this neighborhood recreation area located alongside a "single-loaded" section of one of the streets in Hunter's Pointe. Provision of such facilities typically reduces the need to spend public tax dollars on such items.

Figure 7-9c. A gazebo overlooks a large wetland constituting part of the subdivision open space at Hunter's Pointe, providing a place for quiet contemplation and wildlife observation at this sanctuary.

quality woodlands plus open fields that had formerly been used for baseball by a summer camp that had previously occupied the site. As with Hunter's Pointe, about one-third of the street system opens onto the conservation land on one side, reinforcing the green design concept. It too provides a rustic trail network connecting different parts of the neighborhood with the ball field and soccer field, and a viewing platform offers a vantage point for surveying the wetlands and its small expanse of open water. Part of the conservation land at Solitude Point adjoins and connects with the Pine Hills Camp, extending the open space system.

The Ranch at Roaring Fork

Location: Carbondale, Garfield County, Colorado
Development Period: 1965–1971
Site Designer: Leitch & Kyotaki, Newport Beach, California
Developer: Jay Kee Jacobson

This very attractive site, located several miles outside Carbondale, Colorado, encompasses nearly 420 acres of land on both sides of a two-mile-long stretch of the Roaring Fork River, providing some of the best fly-fishing to be found in the entire state. All but 60 acres, or more than 80 percent of the property, remains in permanent, undivided open space, jointly owned by the 137 lot and condo owners through a neighborhood homeowner association that effectively prevents any further development of the land. Apart from a small neighborhood park with playground equipment and a 25-acre executive par 3 (nine-hole) golf course, the open space remains in grazing lands, meadows, and natural areas providing habitat for the abundant wildlife (including deer, beavers, muskrats, blue heron, and many other types of birds—126 species were counted in one inventory).

The majority of the open space consists of sparsely wooded or open natural lands covered with low vegetation typical of the area and through which courses the Roaring Fork River, fed in part by 26 springs on the property. Prior to its development as a conservation subdivision, the property had for many decades been used as a cattle and alfalfa hobby farm, during which time much of the stream bank had become degraded. In addition, irrigation "improvements" had damaged the quality of the river. These situations were reversed by the developer, who increased the trout habitat by constructing several large ponds linked to the river system.

Water from the river was channeled and regulated through a diversion head gate and then directed into the first of ten lakes to allow silt and debris to settle. The modified habitat includes three stream systems. Water in the upper system flows into a series of interconnected lakes, one to three acres in size, and into a natural spawning raceway. The middle system cuts diagonally across a meadow and connects with the upper system, while the lower system runs parallel to the river. The entire system is eight miles long: two miles of the river itself plus six miles of internal streams connecting the ten lakes, all linked together with trails.

All of the internal streams were modified with new meanders to slow the water movement and with deep holes cut throughout the system and areas dug out under the banks to provide cover. Aided by the natural springs on the property, the stream vegetation is abundant and includes grasses, moss, and watercress (which can provide a tasty addition to salads). Only fly-fishing is allowed and only on a catch-and-release basis.

These improvements were officially recognized in 1998 when The Ranch received an award for having implemented the best fishing improvement plan in Colorado. An early idea to build a full 18-hole golf course was rejected in favor of maintaining the maximum area of this unique property in a more natural state. Now threaded by nearly six miles of walking and bridle trails, this de facto wildlife sanctuary provides nearly continuous opportunities for observing wildlife.

Maintenance of the common areas is supervised by a full-time ranch manager who looks after the common land and monitors the community water supply and sewage treatment systems.

Homes are located on lots averaging 12,000 square feet, nearly all of which abut or face onto open space. Houses range from 1,500 to 2,500 square feet in floor area, typical for relatively upscale homes built in this area 25 to 30 years ago. Of the 137 dwellings, 77 are single-family detached residences, while 60 are townhouse condominiums attached in groups of two, four, and six units (see Fig. 7-10a). The original plan, which had envisioned a greater proportion of townhouses, was modified in favor of more detached residences on their own house lots in response to market demand. In addition to the fishing, hiking, biking, riding, golfing, and cross-country skiing opportunities, The Ranch includes two tennis courts, a riding arena, and a trap/skeet shooting range. The original late-nineteenth-century homestead house has been preserved as a heritage property and continues to serve as a private residence. The site designers also provided for RV storage in a central area that is enclosed by visual screening.

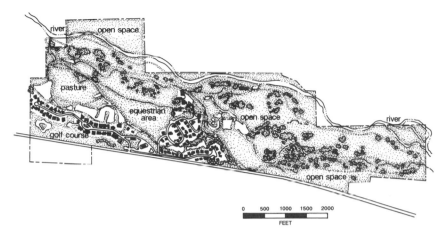

Figure 7-10a. Site plan of the Ranch at Roaring Fork.

Figure 7-10b. Several homes and part of the community's six-mile trail network are located along this tributary of the Roaring Fork River, which provides excellent fly-fishing opportunities. As part of the project, the developer restored extensive areas of streambanks that had been degraded by prior cattle operations on the property.

Figure 7-10c. Many homes such as this one overlook approximately 350 acres of permanent open space in Colorado's first example of a true conservation subdivision.

The Ranch at Roaring Fork was the first planned unit development to be proposed and approved in Garfield County. As a front runner, the developer had to bring county officials up to date with this then-new approach to subdivision design. Years of prior development experience at Del-Webb had prepared him for the task, and after leaving that firm he had decided to create a community laid out with sensitivity and imagination. Although almost entirely rural, the county had adopted urban zoning standards. It only reluctantly agreed to waive its curb-and-gutter requirements upon pleading by the developer, who saw that curbed streets would have spoiled the rural character of the neighborhood he wanted to create. In addition, those urban "improvements" would have channeled all the storm water to central discharge points rather than allowing it to infiltrate into grassy swales and seep into broad, shallow detention areas. In semi-arid climates such as occur frequently in the Inter-Mountain West, stormwater reclamation and infiltration are highly desirable to recharge underground aquifers, helping to maintain base stream flow during dry periods of the year.

Village Homes

Location: Davis, California
Development Period: 1975–1981
Site Designer: Michael Corbett
Developers: Michael and Judith Corbett

Begun in 1975, Village Homes pioneered the concept of green development and set standards that relatively few subsequent projects have equalled to this day. The 60-acre site supports 210 single-family detached dwellings located on lots averaging 4,500 square feet, plus 30 attached rental units. Because of its compact lot sizes, Village Homes has been able to conserve 40 percent of its land area (nearly 28 acres) for a variety of open spaces, including neighborhood greens, community commons, playing fields, greenway corridors, allotment gardens, orchards, and a small vineyard.

Village Homes demonstrates how municipalities can achieve multiple conservation goals through extensions or infilling built at the moderate density of four dwellings per acre. Located in the city of Davis, 14 miles west of Sacramento, the community is situated within easy biking distance of both the University of California campus and a major retail and service center.

Michael Corbett believes that open space in conservation subdivisions must serve four functions or needs: (1) it must be physically attractive; (2) it must attract residents to use it, making it a place of social connections; (3) its landscaping must be largely edible (oranges, figs, grapes, etc.); and (4) nearly all stormwater must be retained on site, recharging the local aquifer.

Regarding the edible landscaping, tree species include oranges, pears, peaches, plums, cherries, figs, almonds, grapes, and persimmons. Residents are allowed to pick the fruit, but the almonds are harvested mechanically and their proceeds (about $3,000 per year) are dedicated to the community's maintenance fund.

The stormwater management system at Village Homes is one of its gems. Corbett essentially sculpted the property, which was originally as flat as a table top, into a series of parallel mini-ridges and mini-valleys. This was accomplished in a very subtle way with the gradients hardly noticeable to the untrained eye. Streets and homes are located along the high points, shedding their runoff toward the greenway corridors adjacent to all the back yards, where the stormwater is absorbed by infiltration trenches backfilled with sand and gravel, recharging the aquifer and reducing summer irrigation costs by one-third. This arrangement successfully reverses the typical approach in which stormwater is directed to streets that have no ability to absorb it but merely channel the water to ungainly pits and craters known as detention basins. Corbett has estimated that eliminating curbs, gutters, and standard drain pipes under the streets saved $800 per lot in 1975, money that was therefore available to be invested in additional landscaping of the common areas. (See Figure 704D-85.)

Streets in Village Homes are 20 feet across, a paved width that works well because adequate off-street parking spaces are provided in driveways and parking bays near garages. Reduced street widths not only cut initial infrastructure costs, they also provide continuing benefits in smaller maintainance costs and less stormwater runoff. The combination of reducing asphalt coverage and planting street trees that can shade a higher proportion of the narrower street surfaces has also lowered summer air temperatures above these streets by 10 to 15 degrees compared with the situation in conventional subdivisions.

Consumer satisfaction at Village Homes is very high, as evidenced by the fact that residents tend to keep thir houses longer than average, typically choosing to remodel and expand them rather than buying larger "move-up" versions elsewhere. House sale prices average

13 percent above those in nearby developments with larger lots but no open space, demonstrating the value added through superior site design. When houses do go on the market, the average sales period is half that for Davis as a whole. However, realtors initially shunned the project in its early days and even discouraged potential buyers from visiting it because they did not really understand the concepts involved. This underscores the need for green developers to educate these critical players in the marketing arena. The strong sales (and resales) enjoyed at Village Homes have, however, earned it the highest accolades from the city's leading realtor (Coldwell Banker), which now describes it as "Davis' most desirable subdivision" (quoted in Wilson 1998).

The site plan is essentially an adaptation of and improvement to the concept pioneered by Clarence Stein and Henry Wright at Radburn, in Fairlawn, New Jersey, in 1928. Vehicular access is provided by twelve cul-de-sacs on the "car side," complemented on the "garden side" by an excellent pedestrian system linking all the homes in the various neighborhoods together via an extensive footpath network located in the greenway areas adjoining every back yard (see Fig. 7-11a). Despite concerns typically expressed by public safety officials about such "single-access" streets being blocked in the event of an emergency, Corbett reports that the absence of second access ways has never presented a problem in the community's 22 years.

Unlike Radburn, the cul-de-sacs at Village Homes were deliberately aligned along approximate east–west axes to assure good solar opportunities for all the houses, which were designed with at least 60 percent of their glazing facing south and with deep roof overhangs on their southern sides to screen summer sun while allowing winter rays to reach the concrete slab floors that absorb solar energy during daylight hours and release it slowly after nightfall. Roofs are more heavily insulated and most are fitted with solar panels that heat the tap water. Because of these features, 50 to 75 percent of heating needs are provided directly by the sun.

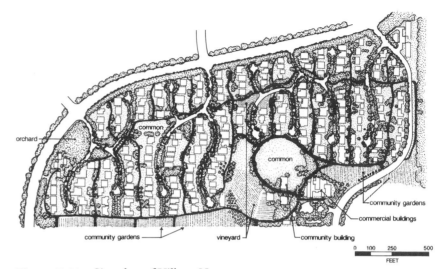

Figure 7-11a. Site plan of Village Homes.

Figure 7-11b. All house lots at Village Homes abut a continuous greenway network with paved paths for pedestrians and cyclists. The boy with the bicycle is standing on one of the many footbridges crossing the infiltration swales that absorb all the precipitation falling onto this development site, irrigating the greenway landscaping and recharging the underlying aquifer. The orange tree and the solar house exemplify two principles advocated by designer Michael Corbett: "edible landscaping" and energy efficiency.

The social aspects of Village Homes are no less impressive than its physical attributes. To encourage and facilitate interaction among community residents, homes are grouped in mini-neighborhoods of eight dwellings, each group arranged around its own semi-common area where landscape features were selected by the first homeowners on a consensus basis. The original landscape option included a variety of fruit-bearing shrubs and trees, fire pits, sandboxes, and gardens for flowers and herbs. More extensive community gardens for vegetables are located at the ends of six cul-de-sacs and provide a buffer along the site's long, western boundary. These open spaces provide casual meeting opportunities and have contributed to a general neighborly feeling among residents of these housing groups, manifested in some cases by regular pot-luck dinners. Community-wide events occur at various times of the year, the most popular being the autumn harvest party. Children of all ages enjoy the many playgrounds and large commons that also serve as playing fields receiving weekly use by local teams. The solar-heated community center provides daycare facilities, a meeting room for homeowners and others who may rent it, and a swimming pool. Other buildings in the complex offer business offices, a dance studio, a restaurant, and second-story apartments.

Community-Wide Map of
Potential Conservation Lands

This design exercise involves creating a Community-Wide Map of Potential Conservation Lands, as described in Chapter 3. This map is a critical part of any municipality's overall strategy to conserve an interconnected network of lands with particular resource values. The second design exercise dovetails with this one in that it shows how an individual parcel that is slated to become a new conservation subdivision fits into the community's overall vision for a greener future, a vision which carefully balances future development and conservation needs.

Unfortunately, this kind of mapping is not always incorporated in municipal Comprehensive Plans and sometimes does not even appear in more detailed Open Space Plans, perhaps because the goal of protecting township-wide conservation networks might be viewed by many people as being unrealistic and unattainable.

Based on the range of land-use planning tools traditionally available to local officials, such a pessimistic assessment of conservation potential is understandable. For decades planners have been coloring maps green and essentially crossing their fingers, hoping that a combination of landowner charity, density incentives for developers, and the occasional state or county grant for land acquisition would enable at least a few properties to be saved, in whole or in part.

However, when a truly comprehensive inventory of natural and cultural resources is combined with an imaginative vision of what could be conserved—and when these two elements are linked with a set of practical regulatory tools providing the means for local officials to implement that vision—a community's long-term future suddenly looks much brighter than the bleak scenario depicted on the "build-out" maps described in Chapter 2 (which should accurately reflect trends that would inevitably continue under current codes).

Just how would a municipality proceed in creating a Map of Potential Conservation Lands? The following paragraphs and illustrations will take the reader through a step-by-step process showing a number of different data layers on which particular resource information is delineated. When these layers are considered together, informed choices must be made as to which elements of the individual resource layers would be the most important to include when integrating them into a composite map depicting the community's future conservation network.

The only absolute limitation is the existing pattern of land that is already developed or fully approved for future development. Where conservation opportunities have been foreclosed by past actions, networks will necessarily be interrupted—at least in terms of possible recreational trail access if not also with regard to wildlife travel corridors (which might survive to a certain degree if the natural areas they traverse are not cleared and graded for lawns). But this should not discourage a community from moving forward and working vigorously to protect the best remaining open space to create whatever kind of network may be possible under the circumstances. This "can-do" spirit has been exemplified in Lower Merion Township which, despite its substantially developed situation, became the first community in Pennsylvania to require 50 to 65 percent conservation lands in virtually all new subdivisions (see Fig. DE1-1).

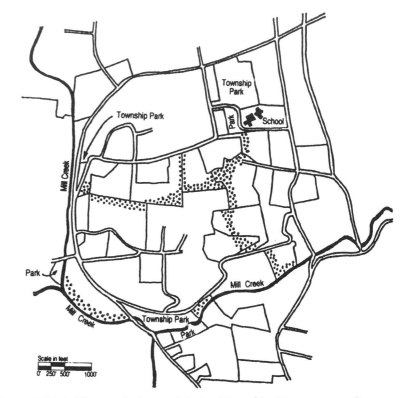

Figure DE1-1. Planners in Lower Merion Township, Montgomery County, Pennsylvania, began to conceptualize a potential open space network in one neighborhood where an elementary school and a municipal park could be connected via a permanently preserved trail system crossing through conservation lands protected by future subdivisions on a number of contiguous estate properties.

Resource Data Layers

In the example provided by this exercise, 11 data layers are examined and analyzed—at least preliminarily. They are then combined and integrated so that the most critical resources will become part of a basic "core" greenway system, supplemented by selected elements from the data layers for second- and third-priority resources.

LAYER 1. BASE MAP

The first of these layers is the base map, consisting of streets and parcel boundaries. The parcel boundary information will help local officials delineate potential greenway lands in a way that would not consume more than half of the otherwise buildable area of any property. (The inherently unbuildable areas are essentially defined by the data layers for floodplains, wetlands, and slopes greater than 25 percent.) At this community-wide mapping stage, it is important to leave approximately half the buildable area of any property outside the greenway system to provide suitable land for accommodating the full development density permitted under the ordinance.

The base map also enables the municipality to identify all parcels over a certain size that would be the threshold above which conservation zoning and subdivision regulations would be required or strongly encouraged to be followed. (In several townships in southeastern Pennsylvania these thresholds vary between five and eight acres.) Certain parcels below that threshold should also be required or strongly encouraged to utilize these flexible site design principles when they occupy strategic positions as critical links in the overall municipal greenway network plan, or if they contain a small but critical resource such as a historic structure or a special tree of significant girth or age. The best approach is not to completely exempt smaller parcels but rather to review them on a case-by-case basis and to issue waivers for those that are not critical to the overall greenway plan and that do not possess any exceptionally special characteristic or feature.

The Core Greenway

The "core greenway" includes only those properties that are already protected and those other lands for which there is a very clear public health or safety justification to exclude all future development. This core area therefore applies to the next three data layers (numbers 2, 3, and 4).

LAYER 2. LANDS THAT ARE EITHER PROTECTED OR EXEMPTED

This data layer shows all public land at the municipal, county, state, and federal levels, such as parks, forests, game lands, and wildlife refuges. In addition, it should show the location of any preserves owned by private conservation organizations, such as land trusts or conservancies. Ideally, the location of properties protected through permanent conservation easements could also be identified as key pieces of the overall network of protected lands, although the opportunity for public trail access on those properties will probably be extremely limited (at least until there is a good track record with local trails for private landowners to evaluate). Far greater trail potential exists along utility rights-of-way, which constitute another type of protected land that should be mapped onto this data layer. As this data layer pertains to lands that would not be subject to design standards for new subdivisions, it makes sense to include those smaller parcels below the size threshold established in the ordinance, which are exempted from the Growing Greener regulations (say, parcels under three or five acres in size) (see Fig. DE1-2).

LAYER 3. CREEKS, FLOODPLAINS, AND WETLANDS

All watercourses should be shown with their associated 100-year floodplains. All wetlands should also be shown on this data layer, as part of the township's hydrologic system (using data from the "medium-intensity" soil survey published by the USDA Natural Resources Conservation Service and wetland maps published by the U.S. Fish and Wildlife Service). Of particular importance are "first-order" streams and streams rated as having exceptional water quality by the state Department of Conservation and Natural Resources. "First-order" streams are the beginning points of drainage systems, typically originating in springs and seeps that provide cold, clear water. Beginning as small, slow-volume streams, the quality of these headwater streams is particularly susceptible to degradation from new construction and development (see Fig. DE1-3).

Publicly Owned Properties

Properties under Conservation Easement

Properties less than 5 Acres Incapable of Subdivision

Figure DE1-2. Lands that are either protected or exempted.

Streams, Floodplains, Wetlands

Figure DE1-3. Streams, floodplains, and wetlands.

LAYER 4. STEEP SLOPES

Generally defined as exceeding 25 percent, steep slopes are inherently unsuitable for house construction, streets, and septic systems because of the extensive (and expensive) grading that is frequently necessary.

Steep Slope Greater than 25%

Figure DE1-4. Steep slopes (greater than 25 percent).

They often occur with shallow bedrock conditions and ledge outcroppings. The environmental reasons for avoiding steep slopes are even more compelling than the economic ones, as these areas are commonly associated with the most mature woodland habitats on any given property. They also have a heightened propensity for soil ero-sion and subsequent siltation of ponds and sedimentation of streams, which progressively degrade those aquatic habitats (see Fig. DE1-4).

Advisory Greenway Areas

The following seven data layers relate to what designers of conservation subdivisions refer to as Secondary Conservation Areas: those places having special features or characteristics meriting careful consideration as elements of the natural or cultural landscape to be "designed around" but that do *not* possess sufficiently severe environmental constraints that would render them unbuildable under conventional land-use regulations. These areas are therefore very much at risk of being cleared, graded, and transformed from a natural to a developed state when there are no clear ordinance standards to protect them through flexible lotting techniques.

These seven data layers are arranged into two groups according to priority for resource protection. Ranking these resources as either second- or third-priority areas is a community decision, and rankings will vary among townships according to their conservation objectives. Priorities may also vary among different zoning districts within the same municipality.

Second-Priority Resource Areas

LAYER 5. RIPARIAN BUFFERS

Numerous studies have shown that wooded buffers along streams, creeks, and rivers are perhaps the single most important element in protecting water quality and aquatic habitat. In addition to filtering runoff from developed areas and providing habitat and travel corridors for terrestrial wildlife, they shade the moving water and help maintain cool water temperatures critical for many species of fish, arthropods (such as crayfish), and some amphibians. Streambanks that have been denuded for agricultural purposes can and generally should be reforested. It is preferable to plant such areas heavily with a variety of native trees and shrubs, but even simply allowing forest succession to occur through a "no-mow" policy would eventually create an adequate buffer. (However, such areas should be managed according to an Operations and Maintenance Plan, specifying the removal of nonnative invasives such as Norway maple, rosa multiflora, japanese knotweed, japanese honeysuckle, and oriental bittersweet.) Buffers should extend at least 50 feet from the top of each watercourse, preferably 100 feet or more. They should also follow watercourses along their entire lengths through the subdivision and ultimately across the municipality (and beyond). Similar buffering and plantings are also highly recommended along the edges of ponds, lakes, wetlands, and bogs (see Fig. DE1-5).

Layer 6. Moderate Slopes and Shallow Bedrock

Areas with moderate slopes (15–25 percent) are typically also characterized by relatively shallow bedrock, both conditions that pose moderate constraints and somewhat higher costs for construction. They are often wooded due to their lesser suitability for agriculture and therefore offer opportunities for buffering the more mature woodland habitats on the steeper slopes with which they are frequently associated. The risk of soil erosion and sedimentation is also greater here than on the flatter terrain (see Fig. DE1-6).

Layer 7. Woodlands

In agrarian areas woodlands represent the only remaining habitat for most species of birds and mammals and should generally be conserved if at all possible. On wooded sites the areas with the oldest or healthiest naturally occurring tree stands should be identified and spared, although this information is usually not available until a subdivision applicant has performed and submitted an Existing Resources/Site Analysis Map. Large blocks of woodland and continuous corridors are the most important to protect at the township scale (although on individual sites that are predominantly open, even hedgerows can be significant features worth designing around) (see Fig. DE1-7).

Riparian Buffers

Figure DE1-5. Riparian buffers.

Layer 8. Soils Rated as "Prime" or "Of Statewide Significance" for Agriculture

Where these soil types coincide with fields, meadows, and pastures, opportunities exist for continuing resource uses such as specialty farming for high-value produce, "community-supported agriculture"

Figure DE1-6. Moderate slopes (15–25 percent) and shallow bedrock.

Figure DE1-7. Woodlands.

(CSA), horticulture, pick-your-own berry operations, wholesale nurseries, tree farms (including Christmas trees), and gentlemen's farms. Although it is generally preferable to conduct traditional agriculture on large blocks of uninterrupted farmland, specialty farming fortunately does not require the same degree of contiguity and can often be conducted on smaller parcels that adjoin developed uses on several sides, especially when some buffering is provided (such as

through ball fields, woodlands, or meadows in conservation subdivisions). For this reason, farmland fragmentation—which is generally unavoidable in suburban situations in any case—need not preclude continued resource uses on the remaining fields and pastures (as attested by five of the examples of creatively designed "flexible subdivisions" featuring various degrees of conservation included in Chapter 7 of this book) (see Fig. DE1-8).

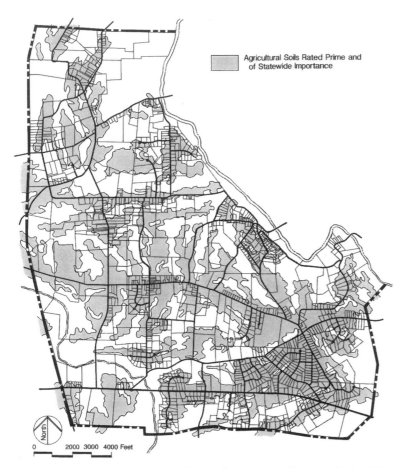

Figure DE1-8. Agricultural soils rated prime or of statewide significance.

Figure DE1-9. Locally important farmland.

Third-Priority Resource Areas

LAYER 9. OTHER FARMLAND

This category includes open lands currently or recently used for agriculture but not classified as being "prime" or "of statewide importance." Although in many cases these areas may provide the most appropriate locations for new development, some of them might be able to be de-

signed around as additional pieces in the overall mosaic of conservation lands in the community. They make excellent parkland, in terms of village greens, ball fields, and community gardens (see Fig. DE1-9).

LAYER 10. SCENIC VIEWSHEDS AND SCENIC ROAD CORRIDORS

By their very nature, scenic viewsheds typically encompass open fields, pastures, and meadows. Their ability to define a community's

Figure DE1-10. Scenic road corridors and historic/cultural elements.

in a community-wide trail network, they may be rated more highly, as second-priority areas (see Fig. DE1-10).

LAYER 11. HISTORIC AND CULTURAL ELEMENTS

These areas typically include structures such as farmhouses, barns, springhouses, and stone walls but may also include places where historic events occurred (such as battles, skirmishes, troop movements, or the birth of a famous person) and abandoned township roads, established footpaths, or trails (see Fig. DE1-10).

The Exercise: Combining Data Layers to Create an Integrated Map

This first design exercise involves combining the various data layers to create an integrated Map of Potential Conservation Lands. Although this is not always as straightforward and simple as it might appear, neither is it terribly complicated or arduous. As happens with site designers processing information compiled on their Existing Resources/Site Analysis Map for a specific property, the most challenging part lies in deciding which resources to design around and protect and which to take for development purposes.

Exercise participants are invited to consider the relative significance of the various second- and third-priority resource types as they pertain to their specific community. Some of these resource types are generally more fragile or vulnerable than others. Decisions about setting priorities for selecting resource types for greater or lesser inclusion in the composite Map of Potential Conservation Lands should be taken on the basis of which would be most important to the community in the context of all its resources and in terms of the community's setting in the regional picture (where linear resources such as creeks, or blocks of prime farmland or significant woodland habitat, might cross municipal boundaries).

Another way of looking at this task is to consider which resource

"rural character" gives such areas additional importance, even if their soils are not particularly productive. However, unless they also possess some feature of special environmental significance (such as wetland vegetation and habitat or floodwater storage), they cannot be considered as constituting first-priority resource areas. To the extent that they include other elements considered significant in the community, such as a historic structure or place of an historic event, or a key link areas would be most deeply missed if they were lost to development. This is clearly an impossible task for any individual to perform alone, but this is only a practice exercise intended to demonstrate the concept. Obviously such decisions should be taken only after a community's resources have been inventoried and evaluated and their significance discussed at meetings to which the public has been invited. In short, the process described here is the one used when preparing Comprehensive Plans, which is logical because Community-Wide Maps of Potential Conservation Lands should be a part of such doc-

uments and should emerge from the local comprehensive planning process.

Readers are encouraged to photocopy Figures DE1-2 through DE1-10, enlarging them if possible, on clear acetate or mylar sheets (available in page size at well-stocked stationers). These clear sheets can then be overlain in various combinations, enabling readers to see the interrelationships and to select those second- and third-priority resource areas that would best complement the inherently unbuildable lands and lands already protected (Figs. DE1-2 through DE1-4).

Laying Out a Conservation Subdivision

The second design exercise involves laying out a conservation subdivision on a parcel of land that also appears on the township-wide Map of Potential Conservation Lands as illustrated in the previous hands-on exercise. Workshop participants are invited to apply the four-step methodology described in Chapter 5 on this mostly wooded site lying along a small creek. In this exercise, participants first locate house sites outside the Primary and Secondary Conservation Areas (which have been pre-identified to facilitate the exercise). Following this step, streets and trail systems are laid out, and then the lot lines are drawn in. In a real-life situation, the Primary Conservation Areas (wet, floodprone, or steep lands) would be pre-identified by the applicant's engineer, and the Secondary Conservation Areas would be strongly suggested by a combination of the township's Map of Potential Conservation Lands and the locational criteria for delineating conservation lands as specified in the subdivision ordinance text (model language for which is contained in Appendix 2).

The Site: Riparian Woodlands and Meadows

Encompassing 85 acres of mixed woodlands, fields, and meadows along a tributary of the state's largest river, this upland site borders a headwaters stream that has been designated as having exceptional water quality by the state Department of Environmental Protection. Marked by both gentle and steep slopes falling generally to the south, the property is distinguished by large areas of mature hardwoods and smaller areas of young hemlock forest, together with a number of meadows and hayfields of varying sizes. Yeager's Mill Inn, an unusual stone farmhouse built in the Federal style around 1810, is situated on the southwest corner of the property and, with its six outbuildings, is believed to be eligible for listing on the National Register of Historic Places. This property is illustrated in "bird's-eye" fashion in Figure DE2-1.

This site contains numerous resources of scenic, natural, and cultural interest that make it valuable to the community; but under conventional development practices few of these would likely be preserved. The entire property is currently listed for sale. With increasing development pressure from rapidly growing urban areas in the southern parts of the county, properties such as this one, with hilltop woodlands, riparian forests, and interior fields and meadows, are becoming highly sought after as potential home sites.

Under ordinary circumstances, the entire property would almost certainly be developed into a checkerboard pattern of "wall-to-wall" house lots, with the historic home located on one of them. Taking into account the township's standard zoning regulations and the site's particular soil and slope conditions, the maximum number of lots that could be achieved on this property is calculated using a "Yield Plan" (see Fig. DE2-2). Based on a minimum lot size of 80,000 square feet (excluding wetlands, floodplains, and steep slopes) and an analysis of soil conditions (as revealed by the medium-intensity soil survey maps published by the USDA Natural Resources Conservation Service), the maximum yield is determined to be 34 lots, with none of the site protected as open space. (A numerical site capacity analysis, applying the "density factors" listed in Chapter 4, produced the same overall yield.)

The Yield Plan clearly illustrates the extent to which the charac-

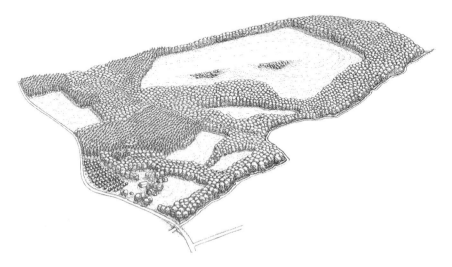

Figure DE2-1. Site before development.

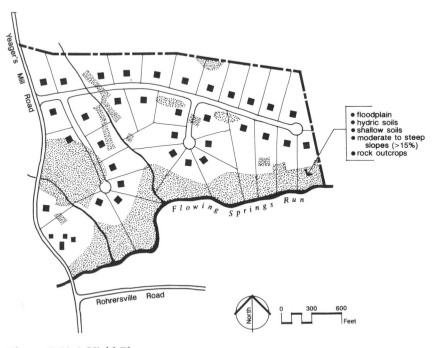

Figure DE2-2. Yield Plan.

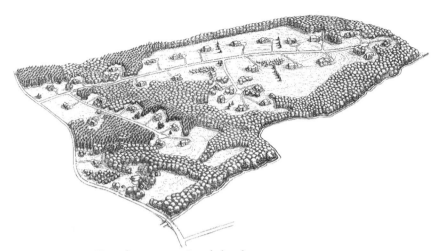

Figure DE2-3. Site after conventional development.

ter of the site could easily be compromised by conventional subdivision practices (see also Fig. DE2-3 for an aerial perspective). The traditional rural landscape on this site has gradually been shaped, over the course of several centuries, by subtle details of the land, with each use fitted to the best slope and soil. Standard subdivisions, by contrast, are shaped by civil engineering standards that do not take subtle, noteworthy, or intrinsically interesting site features into account. Contrary to popular belief, large-lot subdivisions such as this one do not preserve rural character but rather spread their negative impacts over a wider area, turning all the fields, meadows, and woodlands into streets or house lots. An alternative approach, the four-step "conservation subdivision design process" described in this book, allows landowners to meet their financial goals while conserving most of their property's natural and cultural features.

Site Analysis Phase

The first phase in the conservation subdivision design process involves the preparation of an Existing Resources/Site Analysis Map,

whose purpose is to map the special environmental, historic, and scenic elements found on a property so that the land can be profitably developed with minimum damage to those features and resources.

The Yeager's Mill Inn property is typical of many along this creek whose woodlands and steep slopes contain unusually rich natural areas including remnants of plant communities left behind after the last glacial period. The woods are predominantly oak-hickory-beech forest, but variations occur due to the steep slopes, floodplain areas, and differences in the underlying bedrock. Agriculture has traditionally favored the more gentle slopes and drier land, leaving the steeper slopes and moister stream valleys relatively undisturbed.

Two very minor tributary streams cut the site into three land units. The historic house and outbuildings occupy the westernmost one, while fields and meadows cover the flatter portions of the next two land areas. Hardwood forests can be found on the steeper slopes throughout the site and on the floodplain along the creek or run. Small meadows follow the upper edge of the floodplain, linking the house with the large central field that is currently mown for hay. One of the most pleasing visual aspects of the property is its varied sequence of enclosures and open spaces that one encounters while casually walking along old farm paths leading from cool, shady woods through archways of leaves to sunny meadows and fields full of wildflowers and humming insects.

Parts of this property constitute a critical link in an important wildlife corridor identified on maps in the township's Comprehensive Plan and lie within the critical watershed area of the river. In addition, the site also encompasses part of the aquatic habitat that is reported to contain six rare mussel species of national significance and several other rare animal species, including a threatened fish. While the stream corridor itself is subject to an advisory, nonbinding buffer of 100 feet on each side (which is generally ignored by developers), the surrounding woods (which are totally unprotected) play a significant supporting ecological role, enabling connections between unique habitats mentioned above and a large, contiguous woodland area supporting numerous plant and animal species. Fragmentation of these natural areas clearly reduces their wildlife habitat value. An additional risk to native plant communities is the introduction of highly competitive and invasive nonnative plant species that favor disturbed areas such as along road cuts and in clearings.

The rich mix of tree species found in the deciduous woodlands is one of the site's most outstanding features. The leaves of red maple, shagbark hickory, American beech, ash, tulip poplar, white oak, ironwood, sycamore, and hop-hornbeam form an intricately patterned mosaic overhead. Shrubs with memorable names such as sweet pepperbush and Virginia sweetspire commingle with other flowering species such as mountain laurel, viburnum, and winterberry. Shaded by the tall canopy trees of this mature hardwood forest, a variety of wildflowers thrive, including trillium, Dutchman's breeches, and foamflower, along with species more noted for their interesting foliage, such as Christmas fern and wild ginger.

The field edges are home to familiar understory tree species that mark the change of seasons in the rural landscape with their colorful spring blossoms or splendid autumnal foliage: Eastern redbuds, dogwoods, and sassafras. Old red cedars and stands of Eastern white pine stand as witness to fields and pastures that were farmed not so long ago. Several of these old fields are bordered by loose piles of rocks lifted as the land was plowed. Yarrow, fire pink, and andropogon grass can be found in the meadows, along with blackberries and daisies.

These site features, seen individually, occur fairly commonly throughout the county. Yet, taken together, they constitute the unique character of this property and place it firmly within its rural and historic context. The farmhouse and outbuildings are considered to be eligible for nomination to the National Register of Historic Places. But even if historic status is conferred on this farmstead complex, the property as a whole is at risk of being seriously compromised by in-

sensitive development. By quietly eliminating features of local significance, in what has been described as "the daily dwindle," the present pattern of development is gradually eroding the scenic, historic, and natural character of our common rural landscape.

On the other hand, as demonstrated below, these special features could easily be used as the basis for a creative design process that preserves the uniquely rural character of this property, as opposed to being largely ignored through the application of standardized techniques resulting in a generic suburban land-use pattern. The kind of thoughtful site analysis described above should be conducted by an interdisciplinary team so that as many aspects of the site can be recorded as possible. Once this comprehensive background information is collected, the site planners can begin the design process.

Design Phase

Step 1: Identifying Conservation Areas

The design phase of the process through which conservation subdivisions are laid out contains four steps. The first step involves comparing the township's Map of Potential Conservation Lands (contained in its Comprehensive Plan) with the developer's Existing Resources/Site Analysis Map. This comparison will show everyone how the special features on this property relate to (and possibly connect with) resource areas on adjoining lands and will help the applicant and township agree on potential areas for conservation and development.

Ideally this procedure will follow a site visit in which the developer, the site designer, and township officials walk the property with the Existing Resources/Site Analysis in hand. The Primary Conservation Areas (see Fig. DE2-4) are quite simple to identify, consisting of essentially unbuildable lands such as the floodplain and those slopes that are steeper than 25 percent (terrain that rises or falls more than 25 feet over a horizontal distance of 100 feet).

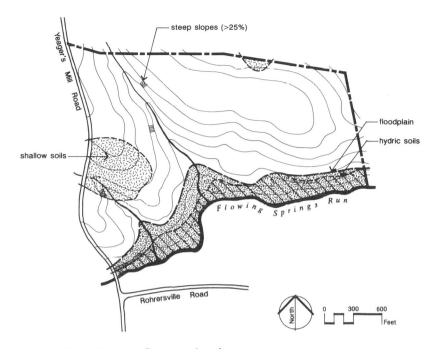

Figure DE2-4. Primary Conservation Areas.

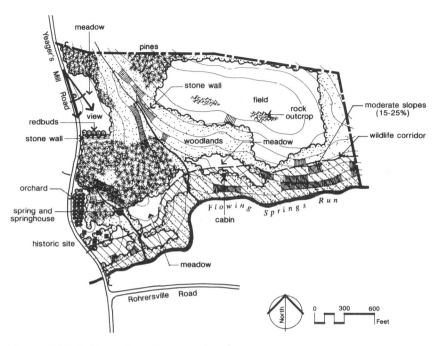

Figure DE2-5. Secondary Conservation Areas.

Secondary Conservation Areas include the historic house, out-buildings, and surrounding orchard, the advisory wildlife corridor and stream buffer, and the woodlands and moderate slopes. Other features adding to the property's rural character include the view of the roadside meadow with its border of redbuds, the small orchard along Yeager's Mill Road, and the old log cabin at the edge of one of the lower meadows down near the creek or run (see Fig. DE2-5). Since the goal is to conserve at least half of the "buildable land" while accommodating full density development, the site designer should initially identify and propose at least that much acreage when sketching potential boundaries for the Secondary Conservation Areas.

Once both kinds of conservation areas have been "greenlined," Potential Development Areas emerge more or less automatically as the remaining land, as shown on Figure DE2-6. In this process, an important goal is to lay out the actual development areas so that they can take maximum advantage of the property's conservation elements. In this case, objectives for arranging development areas are to screen them from the public road, to provide them with access and views to the meadows, and to conserve for them as much undisturbed woodland buffer as is possible. With regard to the property's woodlands and fields, the conservation/development choice is sometimes an "either/or" proposition, depending on whether the forested area or the farmland is deemed to possess greater significance. In this case, a compromise has been judged to be most appropriate, preserving the most critical contiguous areas of woodlands and streamside habitat, while also conserving most of the meadows and fields.

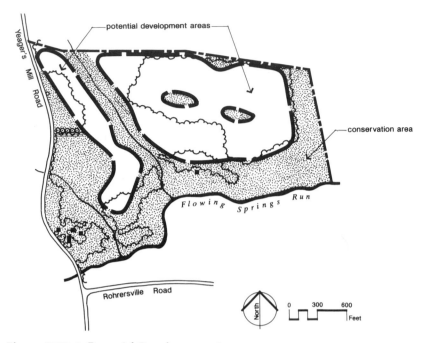

Figure DE2-6. Potential Development Areas.

The Primary and Secondary Conservation Areas shown on the accompanying illustrations have been preselected by the author of this book to expedite and facilitate the hands-on design exercise in which readers are invited to participate.

Once these conservation areas have been identified and selected, the most appropriate locations for the houses, yards, and streets become obvious, as shown in Figure DE2-6.

This concludes the design exercise introduction. The next three steps, which you the readers are being asked to take, are described

only in words in order to refresh your memory of the conservation design process covered in Chapter 5 of this book. Please do not turn to the end of this exercise, where the illustrations of Steps 2, 3, and 4 are reproduced, as worked out by the author, until you have completed this design exercise. The following three paragraphs are provided as general guidance as you proceed through the final three steps of the four-step design process.

Step 2: Locating House Sites

The maximum number of building lots demonstrated through the Yield Plan exercise (34) becomes the target number of homes to be accommodated in the conservation subdivision design. The site designer identifies individual house locations within the Potential Development Areas delineated in Step 1 (see Fig. DE2-6).

Step 3: Aligning Streets and Trails

In the third step, a street and path network is established to link the homes in a manner that also minimizes stream crossings and disturbance to wooded areas.

Step 4: Drawing in the Lot Lines

Finally, lot lines are added, each lot having at least 32,000 square feet to accommodate individual septic fields and wells. Alternatively, individual or shared septic fields (or wells) could be located in adjacent conservation areas just beyond the lot lines, in places designated for this purpose on the Final Plan, in which case lot sizes may be further reduced.

PLEASE DO NOT TURN TO
THE FOLLOWING SECTION UNTIL AFTER
COMPLETING THE DESIGN EXERCISE

One Solution to Design Exercise 2

Step 2: Locating House Sites

In this case, the nine-acre central meadow provides an obvious focal point around which a housing group could logically be arranged. Many homes could be comfortably situated around this expansive central green area, where horses might graze or where children could toss frisbees, fly kites, play catch, engage in informal games of touch football, etc. Since the land falls away at the edges of the field, the higher ground in the middle would help to soften the visual impact of houses seen from across the green. Smaller clusters of homes are located in flat areas of the woods and at the edges of the lower meadows where they will be the least intrusive, while taking full advantage of opportunities for woodland and meadow views. The locations of the 34 house sites are shown in Figure DE2-7.

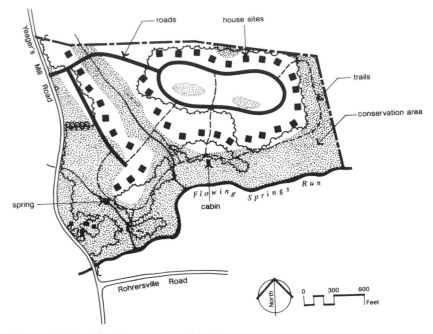

Figure DE2-8. Aligning streets and trails.

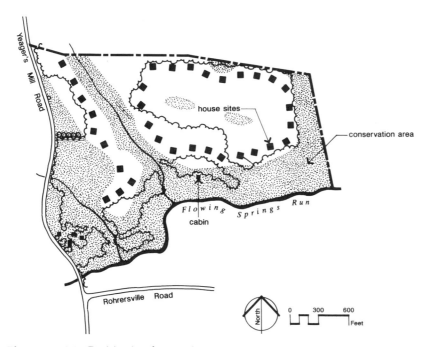

Figure DE2-7. Positioning house sites.

Step 3: Aligning Streets and Trails

Informal footpaths follow the trails and wooded roads that crisscross the farm, thereby conforming to the working structure of the landscape (see Fig. DE2-8).

Step 4: Drawing in the Lot Lines

The stone farmhouse, outbuildings, and orchard remain on their own large parcel to protect their historic integrity and context. Neighborhood access to this historic compound could be limited fairly easily since it is separated from the rest of the property by a small tributary stream and by existing woods.

In this conservation subdivision design, just over 29 acres are taken up by house lots, the average lot size being 36,000 square feet, or 0.85 acres. Street rights-of-way consume an additional 7.3

acres, leaving 48.5 acres as undivided and permanently protected open space. Using the conservation subdivision design process, each and every lot is enhanced by direct views and/or access to the open space, a network of informal neighborhood trails through woods and meadows that is accessible to all residents, and a main entrance that retains the character of the surrounding countryside (see Figs. DE2-9 and DE2-10). In essence, each resident is purchasing access to nearly 50 acres of historic and scenic Piedmont landscape at a fraction of the enormous price that an estate of this magnitude would command. From an investment standpoint, the initial value as well as the resale value of each lot is increased; while from a natural resource and historic preservation viewpoint, the character and integrity of the property is well respected and largely preserved.

Figure DE2-10. Site after conservation design.

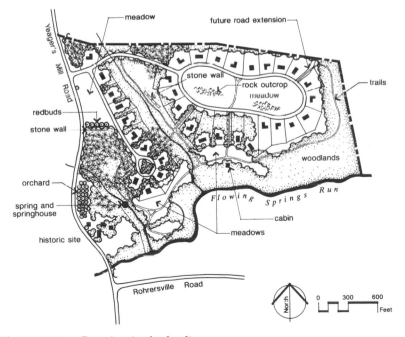

Figure DE2-9. Drawing in the lot lines.

Note on Scale and Density: Applying This Example in Townships with One-Acre Zoning

It should be pointed out that this "conservation subdivision" approach is also viable at higher—and perhaps more typical—densities in other unserviced rural or suburban areas that might lie closer to urban centers. For example, if the illustrations for this site had been drawn at the scale of 1 inch = 300 feet instead of 1 inch = 400 feet, the gross area of the property would have been approximately half the size (about 43 acres instead of 85, with 9 acres being constrained by wetlands, and so on, and 34 acres considered "buildable"). If this property had also been located in another township and zoned for a higher one-acre net density, the same number of conventional house lots (34) could have been created, with lots containing 40,000 square feet of net buildable land per dwelling (instead of 80,000 square feet per dwelling unit). Under this set of circumstances, a practical approach to "conservation subdivision design" would have been to propose half-acre lots with individual wells located in the undivided conservation areas (such as meadows, greens, or ball fields) close to but outside the lots they would serve. It should be noted that these smaller lots could be shaped and arranged in very much the same manner as the lots shown in Figure DE2-9, enabling the advantages and integrity of this layout to be maintained, with every lot facing or backing onto permanent open space. (See also Figure DE2-10 for a bird's-eye view of the property after conservation development.)

Other alternatives, listed in ascending order of complexity, would include:

- locating individual septic systems in the undivided open space instead, with individual wells on each lot (assuming of course that the conservation land adjacent to each lot contains soils suitable for septic systems);
- serving lots from a central well field in the conservation areas; and
- establishing a central sewage disposal facility (such as a community disposal field, or "spray irrigation") on the conservation land.

When individual wells or septic disposal fields are located within the undivided conservation land, the Final Plan must clearly show the specific areas that are being designated for such use by each house lot. These individual systems would normally be owned and maintained by each homeowner and would not, in this arrangement, belong to the homeowner association that owns the conservation land. This is not to suggest that wells or septic disposal facilities should not be owned and maintained by homeowner associations, but rather to point out that such community arrangements would not be necessary for the "conservation subdivision design" approach to work in unserviced areas with one-acre zoning, where half-acre house lots in a "conservation subdivision" would not be large enough to accommodate both wells and septic systems.

———

(*Note:* The author wishes to acknowledge the work of Ann Valentine, who contributed much of the text for this design exercise as a project intern while completing her studies in the landscape architecture program at North Carolina State University under the tutelage of Professor Richard Wilkinson.)

Frequently Asked Questions
About Conservation Subdivision Design

This appendix provides readers with a quick overview of the main concerns typically expressed about conservation subdivision design by local residents and officials. The points on the following several pages have been gleaned from the text of this book and assembled in a format that is easy to photocopy (with the publisher's permission) for distribution at public meetings where this approach is being discussed.

1. Does this conservation-based approach involve a "taking"?

No. People who do not fully understand this conservation-based approach to subdivision design may mistakenly believe that it constitutes "a taking of land without compensation." This misunderstanding may stem from the fact that conservation subdivisions, as described in this book, involve either large percentages of undivided open space or lower overall building densities. There are two reasons why this approach does not constitute a "taking."

First, *no density is taken away.* Conservation zoning is fundamentally fair because it allows landowners and developers to achieve full density under the municipality's current zoning—and even to increase that density significantly—through several different "as-of-right" options. Of the five options permitted under conservation zoning, three provide for either full or enhanced densities. The other two options offer the developer the choice to

135

lower densities and increase lot sizes. Although conservation zoning precludes full-density layouts that do not conserve open space, this is legal because there is no constitutional "right to sprawl."

Second, *no land is taken for public use.* None of the land that is required to be designated for conservation purposes becomes public (or even publicly accessible) unless the landowner or developer wants it to be. In the vast majority of situations, municipalities themselves have no desire to own and manage such conservation land, which they generally feel should be a neighborhood responsibility. For cases in which local officials wish to provide township recreational facilities (such as ball fields or trails) within conservation subdivisions, the municipality must negotiate with the developer for the purchase of that land on a "willing seller/willing buyer" basis. To facilitate such negotiations, conservation zoning ordinances can be written to include density incentives to encourage developers to designate specific parts of their conservation land for public ownership or for public access and use.

2. How can a community ensure permanent protection for conservation lands?

The most effective way to ensure that conservation land in a new subdivision will remain undeveloped forever is to place a permanent conservation easement on it. Such easements run with the chain of title, in perpetuity, and specify the various conservation uses that may occur on the property. These restrictions are separate from zoning ordinances and continue in force even if legal densities rise in future years. Easements are typically held by land trusts and units of government. Since political leadership can change over time, land trusts are the most reliable holder of easements, as their mission never varies. Deed restrictions and covenants are, by comparison, not as effective as easements and are not recommended for this purpose. Easements can be modified only within the spirit of the original agreement and only if the coholders agree. In practice, while a proposal to erect another house or a country club building on the open space would typically be denied, permission to create a small ball field or a single tennis court in a corner of a large conservation meadow or former field might well be granted.

3. What are the ownership, maintenance, tax, and liability issues?

Among the most commonly expressed concerns about subdivisions that conserve open space are questions about who will own and maintain the conservation land and who will be responsible for the potential liability and payment of property taxes. The short answer is that the owner of the conservation land is responsible for all of the above. But who owns this land?

OWNERSHIP CHOICES

There are basically four ownership options, which may be combined within the same subdivision where that makes the most sense.

- *Individual landowner:* At its simplest level, the original landowner (a farmer, for example) can retain ownership of as much as 80 percent of the conservation land to keep it in the family. (At least 20 percent of the open space should be reserved for common neighborhood use by subdivision residents.) That landowner can also pass this property on to sons or daughters or sell it to other individual landowners, with permanent conservation easements running with the land and protecting it from development under future owners. The open space should not, however, be divided among all of the individual subdivision lots because land management and access difficulties are likely to arise.

- *Homeowner associations:* Most conservation land within subdivisions is owned and managed by homeowner associations (HOAs). A few basic ground rules encourage a good performance record. First, membership must be automatic, a precondition of property purchase in the development. Second, zoning should require that bylaws give such associations the legal right to place liens on properties of members who fail to pay their dues. Third, facilities should be minimal (ball fields and trails rather than clubhouses and swimming pools) to keep annual dues low. And fourth, detailed maintenance plans for conservation areas should be required by the municipality as a condition of approval. The municipality has enforcement rights and may place a lien on the property should the HOA fail to perform their obligations to maintain the conservation land.

- *Land trusts:* Although homeowner associations are generally the most logical recipients of conservation land within subdivisions, occasionally situations arise in which such ownership most appropriately resides with a land trust (such as when a particularly rare or significant natural area is involved). Land trusts are private, charitable groups whose principal purpose is to protect land under its stewardship from inappropriate change. Their most common role is to hold easements or fee simple title on conservation lands within new developments, and elsewhere in the community, to ensure that all restrictions are observed. To cover the costs of either maintaining the land that they own or monitoring the land on which they hold easements, land trusts typically require some endowment funding. When conservation zoning offers a density bonus, developers can donate the proceeds from the additional "endowment lots" to such trusts for maintenance or monitoring.

- *Municipality or other public agency:* In special situations, a local government might desire to own part of the conservation land within a new subdivision, such as when that land has been identified in a municipal open space plan as a good location for a neighborhood park or for a link in a community trail network. Developers can be encouraged to sell or donate certain acreage to municipalities through additional density incentives, although the final decision would remain the developer's.
- *Combinations of the above:* As illustrated in Figure A1-1, the conservation land within new subdivisions could involve multiple ownerships, including (1) "noncommon" open space, such as cropland retained by the original farmer; (2) common open space, such as ball fields owned by an HOA; and (3) a trail corridor owned by either a land trust or the municipality.

MAINTENANCE ISSUES

Local officials should require conservation area management plans to be submitted and approved prior to granting final subdivision approval. In Lower Merion Township, Montgomery County, Pennsylvania, the community's "model" management plan is typically adopted by reference by each subdivision applicant. That document identifies a dozen different kinds of conservation areas (from woodlands and pastures to ball fields and abandoned farmland that is reforesting) and describes recommended manage-

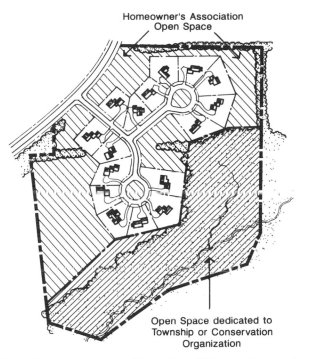

Figure A1-1. Open space ownership options. Various private and public entities can own different parts of the open space within conservation subdivisions.

ment practices for each one. Farmland is typically leased by HOAs and land trusts to local farmers, who often agree to modify some of their agricultural practices to minimize impacts on nearby residents. Although ball fields and village greens require weekly mowing, conservation meadows typically need only annual mowing. Woodlands generally require the least maintenance: trimming bushes along walking trails and removing invasive vines around the outer edges where greater sunlight penetration favors their growth.

TAX CONCERNS

Property tax assessments on conservation subdivisions should not differ, in total, from those on conventional developments. This is because the same number of houses and acres of land are involved in both cases (except when part of the open space is owned by a public entity, which is uncommon). Although the open space in conservation subdivisions is taxed low because easements prevent it from being developed, the rate is similar to that applied to land in conventional subdivisions in which the larger house lots are not big enough to be further subdivided. (For example, the undeveloped back half of a one-acre lot in a one-acre zoning district is subject to minimal taxation because it has no further development value.)

LIABILITY QUESTIONS

Statutes in all but two states protect owners of undeveloped land from liability for negligence if the landowner does not charge a fee to recreational users. A tree root or rock outcropping along a trail that trips a hiker will not constitute landowner negligence. To be sued successfully in Pennsylvania, landowners must be found to have "willfully or maliciously failed to guard against a dangerous condition." This is a much more difficult case for plaintiffs to make. Even so, to cover themselves against such situations, owners of conservation lands routinely purchase liability insurance policies similar to those that most homeowners maintain.

4. How can on-site sewage disposal work with conservation subdivisions?

The conventional view is that the smaller lots in conservation subdivisions make them more difficult to develop in areas without sewers. However, the reverse is true. The flexibility inherent in the design of conservation subdivisions makes them superior to conventional layouts in their ability to provide for adequate sewage disposal. Two examples are discussed in the following sections.

UTILIZING THE BEST SOILS

Conservation design requires the most suitable soils on the property to be identified at the outset, enabling house lots to be arranged to take the best advantage of them. If one end of a property has deeper, better-drained soils, it makes more sense to site the homes in that part of the property rather than to spread them out such that some lots are located entirely on mediocre soils that barely manage to meet minimal standards for septic approval.

LOCATING INDIVIDUAL SYSTEMS WITHIN THE OPEN SPACE

Conventional wisdom also holds that when lots become smaller, central water or sewage disposal is required. That view overlooks the practical alternative of locating individual wells and/or individual septic systems within the permanent open space adjacent to the more compact lots typical of conservation subdivisions, as shown in Figure A1-2. There is no engineering reason to require that septic filter beds must be located within each house lot. However, it is essential that the final approved subdivision plan clearly indicates which parts of the undivided open space are designated for septic disposal, with each lot's disposal area graphically indicated by dotted lines extending out into the conservation land. These filter beds can be located under playing fields or conservation meadows in the same way they typically occupy positions under suburban lawns. (If mound sys-

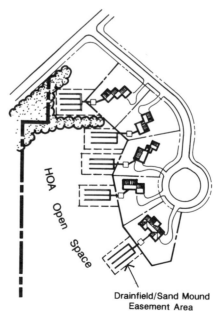

Figure A1-2. Off-lot wells and septics. A practical alternative to central water or sewage disposal facilities consists of individually owned wells and/or septic systems located outside the house lots and within the prescribed conservation areas, in places specifically designated for them on the Final Plan.

tems are required because of marginal soil conditions, they are best located in passive use areas such as conservation meadows where the grass is cut only once a year. Such mounds should also be required to be contoured with gently sloping sides to blend into the surrounding landscape wherever possible.)

Although maintenance and repair of these septic systems remains the responsibility of individual lot owners, it is recommended that HOAs be authorized to pump individual septic tanks on a regular basis (every three or four years) to ensure that the accumulated sludge never rises to a level from which it could flow into and clog the filter beds. This inexpensive, preventive maintenance greatly extends the life of filter beds.

5. How does this conservation approach differ from "clustering"?

The Growing Greener conservation approach described here differs dramatically from the kind of "clustering" that has occurred in many communities over the past several decades. The principal points of difference are as follows.

THE CONSERVATION APPROACH HAS A HIGHER PERCENTAGE AND HIGHER QUALITY OF OPEN SPACE.

In contrast to typical cluster codes, conservation zoning establishes higher standards for both the quantity and the quality of open space that is to be preserved. Under conservation zoning, 50 to 70 percent of the unconstrained land is permanently set aside. This compares with cluster provisions that frequently require only 25 to 30 percent of the gross land area be conserved. That minimal open space often includes all of the most unusable land as open space, and it sometimes also includes undesirable, leftover areas such as stormwater management facilities and land under high-tension power lines.

OPEN SPACE IS PREDETERMINED TO FORM A COMMUNITY-WIDE CONSERVATION NETWORK.

Although clustering has at best typically produced a few small "green islands" here and there in any municipality, conservation zoning can protect blocks and corridors of permanent open space. These areas can be pre-identified on a comprehensive plan Map of Potential Conservation Lands so that each new development will add to rather than subtract from the community's open space acreage.

THE CONSERVATION APPROACH ELIMINATES THE STANDARD PRACTICE OF AWARDING FULL-DENSITY FOR DEVELOPMENTS WITH NO OPEN SPACE.

Under this new system, full density is achievable for layouts in which 50 percent or more of the unconstrained land is conserved as permanent, undivided open space. By contrast, cluster zoning provisions are typically only optional alternatives within ordinances that permit full density, by right, for standard "cookie-cutter" designs with no open space.

Simply put, the differences between clustering and conservation zoning are like the differences between a Model T and a Taurus.

6. How do residential values in conservation subdivisions compare to those in conventional subdivisions?

Another concern of many people is that homes in conservation subdivisions will differ in value from those in the rest of the community. Some believe that because so much land is set aside as open space, the homes in a conservation subdivision will be prohibitively priced and the municipality will become a series of elitist enclaves. Other people take the opposite view, fearing that these homes will be smaller and less expensive than their own because of the more compact lot sizes offered in conservation subdivisions.

Both concerns are understandable, but they miss the mark. Developers will build what the market is seeking at any given time, and they often base their decision about selling price on the character of surrounding neighborhoods and the amount they must pay for the land.

In conservation subdivisions with substantial open space, there is little or no correlation between lot size and price. These developments have sometimes been described as "golf course communities without the golf course," underscoring the idea that a house on a small lot with a great view is frequently worth as much or more than the same house on a larger lot that is boxed in on all sides by other houses.

It is a well-established fact of real estate that people pay more for park-like settings, which offsets their tendency to pay less for smaller lots. Successful developers know how to market homes in conservation subdivisions by emphasizing the open space. Rather than describing a house on a half-acre lot as such, the product is described as a house with twenty and one-half acres, the larger figure reflecting the area of conservation land that has been protected in the development. When that conservation area abuts other similar land, as in the township-wide open space network, a further marketing advantage exists.

7. How does the Growing Greener approach relate to other planning techniques?

Successful communities employ a wide array of conservation planning techniques simultaneously over an extended period of time. Complementary tools that a community should consider adding to its "toolbox" of techniques include the purchase of development rights, donations or sales to conservancies, the transfer of development rights, and "landowner compacts" involving density shifts among contiguous parcels. These other techniques can be effective, but their potential for influencing the "big picture"

is limited. The Growing Greener approach offers the greatest potential because it

- does not require public expenditure,
- does not depend on landowner charity,
- does not involve complicated regulations for shifting rights to other parcels, and
- does not depend on the cooperation of two or more adjoining landowners to make it work.

Of course, municipalities should continue their efforts to preserve special properties in their entirety whenever possible, such as by working with landowners interested in donating easements or fee title to a local conservation group; purchasing development rights or fee title with county, state, or federal grant money; and transferring development rights to certain "receiving areas" with increased density. However, until such time as more public money becomes available to help with such purchases, and until the transfer of development rights mechanism becomes more operational at the municipal level, most parcels of land in any given community will probably eventually be developed. In that situation, coupling the conservation subdivision design approach with multi-optioned conservation zoning offers communities the most practical and feasible way of protecting large areas of land in a methodical and coordinated manner.

Advisory Note for Appendices 2 and 3

The model code language in appendices 2 and 3 is offered to readers as suggested wording that can provide a solid basis for updating their local plans and ordinances. It is not meant to be adopted *verbatim,* even by the Pennsylvania municipalities for which it was originally drafted.

Although the general planning concepts embodied in these provisions could probably be applied in almost every state, it is likely that details in the specific wording may have to be modified to bring it into line with the enabling statutes enacted by your legislature and with the "case law" embodied in relevant decisions rendered by the courts in your state. For that reason, it is recommended that planners and attorneys in your state be asked to review this language and to suggest any refinements before it is formally proposed or adopted.

Other modifications might also be desirable to adapt the recommended provisions in the model ordinance language to suit local political conditions (particularly regarding the underlying "base density" and the minimum required percentage of undivided open space, over and above the acreage that is inherently unfit for development) and to help create the public consensus necessary for its adoption.

The model ordinances contained in these appendices are a joint effort of the author and two of his esteemed colleagues at the Natural Lands Trust: former Trust president Michael Clarke and Ann Hutchinson, who provides superlative assistance in every aspect of the Growing Greener program.

Model Comprehensive Plan Language

DESCRIBING ORDINANCE IMPROVEMENTS NEEDED TO IMPLEMENT CONSERVATION PLANNING OBJECTIVES

Please see the advisory note regarding this appendix on page 141.

A. ZONING ORDINANCE REFINEMENTS

In order to protect the community's existing open space network, municipal officials should consider amending the zoning ordinance to include the following special techniques for "creative development":

A1. *"Menu" of Options Offering a Variety of Densities and Conservation Requirements*

The first zoning technique discussed here provides landowners with a "menu" of options to encourage land-conserving subdivision designs and to discourage land-consumptive layouts that needlessly divide all the acreage into suburban house lots and streets. In its most basic form, this "menu" of five choices consists of two low-density options, one "density-neutral" option, and two higher-density options.

The "density-neutral" option would yield the same number of lots attainable under the preexisting zoning. To attain full density, developers would have to submit a "conservation design," in which lots are reduced in area in order to permanently conserve half the unconstrained land. Developers willing to leave a greater percentage of the unconstrained land as undivided open space would receive a density bonus through a second layout option.

To encourage landowners to consider creating rural "estates" or mini-farms (at one principal dwelling per ten acres, for example), a "Country Properties" option is included. Several incentives are offered for those who choose this alternative, including special street standards for gravel-surfaced "country lanes" and the ability to add two accessory dwellings per lot (subject to certain size limits and design requirements for harmonizing with the rural landscape). Another low-density option of four-acre lots is provided for developers who feel that there is a strong local market for executive homes on lots that are large but are smaller than the ten-acre mini-estates.

The fifth, highest-density option would involve a significant density bonus, doubling the preexisting yield to produce well-designed village layouts in a neo-traditional manner, including architectural standards for all new construction, tree-lined avenues, village greens, parks, playgrounds, and broad perimeter greenbelts or conservancy areas in which mini-farms could be situated. (For additional details about this design option, please refer to section A5 below.)

A2. *Natural Features Conservation Standards*

The zoning technique known as Natural Features Conservation Standards typically excludes certain environmentally sensitive lands from development activities. Depending on the fragility of the resource, restrictions can prohibit construction, grading, and even vegetative clearing (especially when steep slopes occur with highly erodible soils). "Net-outs," which subtract constrained land from the acreage on which building density is calculated, often accompany Natural Features Conservation Standards and effectively reduce the maximum allowable density when environmentally constrained lands occur. The percentage of constrained land that is subtracted typically varies according to the severity of the building limitation imposed by the site feature involved. This variation on Natural Features Conservation Standards is sometimes called "density zoning" or "performance zoning," as described below.

A3. *"Density Zoning"*

This approach, frequently referred to as "performance zoning," was first promoted actively in Bucks County, Pennsylvania, during the early 1970s, and an excellent publication titled *Performance Zoning* is still available from the county planning department in Doylestown. Under "density zoning," the permitted intensity of development directly relates to the ability of the site to safely accommodate it. This tool provides municipalities with a highly defensible way to regulate building density, in contrast to conventional zoning in which entire districts are designated for a single uniform lot size. While the latter "blanket" approach is defensible at higher densities in serviced areas, this more finely grained "performance" approach, which responds to the constraints present on individual parcels, is legally more sustainable in outlying areas where a community wishes to place stricter limits on new development for a variety of sound planning reasons. Courts that have rejected attempts to zone entire districts for two-, three-, or five-acre lots in Pennsylvania have upheld ordinances that place similarly restrictive density limitations on land that is steeply sloping, shallow to bedrock, or underlain by a seasonally high water table. (The definitive court decision on this issue is *Reimer vs. Upper Mt. Bethel Twp.*, 615 Atlantic Reporter, 2nd, 938–946.) For more effective control over the location of house sites and to limit the percentage of the development parcel that is converted from woodland, meadow, or farmland to suburban lawn, either Natural Features Conservation Standards or density zoning must be combined with other land use techniques encouraging or requiring "conservation subdivision design," as described under "Subdivision Ordinance Refinements" below.

A4. "Landowner Compacts"

Although this approach is not currently prohibited, neither is it encouraged (or even mentioned in the zoning as an option for people to consider) in most communities. Simply put, a "landowner compact" is a voluntary agreement among two or more adjoining landowners to essentially dissolve their common, internal lot lines and to plan their separate but contiguous landholdings in an integrated, comprehensive manner. Areas for development and conservation could be located so that they would produce the greatest benefit, allowing development to be distributed in ways that would preserve the best parts of the combined properties. Taking a very simplified example, all the development that would ordinarily occur on two adjoining parcels could be grouped on the one containing the best soils or slopes or having the least significant woodland or wildlife habitat, leaving the other parcel entirely undeveloped. The two landowners would share net proceeds proportionally, based on the number of house lots each could have developed independently. Figure A2-1 shows how a "landowner compact" might occur on two hypothetical adjoining properties.

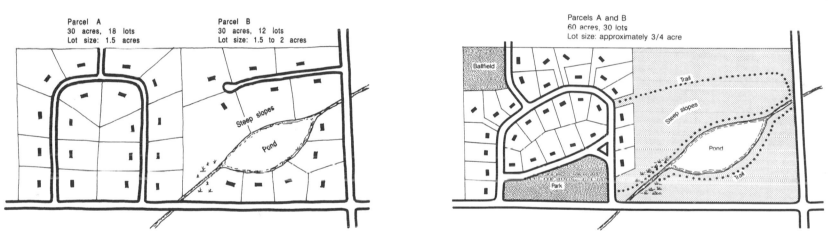

Figure A2-1. Landowner compact. These sketches illustrate contrasting approaches to developing two adjoining parcels, each 30 acres in area. Parcel A contains very few site constraints and could easily be developed into the maximum number of lots permitted under local zoning: 18 lots. Parcel B contains some steep slopes, a pond, and a small wetland area, but it could still be divided into 12 lots. However, much of Parcel B is also covered with some rather special stands of trees—mature hemlock groves around the pond and numerous large beeches on the hillside—that would be completely unprotected under local regulations. The landowner compact would allow the common boundary between the two parcels to be erased so that an overall plan could be created for distributing the house lots in a manner that would preserve all the important natural features on Parcel B. The entire development of 30 homes could be located on Parcel A, together with a natural park/buffer along the public road and a ball field in one corner. Net proceeds would typically be divided in a proportional manner between the two owners; for example, 18/30ths (60 percent) for the owner of Parcel A, and 12/30ths (40 percent) for the owner of Parcel B.

A5. Traditional Neighborhood Model

When it is deemed necessary or desirable to accommodate a diversity of housing sizes and types, including semi-detached and multi-family dwellings at a variety of price ranges, that development can best be handled through the creation of new neighborhoods designed along traditional lines rather than as suburban-style "Planned Residential Developments" with garden apartments and townhouse condominiums (where the central organizing principle typically appears to be large asphalt parking lots). Accordingly, the zoning ordinance should be amended so that higher-density development will be guided by detailed design and layout standards regarding lot size, setbacks, street alignment, streetscape design, on-street parking, and the provision of interior open space as well as surrounding greenbelt areas, etc. Where appropriate, high-density development should be allowed in a manner that reflects the best of traditional villages and small towns in the county. An excellent resource in preparing such zoning design standards can be found in *Visions for a New American Dream* by Anton Nelessen (Planners Press, 1994) and in *Crossroad, Hamlet, Village, Town: Design Characteristics of Traditional Neighborhoods, Old and New* by Randall Arendt (American Planning Association, 1999). Zoning standards for traditional neighborhoods should always include numerous illustrations, such as aerial perspectives, street cross-sections, building elevations, photographs, and streetscape perspectives, so that intending developers will know what the municipality expects before they prepare their proposals.

A6. Transfer of Development Rights (TDRs)

TDR ordinances have proven to be extremely difficult to implement in most states for several reasons. First, when the size of local governmental units having zoning powers is relatively small (towns and townships, as is the case in many states), the ability of those local governments to designate high-density "receiving districts" in appropriate locations (regarding physical infrastructure, environmental limitations, and political acceptability) is severely constrained. Inter-municipal TDRs could alleviate these problems provided that state laws authorize such transfers and assuming that such cooperation and coordination between municipalities could be achieved. Based on past experience, that assumption is not a small one. Second, when

most rural lands are already zoned at suburban densities (one-half to two acres per dwelling), the number of potential units that would need to be accommodated within TDR "receiving districts" becomes extremely high, unless only a small part of the rural area were to be protected in this manner. The experience of TDRs in several Pennsylvania townships is that the "sending districts" (to be preserved) should be relatively modest in scale so that they will not overwhelm the "receiving districts" with more dwelling units than they can reasonably handle. For this reason, *in areas zoned for suburban densities* (e.g., one-half to two dwellings per acre), TDRs are inherently limited to playing only a partial role in conserving a community's undeveloped lands, and they should therefore be viewed as a tool mostly for use on an occasional basis. An exception to this general rule in Pennsylvania is Lancaster County, where numerous townships have—with the political support of their Amish and Mennonite farmers—down-zoned much of the agricultural land to base densities of 20 or more acres per dwelling. Once those local political decisions were made, it became relatively easy to draw "urban growth boundaries" around the remaining parts of those townships and to designate them as TDR "receiving areas." Experience in Maryland, however, suggests that TDRs work best at a county-wide level, and also where rural zoning densities are typically much lower than those in suburban areas (20 or more acres per dwelling).

To gain greater political acceptability at the local level, it is important that the TDR technique be combined with detailed design standards to control the appearance of the areas designated to receive the additional development rights so that they will resemble historic hamlets and villages with traditional streetscapes and neighborhood greens (as advocated in section A5 above) rather than higher-density groupings of attached housing arranged in a suburban manner around cul-de-sacs and large parking lots. The "receiving areas" also represent an excellent opportunity to provide a diversity of housing types that sit comfortably together on the same block because they share a similar architectural style or expression, as was often the case in the older settlements laid out and built prior to World War II.

A7. Purchase of Development Rights (PDRs)

As with TDRs, this technique is inherently limited as an area-wide protection tool by suburban zoning densities, which create land values that are beyond the affordability range of most communities. However, PDRs (like TDRs) provide an excellent way for a municipality to conserve an entire parcel on an occasional basis, and for this reason they can become an important element in protecting individual properties of great local significance from time to time. As with TDRs, PDRs can potentially play critical supporting roles to other techniques that hold more promise as a method for protecting the majority of unbuilt lands in the community, such as conservation subdivision design (see section B5 below). Their advantage is that they typically protect whole properties, while conservation subdivision design (CSD) protects 40–70 percent of each parcel. (However, CSD can protect interconnected networks of open space, while PDRs usually save isolated parcels.)

B. SUBDIVISION ORDINANCE REFINEMENTS

The subdivision and land development ordinance should be specifically amended to include the following six items.

B1. Existing Resources / Site Analysis Maps

Base maps showing fundamental site information (such as topography and the boundaries of floodplains and wetlands) have long been required as part of the subdivision review process. In recent years several municipalities have substantially expanded the list of features to include many resources identified in their open space plans. The new kind of base map that has emerged from this evolution, sometimes called an Existing Resources and Site Analysis Map, identifies, locates, and describes noteworthy features to be designed around through sensitive subdivision layouts. These resources include many otherwise "buildable" areas, such as certain vegetation features (including mature, undegraded woodlands, hedgerows, copses, and trees larger than a certain caliper); farmland soils rated prime or of statewide importance; natural areas listed on the statewide Natural Diversity Inventory that support native flora or fauna known to be threatened or endangered; unique or special wildlife habitats; historic or cultural features (such as farmhouses, barns, springhouses, stone walls, cellar holes, Indian trails, and old country roads); unusual geologic formations; and scenic views into and out from the property.

Even in conventional large-lot subdivisions, a few of these natural and cultural features can occasionally be conserved through sensitive street alignment and by drawing lot lines so that particularly large trees, for example, are located near lot boundaries and not where houses, driveways, or septic systems would likely be sited. However, flexible site design in which lot dimensions can be substantially reduced offers the greatest potential to conserve these special places within new subdivisions. It is recommended that this kind of approach be more strongly and effectively encouraged through updated zoning provisions (such as those that offer a combination of density bonuses for sensitive land-conserving layouts to encourage this conservation design approach, as well as density *dis*incentives to discourage conventional land-consuming layouts).

B2. Pre-Sketch Conference and Site Visit

Subdivision applicants should be encouraged to meet with officials or their staff informally to discuss ideas for their properties prior to the submission of a Preliminary Plan and to walk the land with the Existing Resources/Site Analysis Map in hand at this formative stage. If state law does not specifically authorize Sketch Plans, these steps should be included within the subdivision procedures section as "optional but strongly recommended." Developers interested in expediting the review process will often take advantage of this option because it helps everyone become better acquainted with the issues earlier in the process. Developers can obtain clearer insights into what local officials are looking for, in terms of conserving particular site features, or wanting to avoid, in terms of impacts, by walking the property with them early in the planning process and identifying the noteworthy features.

B3. Voluntary Sketch Plans

Sketch Plans are simple and inexpensive drawings that illustrate conceptual layouts of house lots, streets, and conservation areas. They should ideally be based closely on the Existing Resources/Site Analysis Map and comments received from local officials during the pre-sketch conference and on-site visit. As with that conference and visit, municipalities in many states lack legal authority to require that applicants submit Sketch Plans per se because such a requirement would expand the subdivision process from a two-stage procedure (with 90 days each for the Preliminary and Final Plans) to one involving a third stage and additional time. However, some developers have found the sketch plan process to be time well spent because it helps them to identify and address community concerns prior to spending large sums on detailed engineering typically required for so-called "Preliminary Plans" (on which about 90 percent of the total engineering effort is often expended). The voluntary Sketch Plan helps all parties avoid the extremely common situation in which developers first pay to engineer expensive Preliminary Plans and then understandably refuse to modify their layouts in any substantial manner. The final nature of the highly engineered Preliminary Plan as the first document that local officials see deeply flaws the subdivision review process by limiting dialogue and information exchange at the very point when it is most needed—during those first crucial months when the overall layout should be examined and be open to modification.

B4. Two-Stage Preliminary Plans (Conceptual and Detailed)

Many developers perceive sketch plans as adding to their time and costs (which is generally true only in the short run), and thus they generally forgo this opportunity to start the process with an informal sharing of ideas. To ensure that concepts are sketched out and discussed with local officials early in the process, before plans become heavily engineered and "hardened," it is highly recommended that subdivision ordinances be amended to split the 90-day review authorized under Pennsylvania law for Preliminary Plans into two phases. Those applicants who decide *not* to submit voluntary sketch plans would be required to prepare a Conceptual Preliminary Plan during the first 30 days and a Detailed Preliminary Plan during the following 60 days. The former would closely resemble the voluntary sketch plan in its requirements, while the latter would essentially encompass the requirements for the standard Preliminary Plan. By the end of the first 30 days, the planning commission or its staff must complete their informal but detailed review, specifying the kinds of modifications needed to bring the proposal into compliance with the applicable zoning and subdivision ordinance requirements. As with standard Preliminary Plan applications, in those

instances where additional time is needed, a mutually agreed upon extension should be signed by the applicant.

B5. Conservation Subdivision Design

The term *conservation subdivision design* describes a relatively new breed of residential development in which, in addition to wetlands, floodplains, and steep slopes, the majority of flat, dry, and otherwise buildable land is protected from clearing, grading, and construction by reducing lot sizes in order to achieve full-yield density. Conservation subdivision design offers the single most cost-effective way for municipalities to conserve their natural lands and the other significant resources identified in their Comprehensive Plans. It is seen as a potentially very useful tool for augmenting the land protection efforts possible through state and county funding programs, which are quite limited in scope. This design approach avoids the "taking" issue because developers can, as of right, achieve the full density allowed on their properties under the zoning ordinance and because the land not converted to suburban house lots remains privately owned, typically by homeowner associations (although in some instances developers have preferred to donate those portions of their subdivisions to local land trusts).

Conservation subdivision design differs from "clustering" in three important ways. First, it sets much higher standards for the quantity, quality, and configuration of the resulting open space. Where cluster ordinances typically require only 25 or 30 percent open space to be set aside, conservation subdivisions designate at least 40 percent (and usually 50 percent or more) of the land as permanent, undivided open space. Unlike most cluster provisions, this figure is based only on the acreage that is high, dry, flood-free, and not steeply sloped. Following this approach, a significant part of the community's important farmland or woodland resources (including terrestrial habitat) and its historic or cultural features can be protected.

Second, municipalities can exercise greater influence on the design of new conservation subdivisions. Rather than leaving the outcome purely to chance, this flexible design approach can be strongly encouraged or even required where the Comprehensive Plan has identified the location of noteworthy resources. That encouragement could take the form of density bonuses for land-conserving design and could be combined with strong density *dis*incentives to actively discourage land-consuming layouts of large lots. (The "menu of options" approach described earlier, under "Zoning Ordinance Refinements," is an example of that type of control.) In certain special overlay districts with resources that are critically important or particularly sensitive or abundant, the ordinance could be amended to simply *require* all plans to follow the principles of conservation subdivision design. Those principles are described below, in section B6.

Third, the protected land is also configured so that it will, wherever practicable, contribute to creating an interconnected network of open space throughout the community, linking resource areas in adjoining subdivisions and/or providing buffers between new development and preexisting parklands, state forests, game lands, wildlife refuges, or land trust preserves.

B6. Four-Step Approach to Designing Land-Conserving Subdivisions

The majority of subdivisions are prepared by civil engineers and land surveyors whose professional training and experience have typically not included a strong emphasis on conserving the wide range of natural and cultural features essential to the successful design of this new kind of subdivision. Therefore, subdivision ordinances should be updated to explicitly describe the steps involved in designing conservation subdivisions. A simple four-step design approach clarifies the process for all parties involved, including the landowner, the developer, and local officials. (In addition, the ordinance should include a provision requiring that all subdivisions containing more than ___ lots must be prepared by a team including a landscape architect, an engineer, and a surveyor.)

The sequence of these four steps is critical and reflects their relative importance, with the first and most significant one being the identification of conservation areas. These include both the unbuildable lands (wet, flood-prone, steep) that are classified as Primary Conservation Areas, as well as noteworthy site features that would typically not be highlighted as elements to be designed around in conventional subdivisions. Among those Secondary Conservation Areas would be mature woodlands, hedgerows, large trees, prime farmland, natural meadows, upland habitats, historic buildings, geologic formations, and scenic views (particularly from public roads). In other words, this design approach seeks to conserve those special places that make each community a distinctive and attractive place, and, in that regard, it is a tool that is uniquely well-adapted to implementing both the letter and the spirit of the municipal open space plans. Identifying these conservation areas is a fairly easy task, once the Existing Resources/Site Analysis Map (described earlier) has been carefully prepared.

Once the Primary and Secondary Conservation Areas have been identified (the most critical step of the process), house sites are located to enjoy views of, and often direct access to, the protected open space, enhancing their desirability and value. Siting the homes in this manner provides developers with a strong marketing advantage compared with layouts where homes are boxed in on all sides by other house lots. The third step, aligning streets and trails, is almost a matter of "connecting the dots" for vehicular and pedestrian access, while the fourth and final step of drawing in the lot lines typically involves little more than marking boundaries midway between house locations.

It is virtually impossible to design a truly bad subdivision when following this simple four-step approach. Conservation subdivision design and the four-step approach can be institutionalized in municipal ordinances, providing communities with a ready tool to help them implement their open space conservation objectives even when parcels cannot be protected in their entirety, through donations, purchases, or more sophisticated planning techniques such as TDRs.

———

(*Note:* In laying out hamlets, villages, and other forms of traditional neighborhoods, the second and third steps are reversed, signifying the increased importance of streetscapes, terminal vistas, and public squares in traditional neighborhood developments.)

Model Ordinance Language for Conservation Subdivisions

Zoning Ordinance Language

ARTICLE 1: CONSERVATION DESIGN OVERLAY DISTRICT

Please see the advisory note regarding this appendix on page 141.

SECTION 101. Purposes

A. In conformance with the state enabling legislation, the purposes of this Article, among others, are as follows:

1. To conserve open land, including those areas containing unique and sensitive natural features such as woodlands, steep slopes, streams, floodplains, and wetlands, by setting them aside from development;

2. To provide greater design flexibility and efficiency in the siting of services and infrastructure, including the opportunity to reduce length of roads, utility runs, and the amount of paving required for residential development;

3. To reduce erosion and sedimentation by the retention of existing vegetation and the minimization of development on steep slopes;

4. To provide for a diversity of lot sizes, building densities, and housing choices to accommodate a variety of age and income groups, and residential preferences, so that the community's population diversity may be maintained;

5. To implement adopted municipal policies to conserve a variety of irreplaceable and environmentally sensitive resource lands as set forth in the municipality's Open Space Plan, including provisions for reasonable incentives to create a greenway system for the benefit of present and future residents;

6. To implement adopted land use, transportation, and community policies, as identified in the municipality's Comprehensive Plan;

7. To protect areas of the municipality with productive agricultural soils for continued or future agricultural use by conserving blocks of land large enough to allow for efficient farm operations;

8. To create neighborhoods with direct visual access to open land, with amenities in the form of neighborhood open space, and with a strong neighborhood identity;

9. To provide for the conservation and maintenance of open land within the municipality to achieve the above-mentioned goals and for active or passive recreational use by residents;

10. To provide multiple options for landowners in order to minimize impacts on environmental resources (sensitive lands such as wetlands, floodplain, and steep slopes) and disturbance of natural or cultural features (such as mature woodlands, hedgerows and tree lines, critical wildlife habitats, historic buildings, and fieldstone walls);

11. To provide standards reflecting the varying circumstances and interests of individual landowners and the individual characteristics of their properties; and

12. To conserve scenic views and elements of the municipality's rural character, and to minimize perceived density, by minimizing views of new development from existing roads.

B. In order to achieve these purposes, this Article provides for flexibility in designing new residential subdivisions by allowing four forms of "by-right" development referred to as "options," as summarized below:

1. *Option 1: Neutral Density and Basic Conservation,* providing for residential uses at the density permitted by the underlying zoning. Greenway lands constitute approximately half the tract. The flexibly designed layouts work well with either individual wells and septic systems located in the open space or with central wells and sewage treatment facilities.

2. *Option 2: Enhanced Density with Greater Conservation,* providing for higher density residential uses and a larger percentage (60 percent or more) of greenway land in more flexibly designed layouts with other improvements serving the community, such as central wells and sewage treatment facilities.

3. *Option 3: Estate Lots,* providing for rural-suburban residential uses at lower densities in conventional layouts of standard house lots, where homes and streets are located carefully to minimize impacts on resource lands.

4. *Option 4: Country Properties,* providing for very low densities appropriate to rural situations, with flexible and reduced design standards for instances in which a permanent conservation easement is offered to maintain such uses.

C. In addition, this Article provides for a fifth option, available through the Conditional Use permitting process, as described below:

1. *Option 5: Hamlets and Villages,* allowing for higher density development designed according to special guidelines to ensure that the resulting form incorporates the design principles of traditional villages and hamlets.

D. Section 104 sets forth the development densities and required open space percentages.

SECTION 102. General Regulations

The design of all new subdivisions in the Conservation Design Overlay District shall be governed by the following minimum standards:

A. **Ownership:** The tract of land may be held in single and separate ownership or in multiple ownership. However, when a tract is held in multiple ownership, it shall be planned as a single entity with common authority and common responsibility.

B. **Site Suitability:** As evidenced by the Existing Resources/Site Analysis Map, the conceptual Preliminary Plan, and the detailed Final Plan, the tract incorporating this design option shall be suitable for supporting development in terms of environmental conditions, its size, and its configuration.

C. **Combining the Design Options:** The various layout and density options described in this Article may be combined at the discretion of the Board, based upon demonstration by the applicant that such a combination would better fulfill the intent of this Ordinance, in particular the stated purposes of this Article, as compared with applying a single option to the property.

D. **Intersections and Access:** New intersections with existing public roads shall be minimized. Although two access ways into and out of subdivisions containing more than fifteen (15) dwellings are generally required for safety, proposals for more than two entrances onto public roads shall be discouraged if they would unnecessarily disrupt traffic flow.

E. **Sensitive Area Disturbance:** The proposed design shall strictly minimize disturbance of environmentally sensitive areas, as shown on the Existing Resources and Site Analysis Map. Lands within the 100-year floodplain, or having slopes in excess of 25 percent, and rock outcroppings constitute such environmentally sensitive areas, where disturbance shall be strictly minimized. Demonstration by the applicant that these features will be protected by the proposed application shall be prerequisite to approval of both the conceptual Preliminary Plan and the detailed Final Plan.

F. **Community Wastewater Systems:** In developments that are proposed to be served by community wastewater disposal systems, the selection of wastewater treatment technique shall be based upon the municipality's "Ordered List of Preferred Alternative Types of Community Wastewater Systems" (from its Sewage Facilities Plan) contained in the Appendix to this ordinance.

SECTION 103. Use Regulations

Land in the Conservation Design Overlay District may be used for the following purposes:

A. Single-family detached dwellings in Options 1, 2, 3, and 4 subdivisions:

1. On tracts of six acres or more, single-family detached dwellings are permitted under the standards found in Sections 104 and 105 herein.

2. On tracts of less than six acres, existing on the effective date of this ordinance, single-family detached dwellings are permitted under the standards for Options 1 and 2 found in Sections 104 and 105, with conventional 60,000-square-foot lots with no required greenway land, as formerly permitted throughout the district under the prior zoning ordinance.

B. Residential buildings for two, three, and four households in Option 5 subdivisions, according to the standards in Sections 104 and 105.

C. Greenway land composing a portion of residential development, as specified above and according to requirements of Section 106.

D. The following nonresidential uses in accordance with the standards of Section 108.

1. Agricultural uses, including horticultural, wholesale nurseries, and the raising of crops, and buildings related to the same.

2. Woodlots, arboreta, and other similar silvicultural uses.

3. Woodland preserve, game preserve, wildlife sanctuary, or other similar conservation use.

4. Municipal or public uses; public park or recreation area owned and operated by a public or private nonprofit agency; governmental or public utility building or use; not to include business facilities, storage of materials, trucking or repair facilities, the housing of repair crews, private or municipal sanitary landfills.

E. **Accessory Uses:** Accessory uses shall be permitted on the same lot with and customarily incidental to any permitted use and not conducted as an independent principal use.

1. Accessory dwelling units (including elder cottages and tenant houses) proposed in Option 4 subdivisions (Country Properties) are subject to the following provisions:

    a. Accessory dwelling units in principal residences or in new traditional outbuildings (such as barns, stables, carriage houses, and spring houses) shall be designed to harmonize with vernacular rural buildings in the municipality's historic landscape.

    b. There shall be a maximum of one accessory dwelling unit (ADU) on any legal building lot in an Option 4 subdivision and a maximum of two accessory dwelling units (ADUs) on any legal building lot containing ten (10) or more acres in an Option 4 subdivision, provided all performance standards of this ordinance are met.

    c. The gross floor area in the first ADU shall not exceed 900 square feet. In the second ADU, where permitted, the maximum area shall be 750 square feet. However, on lots exceeding fifteen (15) acres, the second ADU may take the form of a tenant house containing up to 2,000 square feet of floor space. Under this section, existing historic accessory buildings more than 75 years old that exceed these floor space limits may be permitted by the Board to be used as ADUs without having to meet the dimensional setback requirements of this ordinance.

    d. Building permits for ADUs shall not be issued until the applicant demonstrates to the Board that a restrictive easement has been placed on the subject property prohibiting future enlargement of the ADUs or the creation of additional ADUs beyond the limits described above. Issuance of permits for ADUs shall be contingent upon County Health Department approval for any on-site septic sewage disposal systems needed.

F. **Additional Uses in Option 5 Subdivisions: Hamlets and Villages**

1. General

    a. Residential Diversity: A primary objective of the hamlet and village options is to provide for a diversity of household types, age groups, and income levels, in a manner consistent with the variety of existing homes in the municipality and with traditional village building and site development patterns. Within the overall residential density figures for villages and hamlets, new construction is to be predominantly single-family residential on a variety of compact village-scale lot sizes, which should range in area from 6,000 to 12,000 square feet with an average lot size of 10,000 square feet. This component should constitute between 75 and 100 percent of the residential development allowed in villages and may constitute 100 percent of the development in hamlets. However, in both villages and hamlets, the concept of large "Country Properties" of ten acres or more shall be encouraged, in which part of the required open space may be incorporated within lot boundaries, as "mini-farms," consistent with regulations pertaining to active and passive agriculture in other parts of this Ordinance.

    b. Housing Types: Within villages up to 12 percent of all new units may be designed as semi-detached dwellings, and a further 8 percent may be designed as three-or four-family dwellings. These percentages should be interpreted as guidelines. If an applicant elects to pursue the option for semi-detached and/or multi-family dwellings, such dwellings shall be designed to reflect the county's vernacular building tradition for such building types. When different housing types are proposed in either villages or hamlets, they shall be integrated architecturally and in scale so that they can be physically incorporated within the same streetscape as single-family dwellings and nonresidential buildings and not isolated from each other in separate areas. *(Note: Provisions for modifying the above percentages are contained in Section 703 of the Model Subdivision and Land Development Ordinance, in Article 7 pertaining to Option 5 Hamlets and Villages, which authorizes the Board, upon a positive recommendation of the Planning Commission, to modify these percentages within the spirit of that Article, when the applicant demonstrates that such waivers would not substantially diminish the traditional character of the proposed development.)*

    c. Locational Considerations for Hamlet and Village Uses: Residential lots in villages and hamlets shall generally not be located within five hundred (500) feet of any arterial highway having four or more lanes nor within two hundred fifty (250) feet of any two-lane state-numbered highway, unless effectively screened from the public viewshed by virtue of topography, dense vegetation, or other physical or visual barriers. Commercial/Mixed-Use Areas in villages shall be located so they are easily accessible by pedestrians from as much of the residential areas as possible (preferably within 1,500 feet—a five-minute walk). Nonresidential uses that are intended to serve an area beyond the village itself shall be located to permit vehicular access from outside the village without passing through residential streets. This part of the village may be located close to state-numbered highways.

d. <u>Hamlet Uses:</u> Hamlets shall consist of residential uses only, but greater housing variety is permitted, as described above.

e. <u>Village Uses:</u> Villages are intended to provide for a range of complementary uses and may consist of two areas: Residential and Mixed Use/Commercial. These areas are intended to provide for the diversity necessary for traditional village life while maximizing the interactions among related uses and minimizing the adverse impacts of different uses upon each other. The Village Residential Area is intended to contain a variety of housing options and related uses. The Village Mixed Use/Commercial Area is intended primarily to provide uses that meet the retail and service needs of a traditional village center and its vicinity within one- and two-story buildings, and it may contain other compatible uses such as civic and institutional uses of community-wide importance, specifically including second-floor residential uses. The Village Mixed Use/Commercial Area may be located either at the approximate center of the village or at the edge near an existing Major or Minor Collector (including all state-numbered highways). If the Village Mixed Use/Commercial Area is located along such a thoroughfare, parking areas shall be screened from view, preferably by locating them behind the commercial buildings, as seen from the Collector.

2. Conditional Uses in Both Hamlets and Villages

The following uses are classified as Conditional Uses in the Hamlet Option and in the Village Residential Area of the Village Option.

a. Hamlets and the Village Residential Area

1) Single-family detached dwellings (including both site-built and factory-built housing units meeting the minimum width design standards of this ordinance)

2) Two-, three-, and four-family dwellings designed to resemble traditional multi-family homes built in the boroughs and villages of the county prior to 1930 and sited so they front directly onto streets (rather than parking areas)

3) Accessory dwelling units that are architecturally integrated (as allowed in Option 4 subdivisions)

4) Uses accessory to residential uses (including home occupations)

5) Small neighborhood retail (not exceeding 1,000 square feet of floor space if in a single-story building and 1,500 square feet if located in a two-story building in which the second story may be in residential use).

b. Standards setting upper limits on the percentage of dwellings that may be other than single-family detached, and other standards limiting the percentage of the net developable land within the village or hamlet, are provided in Section 701 of the Subdivision Ordinance.

3. Conditional Uses in Village Option Subdivisions

The following additional uses are classified as Conditional Uses in the Village Option, according to area:

a. Village Residential Area:

1) elderly congregate housing; and

2) neighborhood retail uses occupying not more than 1,000 square feet of floor space.

b. Village Mixed-Use/Commercial Area:

1) retail uses, professional offices, and personal or professional services in buildings of 2,000 square feet or less (but up to 3,500 square feet if in buildings of two or more stories facing the street);

2) bed-and-breakfast establishments;

3) schools, daycare centers, libraries, churches and other houses of worship;

4) single-family detached dwellings, two-, three-, and four-family dwellings designed to resemble traditional multi-family homes built in the boroughs and villages of the county prior to 1930 and sited so they front directly onto streets (rather than parking areas);

5) second-story residential uses and shared parking arrangements (according to standards such as those advocated by the Urban Land Institute);

6) artisan living/working uses, public utilities facilities, including substations, pumping stations, and waste treatment facilities, and gasoline stations (outside the core area), and uses accessory to the above; and

7) sites for active recreation, such as organized games

Specifically *excluded* from the category of "retail uses" and service businesses allowed in this subdistrict are flea markets, indoor/outdoor amusement businesses, automotive sales, car washes, gasoline stations, betting parlors, building supply stores, adult bookstores, massage parlors, mini-storage facilities, and similar uses.

SECTION 104. Dimensional Standards and Density Determination

(Note: The model zoning provisions described below for the "Conservation Design Overlay District" offer five options for varying intensities of development linked to different percentages of open space. In this hypothetical rural district with no public water or sewer, the overall "base density" is 80,000 square feet of net usable land per dwelling. When more than the minimum 50 percent open space is provided, a larger number of homes would be permitted, and fewer homes would be allowed when that 50 percent open space minimum is not met. However, in other types of zoning districts, where public water is available, or where both public water and sewer are available, or where there is also an established pattern of higher-density housing, the "model" provisions for the "Conservation Design Overlay District" reproduced below would be entirely inappropriate. Readers interested in seeing how the five options described below for use in the "Conservation Design Overlay District" could be adapted to reflect conditions in less rural districts are referred to Table 4-2 in Chapter 4.)

A. **Dimensional Standards for Option 1:** *Neutral Density and Basic Conservation*

1. Density Factor: One dwelling unit per 80,000 square feet as determined through the Adjusted Tract Acreage approach or Yield Plan described in Section 104C herein. This is "density-neutral" with the pre-existing zoning provisions for this district.

2. Minimum Required Greenway Land:

a. The subdivision must include at least 50 percent of the Adjusted Tract Acreage as greenway land. Greenway land shall not be used for residential lots, except as provided below.

b. Large "conservancy lots" of at least ten acres, conforming to the standards for Option 4 subdivisions found in Section 104E and owned by individuals, may occupy up to 80 percent of the Greenway land, with the remainder (not less than 20 percent) deeded to a homeowner association, land trust, or the Township. However, the Greenway land within each conservancy lot remains subject to the standards for Greenway land in Section 106 herein.

3. Average Minimum Lot Area: 15,000 square feet, on average. Up to twenty (20) percent of the lots may be reduced to a minimum of 10,000 square feet. *(Note: The typical lot area is likely to be much closer to 40,000 square feet because that lot size can be delivered by developers at the 80,000-square-foot density while still meeting the 50 percent minimum conservation land requirement.)*

4. Minimum Lot Width at Building Line: 80 feet

5. Minimum Street Frontage: 20 feet

6. Yard Regulations: The builder or developer is urged to consider variations in the principal building position and orientation but shall observe the following minimum standards:

Front: 20 feet

Rear: 40 feet

Side: 30-foot separation for principal buildings, with no side yard less than 5 feet

7. Maximum Impervious Coverage: 25 percent limit on each lot

8. Maximum Height Regulations: 35 feet

B. **Dimensional Standards for Option 2:** *Enhanced Density with Greater Conservation*

1. Density Factor: One dwelling unit per 60,000 square feet as determined through the Adjusted Tract Acreage approach or Yield Plan described in Section 104C herein.

2. Minimum Required Greenway Land:

a. The subdivision must include at least 60 percent of the Adjusted

Tract Acreage as greenway land. Greenway land shall not be used for residential lots, except as provided below.

b. Large "conservancy lots" of at least ten acres, conforming to the standards for Option 4 subdivisions found in Section 104E and owned by individuals, may occupy up to 80 percent of the Greenway land, with the remainder (not less than 20 percent) deeded to a homeowner association, land trust, or the municipality. However, the greenway land within each conservancy lot remains subject to the standards for Greenway land in Section 106 herein.

3. Average Minimum Lot Area: 10,000 square feet, on average. Up to twenty (20) percent of the lots may be reduced to a minimum of 7,500 square feet. *(Note: The typical lot area is likely to be closer to 24,000 square feet because developers can deliver lots at that size and still meet the minimum 60 percent greenway land requirement.)*

4. Minimum Lot Width at Building Line: 80 feet

5. Minimum Street Frontage: 20 feet

6. Yard Regulations: The builder or developer is urged to consider variations in the principal building position and orientation but shall observe the following minimum standards:

    Front: 20 feet

    Rear: 40 feet

    Side: 25-foot separation for principal buildings, with no side yard less than 5 feet

7. Maximum Impervious Coverage: 30 percent limit on each lot

8. Maximum Height Regulations: 35 feet

C. Density Determination for Option 1 and 2 Subdivisions

Applicants shall have the choice of two methods of determining the maximum permitted residential building density on their properties. They are as follows:

1. Adjusted Tract Acreage Approach: Determination of the maximum number of permitted dwelling units on any given property shall be based upon the Adjusted Tract Acreage of the site. The Adjusted Tract Acreage shall be determined by multiplying the acreage classified as being in the categories of constrained land (described below) by the numerical "density factor" for that category of constrained land.

a. The following areas of constrained land shall be *deducted* from the total (gross) tract area:

1) All land within the rights-of-way of existing public streets or highways, or within the rights-of-way for existing or proposed overhead rights-of-way of utility lines; and

2) All land under existing private streets.

3) Wetlands: multiply the acreage of designated wetlands by 0.95.

4) Floodway: multiply the acreage within the floodway by 1.0

5) Floodplains: multiply the non-wetland portion of the 100-year floodplain by 0.50.

6) Steep Slopes: multiply the acreage of land with natural ground slopes exceeding 25 percent by 0.75.

7) Extensive Rock Outcroppings: multiply the total area of rock outcrops and boulder fields more than 1,000 square feet by 0.90.

8) Moderately Steep Slopes: multiply the acreage of land with natural ground slopes of between 15 and 25 percent by 0.25.

b. If a portion of the tract is underlain by more than one natural feature subject to a deduction from the total tract acreage, that acreage shall be subject to the most restrictive deduction only.

c. Since acreage that is contained within the public or private rights-of-way, access easements, or access strips is excluded from developable lot area, any portion of these items that also contains a natural feature subject to a deduction from the total tract acreage should not be included when calculating the adjusted tract acreage.

2. Yield Plan Approach: Determination of density, or maximum number of permitted dwelling units, shall be based upon the density factor of the chosen option (i.e., Option 1 or 2) applied to the gross tract acreage, as demonstrated by an actual Yield Plan. Yield Plans shall meet the following requirements:

a. Yield Plans must be prepared as conceptual layout plans in accordance with the standards of the Subdivision Ordinance, containing proposed lots, streets, rights-of-way, and other pertinent features. Although it must be drawn to scale, it need not be based on a field survey. However, it must be a realistic layout reflecting a development pattern that could reasonably be expected to be implemented, taking into account the presence of wetlands, floodplains, steep slopes, existing easements or encumbrances and, if unsewered, the suitability of soils for subsurface sewage disposal.

b. Yield Plans should also reflect the dimensional standards for 80,000-square-foot lots when Option 1 is chosen and 60,000-square-foot lots when Option 2 is chosen, found in Section 104C2d below. The Yield Plan must identify the site's primary and secondary resources, as identified in the Existing Resources/Site Analysis Map, and demonstrate that the primary resources could be successfully absorbed in the development process without disturbance, by allocating this area to proposed single-family dwelling lots that conform to the density factory of the chosen option.

c. On sites not served by central sewage disposal, density shall be further determined by evaluating the number of homes that could be supported by individual septic systems on conventional lots. Based on the primary and secondary resources, identified as part of the inventory and analysis, and observations made during an on-site visit of the property, the Planning Commission shall select a ten (10) percent sample of the lots considered to be marginal for on-lot sewage disposal. The applicant is required to provide evidence that these lots meet the standards for an individual septic system, at which time the applicant shall be granted the full density determined by the Yield Plan. Should any of the lots in a sample fail to meet the standard for individual septic system, those lots shall be deducted from the Yield Plan and a second ten (10) percent sample shall be selected by the township planning commission and tested for compliance. This process shall be repeated until all lots in a given sample meet the standard for an individual septic system.

d. Yield Plan Dimensional Standards: The following dimensional standards shall be used in the development of Yield Plans for Option 1 and 2 subdivisions. These minimum areal dimensions are exclusive of all wetlands, slopes greater than 25 percent, and land under high-tension electrical transmission lines (69 kilovolts or greater). No more than 25 percent of the minimum required lot area may consist of land within the 100-year floodplain, and only then if it is free of wetlands.

Standard	*Option 1*	*Option 2*
Minimum lot area	80,000 square feet	60,000 square feet
Minimum street frontage	250 feet	200 feet
Front yard setback	60 feet	60 feet
Rear yard setback	60 feet	60 feet
Side yard setback	40 feet with both side yards totaling 100 feet	40 feet with both side yards totaling 100 feet

D. **Dimensional Standards for Option 3 Subdivisions:** *Estate Lots*

1. Maximum Density: One dwelling unit per four acres, Adjusted Tract Acreage.

2. Minimum Lot Area: One acre. All lots created under Option 3 that are less than four acres shall be permanently restricted through a conservation easement from the development of more than one dwelling.

3. Minimum Street Frontage: 150 feet.

4. Yard Regulations: The builder or developer is urged to consider variations in the principal building position and orientation, but shall observe the following minimum standards:

   Front: 150 feet from the right-of-way of existing Township roads, but 40 feet from the right-of-way of new subdivision streets, country lanes, or common driveways (where applicable).

   Rear: 50 feet minimum for principal buildings and 10 feet for accessory buildings (except that accessory buildings with a ground-floor area exceeding 500 square feet shall conform to the setback requirements for principal structures).

   Side: 50 feet

5. Maximum Impervious Coverage: 4 percent limit on entire subdivision tract.

6. Maximum Height Regulations: 35 feet

E. **Dimensional Standards for Option 4 Subdivisions:** *Country Properties*

1. Maximum Density: One dwelling unit per ten acres (gross).

2. Minimum Lot Area: Ten acres. The lot shapes shall not be irregular, except as allowed for "flag lots," and shall not have a lot depth-width ratio exceeding 5:1 unless such lots are deed restricted from the de-

velopment of more than one dwelling. The minimum lot size may be reduced to one contiguous acre in subdivisions of two or more principal dwelling units provided that all remaining land (a minimum of nine acres per principal dwelling) is permanently protected from future development through a conservation easement.

3. Minimum Lot Width at Building Line: 200 feet

4. Yard Regulations:

   Front: 150 feet from the right-of-way of existing Township roads, but 40 feet from the right-of-way of new subdivision streets, country lanes, or common driveways (where applicable).

   Rear: 50 feet minimum for principal buildings and 10 feet for accessory buildings (except that accessory buildings with a ground-floor area exceeding 500 square feet shall conform to the setback requirements for principal structures).

   Side: 25 feet.

5. Maximum Impervious Coverage: 4 percent limit on entire subdivision tract.

6. Maximum Height Regulations: 35 feet

F. **Scale Criteria for Option 5:** *Hamlets and Villages*

1. Hamlets shall include at least four (4) dwelling units but may not contain more than twenty-five (25) within the Conservation Design Overlay District. The minimum land area required for a hamlet shall be four acres, Adjusted Tract Acreage.

2. Villages shall range in size from 26 to 100 dwelling units, within the Conservation Design Overlay Zoning District. The minimum land area required shall be 26 acres, Adjusted Tract Acreage.

G. **Dimensional Standards for Residential Uses in Option 5:** *Hamlets and Villages*

1. Density Factor: One dwelling unit per 40,000 square feet as determined through the Adjusted Tract Acreage approach or Yield Plan described in Section 104C herein.

2. Minimum Required Greenway Land:

   a. The subdivision must include at least 70 percent of the Adjusted Tract Acreage as greenway land. Not less than one-sixth of this greenway land shall be in a form usable to and accessible by the residents, such as a central green, neighborhood squares or commons, recreational playing fields, woodland walking trails, other kinds of footpaths, a community park, or any combination of the above. In addition, no more than 50 percent of the minimum required greenway land may comprise active recreation facilities such as playing fields, golf courses, or tennis courts. Greenway land shall not be used for residential lots, except as provided below.

   b. Large "conservancy lots" of at least ten acres, conforming to the standards for Option 4 subdivisions found in Section 104E and owned by individuals, may occupy up to 50 percent of the Greenway land, with the remainder deeded to a homeowner association, land trust, or the Township. However, the greenway land within each conservancy lot remains subject the standards for greenway land in Section 106 herein.

   c. The required greenway land shall be located and designed to add to the visual amenities of villages and hamlets and to the surrounding area by maximizing the visibility of internal open space as *terminal vistas* at the ends of streets (or along the outside edges of street curves) and by maximizing the visibility of external open space as perimeter greenbelt land. Greenbelt land shall be designated to provide buffers and to protect scenic views as seen from existing roadways and from public parks.

   d. Traditional villages and hamlets shall include multiple greens or commons measuring a total of at least 1,000 square feet for each dwelling unit.

3. Average Minimum Lot Area: 6,000 square feet, on average. Up to twenty (20) percent of the lots may be reduced to a minimum of 5,000 square feet. *(Note: The typical lot area is likely to be closer to 10,000 square feet because developers can deliver lots at that size and still meet the minimum 70 percent greenway land requirement.)*

4. Minimum Lot Width at Building Line: 40 feet.

5. Yard Regulations: The builder or developer is urged to consider variations in the principal building position and orientation but shall observe the following minimum standards:

   a. Front yard: Principal buildings: 12 feet minimum (6 feet to front porches/steps); attached garages (front-loaded): minimum 10 feet behind plane of house; attached garages (side-loaded): minimum 10 feet from street right–of–way; detached garages (front-loaded): minimum 40 feet from street.

b. Rear yard: 30 feet minimum for principal buildings and 5 feet for accessory buildings (excluding garages); detached garages (rear-loaded): minimum 10 feet from alley or lane.

c. Side yard: 20-foot separation for principal buildings, no side yard less than 5 feet.

6. Maximum Impervious Coverage: 50 percent limit on each lot.

7. Minimum Street Frontage: Lots must have frontage either on a street or on a back lane or shared driveway. Houses served by rear lanes may front directly onto parks or greens, which shall be designed with perimeter sidewalks.

8. Maximum Height Regulations: 35 feet

H. Dimensional, Intensity, and Design Standards for Option 5: *Village Mixed Use/Commercial Areas*

1. Use Intensity Standards

a. New commercial buildings in the Mixed Use/Commercial Area and their associated parking spaces shall not occupy more than 5 percent of the net developable land area of the entire Village. However, they may occupy up to 10 percent if they include second-story office uses and up to 15 percent if they include second-story residential units. In order to qualify for the 15 percent figure, at least half of the new commercial building coverage (foundation footprint) shall be of two-story construction, and at least 25 percent of the second-story space shall be designed for residential uses.

b. Floor area ratios shall be reduced by the Board on a case-by-case basis because village shop buildings and their parking areas should typically be allowed to occupy up to 80 percent of their building sites, with relatively little land between structures or between structures and the sidewalk. Parking areas shall generally be located behind shops (and occasionally to one side, if adequately screened from the street) and should be the primary focus of landscaping and buffering efforts (particularly where they abut adjoining residential lots).

2. Minimum Lot Size

a. The minimum lot size for nonresidential uses in Village Mixed Use/Commercial Subdistrict shall be determined by adding 20 percent to the land area needed for the structure, on-lot parking, ingress/egress, and any on-site infrastructure that is required (e.g., septic disposal areas and stormwater management areas). The additional 20 percent shall be constituted by setbacks and landscaped buffers.

3. Minimum Street Frontage: 50 feet

4. Setback Regulations:

Front: No minimum required; maximum setback 15 feet
Rear: 20 feet minimum
Side: 5 feet

5. Maximum Height Regulations: 35 feet (but 75 feet for church steeples)

6. Additional Design Standards

a. New buildings in this subdistrict shall be subject to a maximum front setback (the "build-to" line) in order to maintain a strong sense of streetscape. Such buildings shall generally be of two-story construction (to the so-called build-up line, as shown in the illustrated design guidelines in the subdivision ordinance) and shall be designed in accordance with the design standards set forth below. Maximum building height and coverage are controlled by other provisions in this ordinance governing maximum height and minimum parking standards.

b. Groundfloor space shall generally be reserved for pedestrian-oriented retailing and services, with offices and housing above.

c. Each Village Mixed Use/Commercial Area shall have a primary common or green of at least 10,000 square feet, which should ideally be surrounded by two-story development that may include commercial, residential, civic, and institutional uses. This primary common shall border on the principal street running through the Mixed Use/Commercial Area or be located so as to constitute the "terminal vista" of that street. This central green shall be located within 1,500 feet of 80 percent of all dwelling units in the village. (Alternatively, two greens of at least 6,000 square feet may be substituted for the central green, in order to meet the distance/proximity standard.) The type of trees and shrubs used shall be such that vistas through the open space are largely unobstructed. Greens shall be landscaped using elements of formal gardens, walkways, monuments, statues, gazebos, fountains, park benches, and pedestrian-scale lamp posts. They shall be designed as attractive gathering places for all village residents in both day and evening. No green shall contain more than 10 percent coverage by impervious surfaces.

   d.   Readers are referred to the Subdivision Ordinance, Section 704, Illustrated Design Principles.

  7. Parking

   a.   Nonresidential off-street parking shall be to the side or rear or located within internal parking areas not visible from the street.

   b.   On-street parking spaces along the street frontage of a lot (except where there are driveway curb-cuts) shall be counted toward the minimum number of parking spaces required for the use on that lot.

   c.   On-street parking spaces shall be designed to be parallel to the curb.

   d.   Off-street parking may be located within 600 feet (measured along a publicly accessible route) from the lot containing the use to which the parking is accessory. Said lot containing the parking shall be owned or leased to the owner of the principal use, or the lot containing the parking shall be dedicated to parking for as long as the use to which it is accessory shall continue and it is owned by an entity capable of assuring its maintenance as accessory parking.

SECTION 105. Design Standards for Option 1, 2, and 5 Subdivisions

A. House lots shall not encroach upon Primary Conservation Areas as identified in Section 402 of the Subdivision Ordinance, and their layout shall respect Secondary Conservation Areas as described in both the Zoning Ordinance and in the Subdivision Ordinance.

B. All new dwellings shall meet the following setback requirements:

  1. From all external roads ultimate right-of-way: 100 feet

  2. From all other tract boundaries: 50 feet

  3. From cropland or pasture land: 100 feet

  4. From buildings or barnyards housing livestock: 300 feet

  5. From active recreation areas, such as courts or playing fields (not including tot-lots): 150 feet

C. Views of house lots from exterior roads and abutting properties shall be minimized by the use of changes in topography, existing vegetation, or additional landscaping that meets the landscaping requirements of the Subdivision and Land Development Ordinance.

D. House lots shall generally be accessed from interior streets rather than from roads bordering the tract.

E. At least three-quarters of the lots shall directly abut or face conservation land or greenway land across a street (except that in Option 5, Hamlets and Villages, this fraction shall be one-half).

F. Standards pertaining to the quantity, quality, configuration, ownership, and maintenance of the greenway land created under this Article are contained in Sections 106 through 109 of this Ordinance.

SECTION 106. Greenway Land Use and Design Standards

Protected greenway land in all subdivisions shall meet the following standards:

A. **Uses Permitted on Greenway Lands**

The following uses are permitted in greenway land areas:

  1. Conservation of open land in its natural state (for example, woodland, fallow field, or managed meadow).

  2. Agricultural and horticultural uses, including raising crops or livestock, wholesale nurseries, and associated buildings, excluding residences that are specifically needed to support an active, viable agricultural or horticultural operation. Specifically excluded are commercial livestock operations involving swine, poultry, mink, and other animals likely to produce highly offensive odors.

  3. Pastureland for horses used solely for recreational purposes. Equestrian

facilities shall be permitted but may not consume more than 3/4 of the minimum required greenway land.

4. Silviculture, in keeping with established standards for selective harvesting and sustained-yield forestry.

5. Neighborhood open space uses such as village greens, commons, picnic areas, community gardens, trails, and similar low-impact passive recreational uses specifically excluding motorized off-road vehicles, rifle ranges, and other uses similar in character and potential impact as determined by the Board.

6. Active noncommercial recreation areas, such as playing fields, playgrounds, courts, and bikeways, provided such areas do not consume more than half of the minimum required greenway land or five acres, whichever is less. Playing fields, playgrounds, and courts shall not be located within 100 feet of abutting properties. Parking facilities for the same shall also be permitted, and they shall generally be gravel-surfaced, unlighted, and properly drained; provide safe ingress and egress; and contain no more than ten parking spaces.

7. Golf courses may constitute up to half of the minimum required greenway land but shall not include driving ranges or miniature golf. Their parking areas and any associated structures shall not be included within the 50 percent minimum greenway requirement; their parking and access ways may be paved and lighted.

8. Water supply and sewage disposal systems and stormwater detention areas designed, landscaped, and available for use as an integral part of the greenway.

9. Easements for drainage, access, sewer or water lines, or other public purposes.

10. Aboveground utility rights-of-way. Above-ground utility and street rights-of-way may traverse conservation areas but shall not count toward the minimum required greenway land.

B. Greenway Design Standards

1. Greenway lands shall be laid out in general accordance with the municipality's Map of Potential Conservation Lands (in the Comprehensive Plan) to ensure that an interconnected network of open space will be provided. The required greenway land consists of a mixture of Primary Conservation Areas (PCAs), all of which must be included, and Secondary Conservation Areas (SCAs). PCAs comprise those areas listed in Section 104C as being subtracted from the total parcel acreage to produce the Adjusted Tract Acreage. SCAs should include special features of the property that would ordinarily be overlooked or ignored during the design process. Examples of such features are listed and described in Section 603 (Greenway Design Review Standards) in the Subdivision Ordinance.

2. In Option 1 and 2 subdivisions, the greenway land constitutes a minimum of 50 percent and 60 percent of the Adjusted Tract Acreage, respectively. This land shall generally remain undivided and may be owned and maintained by a homeowner association, land trust, another conservation organization recognized by the municipality, or a private individual (typically as part of the original farmhouse). However, in no case shall less than 20 percent of the Adjusted Tract Acreage be available for the common use and passive enjoyment of the subdivision residents. These ownership options may be combined so that different parts of the greenway land may be owned by different entities.

3. In Option 3 subdivisions, the required greenway land constitutes all of the PCAs within the total tract and may lie within the Estate Lots. However, because the minimum lot size is one acre, up to 80 percent of the Secondary Conservation Area land may be included within undivided open space, if the developer so chooses.

4. Greenway lands in Option 4 developments may be contained within the Country Property lots, or up to 80 percent may be set aside as undivided land with common rights of usage among the subdivision residents.

5. Up to 5 percent of the total tract acreage in any of the options may be subject to the municipality's public land dedication requirement (typically to provide potential connections with the municipal long-range trail network).

6. Buffers for Adjacent Public Parkland: Where the proposed development adjoins public parkland, a natural greenway buffer at least one hundred fifty (150) feet deep shall be provided within the development along its common boundary with the parkland, within which no new structures shall be constructed nor shall any clearing of trees

or understory growth be permitted (except as may be necessary for street or trail construction). Where this buffer is unwooded, the Board may require that vegetative screening be planted or that it be managed to encourage natural forest succession through "no-mow" policies and the periodic removal of invasive alien plant and tree species.

C. **Other Requirements**

1. No portion of any building lot may be used for meeting the minimum required conservation land, except as permitted within Country Properties (or within "conservancy lots" of at least ten acres, designed as an integral part of Option 5, Hamlets and Villages). However, active agricultural land with farm buildings, excluding areas used for residences, may be used to meet the minimum required greenway land.

2. Pedestrian and maintenance access, excluding those lands used for agricultural or horticultural purposes in accordance with Section 103 herein, shall be provided to greenway land in accordance with the following requirements:

    a. Each neighborhood shall provide one centrally located access point per 15 lots, a minimum of thirty-five (35) feet in width.

    b. Access to greenway land used for agriculture may be appropriately restricted for public safety and to prevent interference with agricultural operations.

3. All greenway land areas that are not wooded, farmed, or managed as meadows shall be landscaped in accordance with the landscaping requirements of the Subdivision and Land Development Ordinance.

SECTION 107. Permanent Greenway Protection Through Conservation Easements

A. **Option 1, 2, 3, and 5 Subdivisions**

1. In Option 1, 2, 3, and 5 subdivisions, the greenway land that is required to be reserved and created through the subdivision process shall be subject to permanent conservation easements prohibiting future development and defining the range of permitted activities. For example, the clearing of woodland habitat shall generally be prohibited, except as necessary to create trails and active recreation facilities or to install subsurface septic disposal systems or spray irrigation facil-

ities. The determination of necessity shall lie with the Board. A list of permitted and conditional uses of greenway lands is contained in this Article in Sections 103 and 106.

B. **Option 4 Subdivisions (Country Properties)**

1. In Option 4 subdivisions (Country Properties), where applicants voluntarily opt to develop their properties at densities conforming with Option 4 standards (minimum ten acres per principal dwelling) and offer to place a restrictive conservation easement preventing future subdivision of the newly created parcels, the Board shall review the proposed easements and shall accept them, provided their wording accomplishes the purposes of this Ordinance and is consistent with the Comprehensive Plan and the Open Space Plan.

SECTION 108. Discretionary Density Bonuses

Additional density may be allowed by the Board when one of the following public benefits is proposed:

A. **Public Usage of Greenway Land**

1. The Board may encourage the dedication of land for public use (including active and passive recreation areas, spray irrigation areas, and municipal buildings) according to the following standards: *A density bonus for greater public usage of greenway land in new subdivisions shall be computed on the basis of a maximum of one dwelling unit per five acres of greenway land or per 2,500 feet of trail that becomes publicly accessible.* The decision whether to accept an applicant's offer to dedicate greenway land to public usage within a proposed subdivision shall be at the discretion of the Board, which shall be guided by the recommendations contained in the Open Space Plan, particularly those sections dealing with active recreational facilities and passive trail networks.

B. **Endowment for Greenway Maintenance**

1. When greenway land is to be donated to a land trust or to the municipality, the Board may allow up to a 10 percent density bonus to generate additional income to the applicant for the sole purpose of endowing a permanent fund to offset continuing costs of maintaining the greenway land (involving activities such as mowing meadows, removing invasive vines, paying insurance premiums and local taxes), in-

cluding costs associated with active or passive recreation facilities. Spending from this fund should be restricted to expenditure of interest so that the principal may be preserved. Assuming an annual average interest rate of 5 percent, the amount designated for the Endowment Fund shall be at least twenty (20) times the estimated annual maintenance costs. Such estimate shall be prepared by an agency, firm, or organization acceptable to the Board and with experience in managing conservation land and recreational facilities.

2. Because additional dwellings, beyond the maximum that would ordinarily be permitted, may reasonably be considered to be net of development costs and represent true profit, 75 percent of the net selling price of the endowment lots shall be donated by the applicant to the Greenway Maintenance Endowment Fund for the greenway lands within the subdivision. This fund shall be transferred by the developer to the designated entity with ownership and maintenance responsibilities at the time this entity is created.

3. When estimating the projected maintenance costs of the greenway land, greenway land that is not accessible by the subdivision residents for their common enjoyment need not be included in the calculations. Such lands would typically include areas designated on the Final Plan for Conservancy Lots or as land reserved for future agricultural, horticultural, silvicultural, or equestrian uses, which may be leased or sold to another party for those express purposes, and which are protected from future development by a permanent conservation easement. In such cases, the density bonus shall be adjusted proportionately to reflect only the acreage that is accessible to residents for their passive or active recreation.

C. **Provision of Affordable Housing**

1. A density increase is permitted where the subdivision proposal provides on-site or off-site housing opportunities for low- or moderate-income families. When such housing provision is proposed, the Board shall require evidence that these units will in fact be constructed by a certain date. The amount of density increase shall be based on the following standard: *For each affordable housing unit provided under this section, one additional building lot or dwelling unit shall be permitted, up to a maximum 15 percent increase in dwelling units. Affordable housing is herein defined as units sold or rented to families earning 70 to 120 percent of the county median income, adjusted for family size, as determined by the U.S. Department of Housing and Urban Development.*

D. **Implementation**

1. For each of the above categories of public purposes, density bonuses may be implemented by reducing the amount of required greenway land by up to 10 percent, reducing the minimum lot area requirements by up to 10 percent, or by a combination of these approaches, at the discretion of the Board. The cumulative reductions may total up to 30 percent, if the board is satisfied that the public purposes are being served.

SECTION 109. Ownership and Maintenance of Greenway Land and Common Facilities

A. All greenway land shall be permanently restricted from future subdivision and development. Under no circumstances shall any development be permitted in the open space at any time, except for those uses listed in Section 106.

B. **Ownership Options**

The following methods may be used, either individually or in combination, to own common facilities; however, greenway land shall be initially offered for dedication to the municipality. Common facilities shall not be transferred to another entity except for transfer to another method of ownership permitted under this section, and then only when there is no change in the common facilities or in the open space ratio of the overall development. Ownership methods shall conform to the following:

1. <u>Fee Simple Dedication to the Municipality:</u> The municipality may, but shall not be required to, accept any portion of the common facilities, provided that:

  a. There is no cost of acquisition to the municipality; and,

  b. The municipality agrees to and has access to maintain such facilities.

2. <u>Condominium Association:</u> Common facilities may be controlled

through the use of condominium agreements. Such agreements shall be in accordance with relevant state law. All open land and common facilities shall be held as "common elements."

3. <u>Homeowner Association:</u> Common facilities may be held in common ownership by a homeowner association, subject to all of the provisions for homeowner associations set forth in state regulations and statutes. In addition, the following regulations shall be met:

   a. The applicant shall provide the municipality a description of the organization of the proposed association, including its bylaws, and all documents governing ownership, maintenance, and use restrictions for common facilities.

   b. The proposed association shall be established by the owner or applicant and shall be operating (with financial subsidization by the owner or applicant, if necessary) before the sale of any dwelling units in the development.

   c. Membership in the association shall be automatic (mandatory) for all purchasers of dwelling units therein and their successors in title.

   d. The association shall be responsible for maintenance and insurance of common facilities.

   e. The bylaws shall confer legal authority on the association to place a lien on the real property of any member who falls delinquent in dues. Such dues shall be paid with the accrued interest before the lien may be lifted.

   f. Written notice of any proposed transfer of common facilities by the association or the assumption of maintenance for common facilities must be given to all members of the association and to the municipality no less than thirty (30) days prior to such event.

   g. The association shall have adequate staff to administer, maintain, and operate such common facilities.

4. <u>Private Conservation Organization or the County:</u> With permission of the municipality, an owner may transfer either fee simple title of the open space or easements on the open space to a private nonprofit conservation organization or to the County provided that:

   a. The conservation organization is acceptable to the municipality

and is a bona fide conservation organization intended to exist indefinitely;

   b. The conveyance contains appropriate provisions for proper reverter or retransfer in the event that the organization or _____ County becomes unwilling or unable to continue carrying out its functions;

   c. The greenway land is permanently restricted from future development through a conservation easement and the municipality is given the ability to enforce these restrictions; and

   d. A maintenance agreement acceptable to the municipality is established between the owner and the organization or _____ County.

5. <u>Dedication of Easements to the Municipality:</u> The municipality may, but shall not be required to, accept easements for public use of any portion of the common land or facilities. In such cases, the facility remains in the ownership of the condominium association, homeowner association, or private conservation organization while the easements are held by the municipality. In addition, the following regulations shall apply:

   a. There shall be no cost of acquisition to the municipality.

   b. Any such easements for public use shall be accessible to the residents of the municipality.

   c. A satisfactory maintenance agreement shall be reached between the owner and the municipality.

6. <u>Noncommon Private Ownership:</u> Up to 80 percent of the required greenway land may be included within one or more large "conservancy lots" of at least ten acres provided the open space is permanently restricted from future development through a conservation easement, except for those uses listed in Section 106, and that the municipality is given the ability to enforce these restrictions.

C. **Maintenance**

1. Unless otherwise agreed to by the Board, the cost and responsibility of maintaining common facilities and greenway land shall be borne by the property owner, condominium association, homeowner association, or conservation organization.

2. The applicant shall, at the time of preliminary plan submission, provide a Plan for Maintenance of Greenway Lands and Operation of Common Facilities in accordance with the following requirements. (This plan may be based on the model prepared for Lower Merion Township, Montgomery County, Pennsylvania, by the Natural Lands Trust, which has been routinely adopted by developers of conservation subdivisions in that municipality.)

   a. The plan shall define ownership;

   b. The plan shall establish necessary regular and periodic operation and maintenance responsibilities for the various kinds of open space (i.e., lawns, playing fields, meadows, pastures, croplands, woodlands, etc.);

   c. The plan shall estimate staffing needs, insurance requirements, and associated costs and define the means for funding the maintenance of the greenway land and operation of any common facilities on an ongoing basis. Such funding plan shall include the means for funding long-term capital improvements as well as regular yearly operating and maintenance costs;

   d. At the municipality's discretion, the applicant may be required to escrow sufficient funds for the maintenance and operation costs of common facilities for up to one year; and

   e. Any changes to the maintenance plan shall be approved by the Board.

3. In the event that the organization established to maintain the greenway lands and the common facilities, or any successor organization thereto, fails to maintain all or any portion thereof in reasonable order and condition, the municipality may assume responsibility for maintenance, in which case any escrow funds may be forfeited and any permits may be revoked or suspended.

4. The municipality may enter the premises and take corrective action, including extended maintenance. The costs of such corrective action may be charged to the property owner, condominium association, homeowner association, conservation organization, or individual property owners who make up a condominium or homeowner association and may include administrative costs and penalties. Such costs shall become a lien on said properties. Notice of such lien shall be filed by the municipality in the office of the Prothonotary of the County.

Additional Definitions

Conservancy Lot. A large, privately owned lot constituting part of an area of open land. The purpose of the conservancy lot is to provide surrounding residents with visual access to greenway land while keeping the land under private ownership and maintenance. Only a small portion of such lots may be developed; the remainder must be protected through conservation easements and used in conformance with standard for greenway land. Public access to conservancy lots is not required.

Greenway Land. That portion of a tract that is set aside for the protection of sensitive natural features, farmland, scenic views, and other unique features. Greenway land may be accessible to the residents of the development and/or the municipality, or it may contain areas of conservancy lots that are not accessible to the public.

Appendix. Community Wastewater Systems: Ordered List of Preferred Alternative Types

The following six types of wastewater treatment systems are ranked in descending order reflecting the municipality's official preferences, as stated in its Sewage Facilities Plan. Applicants for new development proposals involving community sewage treatment systems shall be required to demonstrate to the Board of Supervisors that they cannot utilize preferred types of wastewater treatment before they may be permitted to utilize a less-preferred alternative that ranks lower on the ordered list below:

1. Lagoon treatment/spray irrigation
2. Package treatment/spray irrigation
3. Community septic tank/sand filter/subsurface
4. Package plant/sand filter/spray irrigation
5. Package plant/direct discharge to groundwater
6. Package plant/seasonal spray—discharge

SUBDIVISION ORDINANCE LANGUAGE

ARTICLE 4: PLAN CONTENT REQUIREMENTS

SECTION 400. Purposes and Applicability

The provisions of this Article shall apply to all subdivision and land development applications in this municipality. For the convenience of applicants, the municipality provides a complimentary Plan Requirements Checklist listing all the documents that this Ordinance requires to be submitted at each step of the review process. Copies of this checklist are available from the Municipal Office. The checklist also facilitates review by staff and officials, as they review each application for completeness and conformance with relevant ordinance provisions.

SECTION 401. Sketch Plan Overlay Sheet

A. A Sketch Plan may be submitted by the applicant as a diagrammatic basis for informal discussion with the Board, the Planning Commission, and the County Planning Commission regarding the design of a proposed subdivision or land development. Sketch Plan submission is *strongly encouraged* by the municipality as a way of helping applicants and officials develop a better understanding of the property and to help establish an overall design approach that respects its special or noteworthy features while providing for the density permitted under the zoning ordinance.

B. To provide a full understanding of the site's potential and to facilitate the most effective exchange with the Planning Commission, the Sketch Plan should include the information listed below. *Many of these items can be taken from the Existing Resources and Site Analysis Map, a document that must in any case be prepared and submitted no later than the date of the Site Inspection,* which precedes the Conceptual Preliminary Plan (see Section 402C2). In fact, the diagrammatic Sketch Plan may be prepared as a simple overlay sheet placed on top of the Existing Resources and Site Analysis Map.

1. Name and address of the legal owner, the equitable owner, and/or the applicant;

2. Name and address of the professional engineer, surveyor, planner, architect, landscape architect, or site designer responsible for preparing the plan;

3. Graphic scale (not greater than 1 inch = 200 feet; however, dimensions on the plan need not be exact at this stage) and north arrow;

4. Approximate tract boundaries, sufficient to locate the tract on a map of the municipality;

5. Location map;

6. Zoning district;

7. Streets on and adjacent to the tract (both existing and proposed);

8. 100-year floodplain limits, and approximate location of wetlands, if any;

9. Topographic, physical, and cultural features including fields, pastures, meadows, wooded areas, trees with a diameter of 15 inches or more, hedgerows and other significant vegetation, steep slopes (over 25 percent), rock outcrops, soil types, ponds, ditches, drains, dumps, storage tanks, streams within two hundred (200) feet of the tract, existing rights-of-way and easements, and cultural features such as all structures, foundations, walls, wells, trails, and abandoned roads;

10. Schematic layout indicating a general concept for land conservation and development (*"bubble" format is acceptable* for this delineation of Step One of the four-step design process described in Section 602B of this ordinance);

11. Proposed general street and lot layout;

12. In the case of land development plans, proposed location of buildings and major structures, parking areas, and other improvements; and

13. General description of proposed method of water supply, sewage disposal, and stormwater management.

SECTION 402. Documents Required for the Conceptual Preliminary Plan

(Note: The approach advocated in this Article is to return to the original intent of the state enabling legislation, in which "Preliminary Plans" were much more conceptual in nature than they have evolved into in recent years in many municipalities. The following model provisions strike a balance between the municipality's need for certain kinds of information prior to vesting, while at the same time avoiding the situation in which applicants become "locked into" highly detailed and so-called preliminary plans that cost them tens of thousands of dollars to prepare. It is not essential that such a high degree of detail be supplied at this early stage, and the practice of transforming "preliminary" plans into very expensive engineering documents has proven to be counterproductive in many cases, with applicants typically refusing to substantially modify their "preliminary" plans.)

The application for a Conceptual Preliminary Plan shall provide the name and address of the legal owner or equitable owner of the subject property and the name and address of the applicant if not the same party, plus the following four elements listed below. A deed or agreement of sale evidencing that the applicant is the legal or equitable owner of the land to be subdivided or developed shall be shown.

A. **Conceptual Preliminary Plan Application Submission Requirements**

1. The submission requirements for a Conceptual Preliminary Plan shall consist of the following four elements and shall be prepared in accordance with the drafting standards and plan requirements described herein:

   a. Site Context Map

   b. Existing Resources and Site Analysis Map

   c. Preliminary Resource Impact and Conservation Plan

   d. Preliminary Improvements Plan

   e. Preliminary Studies and Reports as set forth in other parts of this ordinance.

B. **Drafting Standards**

1. The plan shall be drawn to a scale of either 1 inch = 100 feet or 1 inch = 200 feet, whichever would fit best on a standard size sheet (24 inches x 36 inches), unless otherwise approved by the Planning Commission.

2. Dimensions shall be set in feet.

3. Each sheet shall be numbered and the plan shall provide an adequate legend indicating clearly which features are existing and which are proposed.

4. All plans submitted shall be made on sheets no larger than 34 inches x 44 inches nor smaller than 17 inches x 22 inches.

C. **Plan Requirements**

The following plans and maps shall bear the name, signature, address, and telephone number of the engineer, land surveyor, or landscape architect responsible for preparing the plan or map.

1. Site Context Map

   A map showing the location of the proposed subdivision within its neighborhood context shall be submitted. For sites under 100 acres, such maps shall be at a scale not less than 1 inch = 200 feet, and shall show the relationship of the subject property to natural and human-made features existing within 1,000 feet of the site. For sites of 100 acres or more, the scale shall be 1 inch = 400 feet, and shall show the above relationships within 2,000 feet of the site. The features that shall be shown on Site Context Maps include topography (from USGS maps), stream valleys, wetland complexes (from maps published by the U.S. Fish & Wildlife Service or the USDA Natural Resources Conservation Service), woodlands over one-half acre in area (from aerial photographs), ridge lines, public roads and trails, utility easements and rights-of-way, public land, and land protected under conservation easements.

2. Existing Resources and Site Analysis Map

   For all subdivisions (except those in which all proposed lots are to be ten or more acres in area), an Existing Resources and Site Analysis Map shall be prepared to provide the developer and the municipality with a comprehensive analysis of existing conditions both on the proposed development site and within 500 feet of the site. Conditions beyond the parcel boundaries may be described on the basis of existing published data available from governmental agencies and from aerial photographs.

The municipality shall review the Map to assess its accuracy, conformance with municipal ordinances, and likely impact upon the natural and cultural resources on the property. Unless otherwise specified by the Planning Commission, such maps shall generally be prepared at the scale of 1 inch = 100 feet or 1 inch = 200 feet, whichever would fit best on a single standard size sheet (24 inches x 36 inches). The following information shall be included on this Map:

a. A vertical aerial photograph enlarged to a scale not less detailed than 1 inch = 400 feet, with the site boundaries clearly marked.

b. Topography, the contour lines of which shall generally be at two-foot intervals, determined by photogrammetry (although ten-foot intervals are permissible beyond the parcel boundaries, interpolated from USGS published maps). The determination of appropriate contour intervals shall be made by the Planning Commission, which may specify greater or lesser intervals on exceptionally steep or flat sites. Slopes between 15 and 25 percent and those exceeding 25 percent shall be clearly indicated. Topography for major subdivisions shall be prepared by a professional land surveyor or professional engineer from an actual field survey of the site or from stereoscopic aerial photography and shall be coordinated with official USGS benchmarks.

c. The location and delineation of ponds, streams, ditches, drains, and natural drainage swales, as well as the 100-year floodplains and wetlands, as defined in the Zoning Ordinance. Additional areas of wetlands on the proposed development parcel shall also be indicated, as evident from testing, visual inspection, or the presence of wetland vegetation.

d. Vegetative cover conditions on the property according to general cover type, including cultivated land, permanent grassland, meadow, pasture, old field, hedgerow, woodland and wetland, trees with a caliper in excess of 15 inches, the actual canopy line of existing trees and woodlands. Vegetative types shall be described by plant community, relative age, and condition.

e. Soil series, types, and phases, as mapped by the U.S. Department of Agriculture, Natural Resources Conservation Service in the published soil survey for the county, and accompanying data published for each soil relating to its suitability for construction (and, in unsewered areas, for septic suitability).

f. Ridge lines and watershed boundaries shall be identified.

g. A viewshed analysis showing the location and extent of views into the property from public roads and from public parks, public forests, and state game lands.

h. Geologic formations on the proposed development parcel, including rock outcroppings, cliffs, sinkholes, and fault lines, based on available published information or more detailed data obtained by the applicant.

i. All existing human-made features, including but not limited to streets, driveways, farm roads, woods roads, buildings, foundations, walls, wells, drainage fields, dumps, utilities, fire hydrants, and storm and sanitary sewers.

j. Locations of all historically significant sites or structures on the tract, including but not limited to cellar holes, stone walls, earthworks, and graves.

k. Locations of trails that have been in public use (pedestrian, equestrian, bicycle, etc.).

l. All easements and other encumbrances of property that are or have been filed of record with the Recorder of Deeds of _____ County shall be shown on the plan.

m. Total acreage of the tract, plus the Adjusted Tract Acreage with detailed supporting calculations.

3. Four-Step Design Process for Subdivisions in the Conservation Design Overlay District

   (Note: This process can also be used in other zoning districts where conservation design is encouraged or required under the Township's ordinance.)

   All Conceptual Preliminary Plans in the Conservation Design Overlay District shall include documentation of a four-step design process in determining the layout of proposed greenway lands, house sites, streets, and lot lines, as described below.

   a. Step 1: Delineation of Greenway Lands

1) The minimum percentage and acreage of required greenway lands shall be calculated by the applicant and submitted as part of the Sketch Plan or Conceptual Preliminary Plan in accordance with the provisions of this ordinance and of the zoning ordinance. Greenway lands shall include all Primary Conservation Areas and those parts of the remaining buildable lands with the highest resource significance, as described below and in Sections 603A and 603B.

2) Proposed greenway lands shall be designated using the Existing Resources and Site Analysis Map as a base map and complying with Section 106B of the Zoning Ordinance and Sections 602 and 603 herein, dealing with Resource Conservation and Greenway Delineation Standards. The municipality's Map of Potential Conservation Lands in the Comprehensive Plan shall also be referenced and considered. Primary Conservation Areas shall be delineated comprising floodplains, wetlands, and slopes over 25 percent. (The definition of Primary Conservation Areas is independent of the "density factors" applied to various categories of constrained lands to calculate Adjusted Tract Acreage in Section 104C1 of the zoning ordinance.)

3) In delineating Secondary Conservation Areas, the applicant shall *prioritize* natural and cultural resources on the tract in terms of their highest to least suitabilities for inclusion in the proposed greenway, in consultation with the Planning Commission and in accordance with Sections 603A and 603B herein ("Prioritized List of Resources to be Conserved" and "Other Design Considerations").

4) On the basis of those priorities and practical considerations given to the tract's configuration, its context in relation to resource areas on adjoining and neighboring properties, and the applicant's subdivision objectives, Secondary Conservation Areas shall be delineated to meet at least the minimum area percentage requirements for greenway lands and in a manner clearly indicating their boundaries as well as the types of resources included within them.

b. Step 2: Location of House Sites

Potential house sites shall be tentatively located using the proposed greenway lands as a base map as well as other relevant data on the Existing Resources and Site Analysis Map, such as topography and soils. House sites should generally be located not closer than 100 feet from Primary Conservation Areas and 50 feet from Secondary Conservation Areas, taking into consideration the potential negative impacts of residential development on such areas as well as the potential positive benefits of such locations to provide attractive views and visual settings for residences.

c. Step 3: Alignment of Streets and Trails

Upon designating the house sites, a street plan shall be designed to provide vehicular access to each house, complying with the standards in Article 7 herein and bearing a logical relationship to topographic conditions. Impacts of the street plan on proposed greenway lands shall be minimized, particularly with respect to crossing environmentally sensitive areas such as wetlands and traversing slopes exceeding 15 percent. Street connections shall generally be encouraged to minimize the number of new cul-de-sacs to be maintained by the municipality and to facilitate access to and from homes in different parts of the tract (and adjoining parcels).

d. Step 4: Drawing in the Lot Lines

Upon completion of the preceding three steps, lot lines are drawn as required to delineate the boundaries of individual residential lots. Applicants shall be prepared to submit four separate sketch maps indicating the findings of each step of the design process, if so requested by the Planning Commission or the Board.

4. Note on the Four-Step Site Design Process for Option 5: Hamlets and Villages

The design process for laying out Option 5, Hamlets and Villages, shall be a variation on the four-step process for conservation subdivisions, as described in Section 402C3 of this Ordinance. In hamlets and villages, where traditional streetscape and "terminal vistas" are of greater importance, Steps 2 and 3 may be reversed so that streets and squares are located during the second step and house sites are located immediately thereafter. The first step is to identify greenway lands, including both Primary and Secondary Conservation Areas.

5. Preliminary Resource Impact and Conservation Plan

a. A Preliminary Resource Impact and Conservation Plan shall be prepared for all major subdivision and land development applications to categorize the impacts of the proposed activities and physical alterations on those resources shown on the Existing Resources and Site Analysis Map (as required under Section 402C2). All proposed improvements, including but not necessarily limited to grading, fill, streets, buildings, utilities, and stormwater detention facilities, as proposed in the other Conceptual Preliminary Plan documents, shall be taken into account in preparing the Preliminary Resource Impact and Conservation Plan, which shall clearly demonstrate that the applicant has minimized site disturbance to the greatest extent practicable.

b. Using the Existing Resources and Site Analysis Map as a base map, impact areas shall be mapped according to the following categories: (1) primary impact areas (i.e., areas directly impacted by the proposed subdivision), (2) secondary impact areas (i.e., areas in proximity to primary areas that may be impacted), and (3) designated protected areas either to be included in a proposed greenway or an equivalent designation such as dedication of a neighborhood park site.

c. This requirement for a Preliminary Resource Impact and Conservation Plan may be waived by the Planning Commission if, in its judgment, the proposed development areas, as laid out in the Sketch Plan or in the Conceptual Preliminary Plan would be likely to cause no more than an insignificant impact upon the site's resources.

6. Preliminary Improvements Plan

This plan shall include the following items:

a. Historic resources, trails, and significant natural features, including topography, areas of steep slope, wetlands, 100-year floodplains, swales, rock outcroppings, vegetation, existing utilities, and other site features, as indicated on the Existing Resources and Site Analysis Map.

b. Existing and *approximate* proposed lot lines, lot areas, any existing easements and rights-of-way. For properties subject to the Conservation Design Overlay District, the boundaries of greenway lands shall be indicated.

c. *Approximate* location, alignment, width, and tentative names of all proposed streets and street rights-of-way, including all street extensions or spurs that are reasonably necessary to provide adequate street connections and facilities to adjoining development or undeveloped areas; preliminarily engineered profiles for proposed streets.

d. *Approximate* location of proposed swales, drainage easements, and stormwater and other management facilities.

e. Where community sewage service is to be permitted, the *conceptual* layout of proposed sewage systems, including but not limited to, the tentative locations of sewer mains and sewage treatment plants, showing the type and degree of treatment intended and the size and capacity of treatment facilities.

f. Where central water service is to be permitted, the *conceptual* layout of proposed water distribution facilities including water mains, fire hydrants, storage tanks, and, where appropriate, wells or other water sources.

g. Location of all percolation tests as may be required under this ordinance, including all failed test sites or pits as well as those approved and including an approved alternate site for each lot requiring a sand mound system. All approved sites shall be clearly distinguished from unapproved sites.

h. Limit-of-disturbance line (must be exact in relation to the retention of existing trees proposed to be saved).

i. *Approximate* location and dimensions of proposed playgrounds, public buildings, public areas, and parcels of land proposed to be dedicated or reserved for public use.

j. If land to be subdivided lies partly in or abuts another municipality, the applicant shall submit information concerning the location and conceptual design of streets, layout, and size of lots and provisions of public improvements on land subject to applicant's control within the adjoining municipalities. The design of public improvements shall provide for a smooth, practical transition where specifications vary between municipalities. Evidence of approval of this information by appropriate officials of the adjoining municipalities also shall be submitted.

k. Where installation of the improvements is proposed to be done in phases, the applicant shall submit with the Conceptual Preliminary Plan a delineation of the proposed sections and a schedule of deadlines within which applications for final approval of each section are intended to be filed.

l. Typical street cross-section drawing(s) for all proposed streets shall be shown, including details relating to thickness, crowning, and construction materials.

m. Utilities and Easements

  1) Exact locations of existing utility easements and *approximate* locations of proposed utility easements.

  2) *Approximate* layout of all proposed sanitary and storm sewers and location of all inlets and culverts and any proposed connections with existing facilities. (These data may be on a separate plan.)

  3) The tentative location of proposed on-site sewage and water facilities.

n. Approximate location of proposed shade trees, plus locations of existing vegetation to be retained.

o. Signature blocks for the Planning Commission, Board, and the County Planning Commission shall be provided on the right-hand side of the Preliminary Improvements Plan.

7. Preliminary Studies and Reports

  When required by the Board, typically in cases involving large subdivision and land development proposals (with more than 25 lots) or smaller development plans where the Board believes that potential impacts could be significant, the Conceptual Preliminary Plan submission shall include one or more of the following studies to assist in determination of the impact of the application on municipal services and facilities:

a. Sewer and Water Feasibility Report

b. Groundwater Protection and Replenishment Study

c. Erosion and Sedimentation Control Plan

d. Traffic Impact Study

e. Community Association Document

  1) A Community Association Document, also known as a Homeowner Association Document or a Condominium Association Document, shall be provided for all subdivision and land devel-opment applications that propose lands or facilities to be used or owned in common by all the residents of that subdivision or land development and not deeded to the municipality.

  2) The elements of the Community Association Document shall include but shall not necessarily be limited to the following:

    a) A description of all lands and facilities to be owned by the Community Association. This description shall include a map of the proposal highlighting the precise location of those lands and facilities.

    b) Statements setting forth the powers, duties, and responsibilities of the Community Association, including the services to be provided.

    c) A Declaration of Covenants, Conditions, and Restrictions, giving perpetual easement to the lands and facilities owned by the Community Association. The Declaration shall be a legal document that also provides for automatic Association membership for all owners in the subdivision or land development and shall describe the mechanism by which owners participate in the Association, including voting, elections, and meetings. Furthermore, it shall give power to the Association to own and maintain the common property and to make and enforce rules.

    d) Statements prescribing the process by which Community Association decisions are reached and setting forth the authority to act.

    e) Statements requiring each owner within the subdivision or land development to become a member of the Community Association.

    f) Statements setting cross covenants or contractual terms binding each owner to all other owners for mutual benefit and enforcement.

    g) Requirements for all owners to provide a *pro rata* share of the cost of the operations of the Community Association.

    h) A process of collection and enforcement to obtain funds from owners who fail to comply.

    i) A process for transition of control of the Community Association from the developer to the unit owners.

j) Statements describing how the lands and facilities of the Community Association will be insured, including limit of liability.

k) Provisions for the dissolution of the Community Association, in the event the Association should become inviable.

(Note: See also Section 109 of the Zoning Ordinance, "Ownership and Maintenance of Greenway Land and Common Facilities.")

D. Preliminary Greenway Ownership and Management Plan

Using the Conceptual Preliminary Plan as a base map, the boundaries, acreage, and proposed ownership of all proposed greenway areas shall be shown. In addition, the applicant shall also submit a Preliminary Greenway Ownership and Management Plan detailing the entities responsible for maintaining various elements of the property and describing management objectives and techniques for each part of the property. Such management plans shall be consistent with the requirements of Section 109 of the zoning ordinance ("Ownership and Maintenance of Greenway Land and Common Facilities").

E. Preliminary Engineering Certification

Prior to approval of the Conceptual Preliminary Plan, the applicant shall submit to the Planning Commission a "Preliminary Engineering Certification" verifying that the approximate layout of proposed streets, house lots, and greenway lands complies with the municipality's zoning and subdivision ordinances, particularly those sections governing the design of subdivision streets and stormwater management facilities. This certification requirement is meant to provide the Planning Commission with assurance that the proposed plan is able to be accomplished within the municipality's current regulations. The certification shall also note any waivers needed to implement the plan as drawn.

SECTION 403. Detailed Final Plan

Final plans shall conform to the Conceptual Preliminary Plan, including any conditions specified by the Board. A Detailed Final Plan shall consist of and be prepared in accordance with the following:

A. Drafting Standards

All drafting standards as required in Section 402B shall apply. Also, final plans shall be prepared at the scale of 1 inch = 100 feet. However, Detailed Final Plans for low-density "Option 4" subdivisions shall generally not be required to be prepared at scales finer than 1 inch = 200 feet, unless special conditions exist on the site.

B. Existing Resources and Site Analysis Map

A plan as stipulated in Section 402C consistent with the terms of Conceptual Preliminary Plan approval and modified as necessary to reflect the proposal for final approval.

C. Final Resource Impact and Conservation Plan

1. This plan shall comply with all of the requirements for the Preliminary Resource Impact and Conservation Plan, as set forth in Section 402C5, to reflect all proposed improvements described in the other Detailed Final Plan documents as required under Section 403 herein.

2. In addition to the requirements of Section 402C5, the applicant shall submit an accompanying Resource Assessment Report divided into the following sections: (1) description of existing resources (as documented in Section 402C2; (2) impacts of the proposed subdivision on existing resources, correlated to the areas depicted in the Final Resource Impact and Conservation Plan; and (3) measures taken to minimize and control such impacts both during and following the period of site disturbance and construction. The qualifications and experience of the preparer of this report shall be provided.

D. Final Improvements Construction Plan

Where public or private improvements other than monuments and street traffic signs are to be required for any subdivision or land development, an Improvements Construction Plan and specifications, prepared by a registered professional engineer, shall be filed, setting forth the precise nature and exact location of the work and all engineering data necessary for completion of the work. The Improvements Construction Plan and specifications shall be subject to approval of the Municipal Engineer and the Board as a prerequisite to approval of the Detailed Final Plan. The Improvements Construction Plan shall conform with the following standards and contain the following information:

1. All information required in Sections 401B and 402C2 relating to existing features and resources on the site.

2. Detailed profile sheets for all proposed streets within the tract.

3. If required, a plan, details, and specifications of street lights to be installed, together with the necessary contract for street light installation for approval by the municipality.

4. Detailed design of any stormwater management facilities that may be required.

5. Where off-site or community sewer service is to be provided, the final detailed design of all facilities, including but not limited to sewer mains, manholes, pumping stations, and sewage treatment facilities.

6. Where off-site or central water service or water supply is to be provided, the final detailed design, including location and size of water service facilities within the subdivision, shall be shown, including wells, storage tanks, pumps, mains, valves, and hydrants.

7. Detailed designs for all other improvements as required by this ordinance.

E. **Final Stormwater Management and Erosion and Sedimentation Control Plan**

F. **Final Greenway Ownership and Management Plan**
   Using the Detailed Final Plan as a base map, the precise boundaries, exact acreage, and proposed ownership of all proposed greenway areas shall be shown. A narrative report shall also be prepared indicating how and by whom such greenway areas will be managed and demonstrating compliance with Article 1 of the Zoning Ordinance.

G. **Final Landscape Plan**

H. **Additional Approvals, Certificates, and Documents**

1. All offers of dedication of realty or structures and all declarations, easements, and covenants governing the reservation and maintenance of undedicated open space, for the Detailed Final Plan shall be in such form as shall be satisfactory to the Board.

2. A copy of such deed restrictions, easements, covenants, and declarations that are to be imposed upon the property to comply with the Detailed Final Plan as approved by the Board. All such documents shall be in such form as is satisfactory to the Board.

ARTICLE 5: PLAN PROCESSING PROCEDURES

SECTION 500. General

A. All preliminary and final subdivision or land development plans shall be referred to and reviewed by the Planning Commission and shall be approved or disapproved by the Board of Supervisors in accordance with the procedures specified in this Article and in other sections of this ordinance. Any application not processed as required herein shall be null and void unless it was made prior to the adoption of these regulations.

B. **Overview of Procedures:** Items 1–4 and 6–10 below are required under this Ordinance. Item 5 (Sketch Plan Submission and Review) is optional but strongly encouraged as an important, valuable, and highly recommended step that will speed the review process and may result in lower costs for the project. These steps shall be followed sequentially and may be combined only at the discretion of the Municipality:

1. Pre-Application Meeting

2. Existing Resources and Site Analysis Map, as described in Section 402C2 of this Ordinance

3. Site Inspection by Planning Commission and Applicant

4. Pre-Sketch Plan Conference

5. Sketch Plan Submission and Review (diagrammatic sketch, optional step)

6. Conceptual Preliminary Plan: Determination of Completeness; Preliminary Resource Conservation Plan and Sewage Planning Module Submission. Review by Municipal and County Planning Commissions, Township Engineer, and County Health Department; and Approval by Supervisors on advice of the Municipal Planning Commission. (In the Conservation Design Overlay District, the Four-Step Design Process described in Section 402C3 of this Ordinance must be followed.)

7. Detailed Final Plan, Preparation: Incorporation of all Conceptual Preliminary Plan Approval Conditions, Documentation of all other agency approvals, as applicable.

8. Detailed Final Plan, Submission: Determination of Completeness, Review, and Approval

9. Supervisors' signatures

10. Recording of approved Detailed Final Plan with County Recorder of Deeds

SECTION 501. Plan Classification for Major and Minor Subdivisions

A. Classification

For purposes of procedure, all applications shall be classified as either major or minor:

1. Minor: Any subdivision in which

   a. No public or private street is constructed or is required to be widened;

   b. No other completion of public improvement or guarantee thereof is required other than individual on-lot stormwater management systems;

   c. No earthmoving activities will take place except those incidental to construction of a single-family dwelling on each lot; and

   d. No more than three (3) lots are created.

2. Major: Any land development or subdivison application not in compliance with Section 501A1 or any part thereof, or for any use other than single-family residential, shall be considered a major use plan.

B. Review

1. Major applications shall be subject to all review procedures specified in this article.

2. When an application includes only a portion of a landowner's entire tract, or when such portion is contiguous to an adjoining tract of the landowner, a sketch layout shall be included showing future potential subdivision of all the contiguous lands belonging to the landowner to ensure that subdivision may be accomplished in accordance with current codes and with appropriate access. Submission and review of the sketch plan described in this section shall not constitute approval of the future subdivision shown thereon.

SECTION 502. Submission and Review of Sketch Plan

(Note: Municipalities shall determine whether an optional or mandatory Sketch Plan best suits their needs. The language below provides for optional Sketch Plans only because Pennsylvania law does not specifically provide for more than two 90-day review periods for subdivision plans. Municipalities that adopt the optional approach should evaluate, at the end of one year, whether applicants are generally choosing to follow the Sketch Plan process. If they are not, the municipality should consider requiring Sketch Plans, as a large number of municipalities in southeastern Pennsylvania have done. If the requirements are not onerous and are seen by applicants as a way to help them avoid delays, or to avoid situations in which they must substantially modify their original plans to comply with ordinance requirements, experience has shown that applicants will not litigate over a Sketch Plan requirement.)

A. Applicability

A diagrammatic sketch plan is *very strongly encouraged* for all proposed minor or major subdivisions. Sketch Plans, as described in Section 401, shall be submitted to the Board of Supervisors for review by the Planning Commission. Such plans are for informal discussion only. Submission of a Sketch Plan does not constitute formal filing of a plan with the Municipality, and shall not commence the statutory review period as required by the Municipalities Planning Code. The procedures for submission of a diagrammatic Sketch Plan are described in Section 502F below and may be altered only at the discretion of the Municipality.

B. Pre-Application Meeting

A Pre-Application meeting is encouraged between the applicant, the site designer, and the Planning Commission (and/or its planning consultant) to introduce the applicant to the municipality's zoning and subdivision regulations and procedures, to discuss the applicant's objectives, and to schedule site inspections, meetings, and plan submissions as described below. Applicants are also encouraged to present the Existing Resources and Site Analysis Map at this meeting.

C. Existing Resources and Site Analysis Map

Applicants shall submit an Existing Resources and Site Analysis Map, in its context, prepared in accordance with the requirements contained in Section 402C2. The purpose of this key submission is to familiarize officials with existing conditions on the applicant's tract and within its immediate vicinity and to provide a complete and factual reference for them in making a site inspection. This Plan shall be provided prior to or at the site inspection and shall form the basis for the development design as shown on the diagrammatic Sketch Plan (or on the Conceptual Preliminary Plan, if the optional Sketch Plan is not submitted).

D. Site Inspection

After preparing the Existing Resources and Site Analysis Map, applicants shall arrange for a site inspection of the property by the Planning Commission and other municipal officials and shall distribute copies of said site analysis plan at that on-site meeting. Applicants, their site designers, and the landowner are encouraged to accompany the Planning Commission. The purpose of the visit is to familiarize local officials with the property's existing conditions and special features, to identify potential site design issues, and to provide an informal opportunity to discuss site design concepts, including the general layout of designated greenway lands (if applicable) and potential locations for proposed

buildings and street alignments. Comments made by municipal officials or their staff and consultants shall be interpreted as being only suggestive. It shall be understood by all parties that no formal recommendations can be offered, and no official decisions can be made, at the Site Inspection.

E. Pre-Sketch Conference

Following the site inspection and prior to the submission of a diagrammatic Sketch Plan, the applicant shall meet with the Planning Commission to discuss the findings of the site inspection and to develop a mutual understanding on the general approach for subdividing and/or developing the tract in accordance with the four-step design procedure described in Sections 402C3 and 602B of this ordinance, where applicable. At the discretion of the Commission, this conference may be combined with the site inspection.

F. Sketch Plan Submission and Review

1. Copies of a diagrammatic Sketch Plan, meeting the requirements set forth in Section 401, shall be submitted to the Municipal Secretary during business hours for distribution to the Board, the Planning Commission, the Municipal Planner, the Municipal Engineer, and applicable municipal advisory boards (such as the Parks Board, the Environmental Advisory Council, the Historic Architectural Review Board, the Shade Tree Commission, and the Open Space Committee) at least seven (7) days prior to the Planning Commission meeting at which the Sketch Plan is to be discussed. The Sketch Plan diagrammatically illustrates initial thoughts about a conceptual layout for greenway lands, house sites, and street alignments and shall be based closely upon the information contained in the Existing Resources and Site Analysis Map. The Sketch Plan shall also be designed in accordance with the four-step design process described in Sections 402C2 and 602B, and with the design review standards listed in Sections 603A and 603B.

2. The Planning Commission shall review the Sketch Plan in accordance with the criteria contained in this ordinance and with other applicable ordinances of the municipality. Their review shall informally advise the applicant of the extent to which the proposed subdivision or land development conforms to the relevant standards of this Ordi-

nance and may suggest possible plan modifications that would increase its degree of conformance. Their review shall include but is not limited to:

a. the location of all areas proposed for land disturbance (streets, foundations, yards, septic disposal systems, storm water management areas, etc.) with respect to notable features of natural or cultural significance as identified on the applicant's Existing Resources and Site Analysis Map and on the Municipality's Map of Potential Conservation Lands;

b. the potential for street connections with existing streets, other proposed streets, or potential developments on adjoining parcels;

c. the location of proposed access points along the existing road network;

d. the proposed building density and impervious coverage;

e. the compatibility of the proposal with respect to the objectives and policy recommendations of the Comprehensive Plan and the Open Space Plan; and

f. consistency with the zoning ordinance.

   The Commission shall submit its written comments to the applicant and the Board. The diagrammatic Sketch Plan may also be submitted by the Board to the County Planning Commission for review and comment. *(Note: Municipalities are advised to discuss the optional Sketch Plan review process with their County planning agency to determine whether the County is willing to conduct such a review and if so, whether fees will be charged.)*

SECTION 503. Submission of Concpetual Preliminary Plan Documents

A. Conceptual Preliminary Plan

1. The Conceptual Preliminary Plan is a preliminarily engineered scale drawing in which layout ideas are illustrated in more than the rough, diagrammatic manner appropriate for Sketch Plans but *before* heavy engineering costs are incurred in preparing detailed alignments and profiles for streets and/or detailed calculations for stormwater management. If an applicant opts not to submit a Sketch Plan, the Conceptual Preliminary Plan shall include all information required for Sketch Plans listed in Section 401, specifically including the Existing Resources and Site Analysis Map plus further details as noted below and in Section 402C2.

2. The applicant shall complete and sign the application form provided by the Township and shall accompany such application form with the type and number of plans, documents, and other submissions required and the appropriate filing fee(s). The applicant must identify the name, address, and telephone number of the record holder of legal title to the land involved (if different from the applicant), the nature of the applicant's interest in the land (whether holder of legal or equitable title or otherwise); and the name, address, and telephone number of the agent, if any. No application shall be deemed filed unless all requirements have been met and all fees therefor paid in full.

3. The Existing Resources and Site Analysis Map shall be presented at the Pre-Application Meeting and distributed to those municipal officials who attend the Site Inspection described in Section 502D (which shall occur at the Conceptual Preliminary Plan stage if it has not already occurred at the Sketch Plan stage).

4. The application "window" and deadline dates for submission of Conceptual Preliminary Plans shall be as follows: Applicants shall submit to the Municipal Secretary, at least twenty-one (21) days but not more than twenty-eight (28) days prior to the date of the next regularly scheduled Planning Commission meeting at which official review is requested, sixteen copies of a complete Conceptual Preliminary Plan and all other required documents and information, including the same number of copies of the Existing Resources and Site Analysis Map drawn at the same scale (generally 1 inch = 100 feet or 1 inch = 200 feet, at the discretion of the Zoning Officer). All applications shall be accompanied by full payment of the required fees and escrow deposits established in accordance with the terms of this ordinance for proposed subdivisions. The Municipal Secretary shall note the date of receipt of the application, fees, and escrow deposit and shall forward copies of the proposed plan to the same individuals and bodies named in Section 502F as recipients of Sketch Plans. The official 90-day re-

view period provided for Preliminary Plans under the Pennsylvania Municipalities Planning Code shall commence at the next scheduled meeting of the Planning Commission at which time the Commission receives the Plan and its related documentation and determines that the Conceptual Preliminary Plan application is complete.

5. The date of receipt is subject to review by the Zoning Officer and the Board of Supervisors to determine if all required materials, fees, and escrow deposits have been submitted by the applicant. If the application is defective or incomplete, the applicant shall be notified in writing within fifteen (15) days of the date of receipt and the application shall be null and void *ad initi,* and shall be deemed withdrawn by the applicant. If no such notice is given to the applicant that the application is defective or incomplete, then the date of filing shall be determined as follows. The review process for the plans required by the municipality shall include no more than ninety (90) days following the date of the next regular meeting of the Planning Commission following the date the application was filed, provided that should said next regular meeting occur more than thirty (30) days following the filing of the application, the said ninety (90) day period shall be measured from the thirtieth day following the day the application was filed. The applicant may agree to waive the time requirement.

SECTION 504. Review of Conceptual Preliminary Plan

A. Planning Commission Review

1. The Planning Commission shall review the plan and any recommendations made by County, State, and Federal agencies and the Municipal Planner and the Municipal Engineer to determine conformance of the Plan to this ordinance, the zoning ordinance, and any other relevant ordinances of the municipality.

2. After such review, the Planning Commission shall submit its report to the Board, containing its findings, recommendations, and reasons, citing specific sections of the statutes or ordinances relied upon. A copy of said report shall be given to the applicant.

3. If the applicant agrees that this review period shall be extended for a period of thirty (30) or more days to provide additional time for submission of all the required materials and for the Planning Commission to review the same, a written agreement to this effect shall be signed in duplicate, with a file copy being retained by the Planning Commission and by the applicant. Such an extension shall be entered in good faith and for specific reasons relating to the review process, including but not limited to providing sufficient time for the municipality to receive the written report of the County Planning Commission, the County Health Department, the Municipal Planner, and the Municipal Engineer, or to allow the applicant additional time in which to revise his/her application documents.

B. Board Review

1. When the recommendations on the Conceptual Preliminary Plan have been officially submitted to the Board of Supervisors by the Planning Commission, such recommendations shall be placed on the Board's agenda for review and action.

2. In acting on the preliminary subdivision or land development plan, the Board shall review the plan and the written comments of the Municipal Planner, the Municipal Engineer, the Planning Commission, the County Planning Commission and Health Department, and all other reviewing agencies, as well as comments from public hearings. The Board may specify conditions, changes, modifications, or additions thereto that it deems necessary or appropriate and may make its decision to grant preliminary approval subject to such conditions, changes, modifications, or additions. Whenever the approval of a Conceptual Preliminary Plan is subject to conditions, the written action of the Board should (1) specify each condition of approval and (2) request the applicant's written agreement to the conditions within ten (10) days of receipt of the Board's written decision.

3. If the Conceptual Preliminary Plan is not approved, the Board's decision shall specify the defects found in the plan, shall describe the requirements that have not been met, and shall cite in each case the provisions of the Ordinance relied upon.

4. Notwithstanding the foregoing procedure, unless the applicant agrees in writing to extend the period for decision, the Board shall render a

decision on all Conceptual Preliminary Plans not more than ninety (90) days from the date of the first regular meeting of the Planning Commission held after the complete application was filed. However, if that regular meeting of the Planning Commission occurred more than thirty (30) days after the complete application was filed, the ninety (90) day period shall be measured from the thirtieth day following the date the complete application was filed.

5. The decision of the Board shall be in writing and shall be communicated to the applicant personally or mailed to the applicant's last known address not later than fifteen (15) days following the decision. The form and content of the decision shall comply with applicable requirements of the Municipalities Planning Code.

6. At the time a revised plan is submitted, it shall be accompanied by the applicant's written and executed agreement of an extension of the period for decision.

7. The decision of the Board shall also be communicated to the governing body of any adjacent municipality, if the plan includes land in that municipality and/or directly abuts its boundaries.

SECTION 505. Submission of Detailed Final Plan Documents

A. Within one year after approval of the Detailed Preliminary Plan, a Detailed Final Plan and all supplementary data, together with an application form provided by the Municipality and filing fees, shall be officially submitted to the Municipal Secretary. The Detailed Final Plan shall conform to the requirements set forth in Section 403. It shall also conform to the Conceptual Preliminary Plan as previously reviewed by the Planning Commission and the Board and shall incorporate all conditions set by the Municipality in its approval of the Conceptual Preliminary Plan. No application shall be deemed filed unless all requirements have been met and all fees paid in full.

B. The Board of Supervisors may permit submission of the Detailed Final Plan in phases, each covering a reasonable portion of the entire proposed development as shown on the approved Conceptual Preliminary Plan; provided that the first Detailed Final Plan phase shall be submitted within one (1) year after approval of the Conceptual Preliminary Plan. Each subsequent phase shall be submitted within one (1) year of approval of the previous phase, provided all phases have been submitted within three (3) years after the date of Preliminary Plan approval.

C. Unless the filing deadline in Section 505A is waived or extended by the Board, failure to make timely submission of final plans renders void a Conceptual Preliminary Plan, and the applicant shall be required to file a new application and fee for Conceptual Preliminary Plan approval.

D. Official submission of the Detailed Final Plan to the Municipal Secretary shall consist of:

1. Three (3) copies of the application for review of final subdivision or land development plan.

2. Sixteen (16) or more copies of the Detailed Final Plan and all supporting plans and information to enable proper distribution and review, as required by the Board.

3. Copies of all applications made or notices provided to Federal, State, and County agencies by or on behalf of the applicant for permits, certifications, approvals, or waivers required or sought for either subdivision or land development as proposed in the Conceptual Preliminary Plan or in the Detailed Final Plan, including but not limited to applications or notices provided to the U.S. Army Corps of Engineers, the U.S. Department of Agriculture Soil Conservation District, the U.S. Environmental Protection Agency, the state Department of Environmental Protection, the state Department of Transportation, or the County Health Department.

4. Payment of application fees and deposit of escrow, if required, for plan review costs.

E. Sixteen (16) or more copies of the Detailed Final Plan and all required supplementary data shall be submitted to the Municipal Secretary together with the required fees and escrow deposit as prescribed by resolution of the Board. The Municipal Secretary shall note the date of receipt and shall then forward:

1. Five (5) copies of the Detailed Final Plan and application to the Planning Commission; and

2. One (1) copy each to the Municipal Planner and the Municipal Engineer;

3. Two (2) copies to the Board;

4. Two (2) copies for the municipal files;

5. One (1) copy to the municipal Historical Commission, where applicable;

6. One (1) copy to the municipal Environmental Advisory Council;

7. One (1) copy to the municipal Parks Board;

8. One (1) copy to the municipal Shade Tree Commission;

9. One (1) copy, referral letter, and sufficient fee to the _____ County Planning Commission, when required by the Board;

10. One (1) copy to other state and county agencies, including the _____ County Health Department, when required by the Board;

11. One (1) copy to the governing body of any adjacent municipality or municipalities if tract to be subdivided abuts or lies partially in that municipality;

12. One (1) copy of the Sedimentation and Erosion Control Plan and application form to the U.S. Department of Agriculture Soil Conservation District, where applicable; and

13. One (1) copy of the Detailed Final Plan showing applicant's correct address to the Municipal Secretary.

F. Where the final plan is for a minor subdivision, the applicant shall submit the plan in accordance with the requirements of Section 503 above.

SECTION 506. Review of Detailed Final Plan

A. General

1. The Detailed Final Plan shall conform in all important respects to the Conceptual Preliminary Plan as previously reviewed and approved by the Board of Supervisors and shall incorporate all modifications and revisions specified by the Board in its approval.

2. The Detailed Final Plan and supporting data (including reports from the Pennsylvania Department of Environmental Protection, the _____ County Board of Health, the _____ County office of

the USDA Natural Resources Conservation Service, and the _____ County Planning Commission) shall comply with the provisions of this Ordinance and those of the zoning ordinance. Failure to do so shall be cause for denying the plan (or, in situations where only minor details are missing and when the official approval deadline allows, tabling the plan).

B. Planning Commission Review

1. The Planning Commission will review the Detailed Final Plan and the recommendations of the Municipal Engineer and any other reviewing agencies to determine its conformance with the requirements of this ordinance and with those of the zoning ordinance.

2. After such review, and prior to any action by the Board within the required ninety (90) day review period, the Planning Commission shall forward its recommendations and its reasons to the Board and the applicant. If the plan includes land in any adjacent municipality and/or directly abuts its boundaries, then such notice and recommendation should also be transmitted to the governing body of the adjacent municipality.

3. No recommendations shall be made by the Planning Commission until the municipality has received the written report of the County Planning Commission, the Municipal Engineer, the state Department of Environmental Protection (DEP), the _____ County Health Department, and the Department of Transportation, if applicable, and the approval of the _____ County Soil Conservation District, provided, however, that if these reports are not received within forty-five (45) days after transmittal of the Detailed Final Plan to these agencies, the Planning Commission may act without having received and considered such report.

C. Board Review

1. Prior to the Detailed Final Plan review process, the Board should complete its review of the proposed Sewage Facilities Planning Module in accordance with DEP and _____ County Health Department regulations and procedures. When approved or adopted by the Board, the Planning Module shall be forwarded to DEP for review and approval.

2. No approval of the Detailed Final Plan shall be granted by the Board until the Municipality receives notification of DEP's approval of the Sewage Facilities Planning Module. Should such notification not be received within the time limitations for Detailed Final Plan approval in accord with the Act, the time limitations shall be extended for not more than ninety (90) days at the written consent of the applicant. If the applicant refuses to provide such written consent, the Detailed Final Plan shall be disapproved.

3. When a recommendation on a Detailed Final Plan has been submitted to the Board by the Planning Commission, such plan shall be placed on the agenda of the Board of Supervisors for its review and action.

4. Upon receipt of the Planning Commission's recommendation and other supporting information, the Board may, at one or more regular or special public meetings, review the Detailed Final Plan and shall, within the time limitations set forth herein below, either approve, approve with conditions, or disapprove the plan. Whenever the approval of a Detailed Final Plan is subject to conditions, the written action of the Board shall (1) specify each condition of approval and (2) request the applicant's written agreement to the conditions within ten days of receipt of the Board's written decision.

5. If the Final Plan is not approved, the decision shall specify the defects found in the plan, shall describe the requirements that have not been met, and shall, in each case, cite the provisions of the Ordinance relied upon.

6. Notwithstanding the foregoing procedure, unless the applicant agrees in writing to extend the time period for decision, the Board shall render a decision on all Detailed Final Plans within the statutory time limitations.

7. The decision of the Board shall be in writing and shall be communicated to the applicant as required by the Act.

8. If at any time the applicant submits a revised Detailed Final Plan, it shall be deemed a new application and shall not be accepted unless it is accompanied by the applicant's written and executed agreement of a ninety (90) day extension of the period required by the Act for de-

cision. No new application fee shall be required for any revision submitted within two years of the first Final Plan application.

9. Copies of the Detailed Final Plan, as finally approved with the appropriate endorsement of the Board, shall be distributed as follows:

   a. At least three (3) copies to the applicant, of which two (2) shall be recorded in accordance with Section ___.

   b. One (1) copy to the Municipal Planning Commission.

   c. One (1) copy to the County Planning Commission.

   d. One (1) copy to the County Health Department.

   e. One (1) copy to be retained in the municipal files.

   f. One (1) copy to the Municipal Engineer. If a new street is proposed, an additional "as built" plan with deed of dedication application shall be submitted.

D. **Conditions of Detailed Final Plan Approval**

Approval of any Detailed Final Plan shall, in addition to any other applicable provisions of this ordinance, be subject to the following conditions:

1. The landowner shall execute a Subdivision Agreement in accordance with Section ___ of this ordinance, verifying that he/she agrees to construct all required improvements and common amenities and further verifying that he/she guarantees completion and maintenance of these improvements and amenities through a type of financial security acceptable to the municipality.

2. Where applicable, the landowner shall execute an Escrow Agreement to cover the cost of all required improvements and common amenities, in accordance with Section ___ of this ordinance.

3. The landowner agrees, if requested, to tender to the municipality a deed of dedication in a form satisfactory to the Municipal Solicitor for streets and improvements thereto, including street paving, water mains, fire hydrants, storm sewers, inlets, pumping stations, and other appurtenances as shall be constructed as public improvements within the public right-of-way and are required for the promotion of public welfare, after all streets and improvements to be dedicated to the municipality are completed and are certified as being satisfactory by the Municipal Engineer. The Board may re-

quire that the applicant provide a certificate from a duly licensed title insurance company certifying that the title to be conveyed is good and marketable and free of all liens and encumbrances, except utility easements, before any property is accepted by the municipality.

4. Whenever the landowner is providing open space as part of the development, an easement in perpetuity restricting such open space against further subdivision or development shall be executed between the landowner and the Township or a conservation organization acceptable to the Township.

5. The landowner shall submit to the municipality all required permits, approvals or waivers from agencies having jurisdiction over ancillary matters necessary to effect the subdivision or land development, such as state Departments of Transportation or Environmental Protection, the Public Utility Commission, U.S. Army Corps of Engineers or Department of Agriculture Soil Conservation District, and the _____ County Health Department.

6. All final approvals or waivers required by Federal, State, and County agencies for development in accord with the Detailed Final Plan including but not limited to approval of the Sewage Facilities Planning Module by the DEP, approval by the U.S. Department of Agriculture Soil Conservation District, and a highway occupancy permit, if required, from the state Department of Transportation shall be presented to the municipality.

―――

ARTICLE 6: RESOURCE CONSERVATION AND GREENWAY DELINEATION STANDARDS

SECTION 600. Applicability

The standards for resource conservation, as set forth in this Article, shall apply to all land subdivision and developments in the municipality. The standards for greenway delineation shall apply to all land subdivision and developments within the Conservation Design Residential Overlay District.

SECTION 601. Planning and Design Standards

A. **General Standards to Minimize Adverse Impacts**

All subdivisions and land developments shall avoid or minimize adverse impacts on the municipality's natural, cultural, and historic resources, as defined below.

B. **Groundwater Resources**

This section is intended to ensure that the municipality's limited groundwater resources are protected for purposes of providing water supplies to its residents and businesses and to protect the base flow of the Municipality's surface waters. These regulations shall be applied in conjunction with those provided for in other sections of this ordinance, dealing with groundwater conservation and replenishment.

1. The proposed subdivision and land development of any tract shall be designed to cause the least practicable disturbance to natural infiltration and percolation of precipitation to the groundwater table through careful planning of vegetation and land disturbance activities and the placement of streets, buildings, and other impervious surfaces in locations other than those identified on the Existing Resources and Site Analysis Map as having the greatest permeability where precipitation is most likely to infiltrate and recharge the groundwater.

C. **Stream Valleys, Swales, Springs, and Other Lowland Areas**

The municipality's Open Space Plan describes and maps stream valleys (which include stream channels and flood plains), swales, springs, and other lowland areas as resources that warrant restrictive land use controls because of flooding hazards to human life and property, their groundwater recharge functions, their importance to water quality and the health of aquatic communities, and their wildlife habitats. They are generally poorly suited for on-site subsurface sewage disposal systems.

1. The following activities shall be minimized:
   a. Disturbance to streams and drainage swales.
   b. Disturbance to year-round wetlands, areas with seasonally high water tables, and areas of surface water concentration.
   c. Because of their extreme limitations, stream valleys, swales, and other lowland areas warrant designation as greenway lands. They may also require adjoining buffer lands to be included in the greenway as determined by an analysis of the protection requirements of such areas on a case-by-case basis. In certain instances, seasonal high water table soils may be excluded from the greenway where it can be demonstrated that they are suitable for low density residential uses and conventional on-site sewage systems.

D. Woodlands

Woodlands occur extensively throughout the municipality, often in association with stream valleys and wet areas, poor and erodible agricultural soils, and moderate to steep slopes.

1. Woodland conditions within the municipality vary with respect to species composition, age, stocking, and health. They range from relatively recent post-agricultural young stands to mature mixed-age forests. Most woodlands in the municipality represent one or more of the following resource values:
   a. As soil stabilizers, particularly on moderate to steep slopes, thereby controlling erosion into nearby streams, ponds, impoundments, and roads. A closely related function is their enhancement of groundwater recharge.
   b. As a means of ameliorating harsh microclimatic conditions, in both summer and winter.
   c. As a source of wood products (i.e., poles, sawtimber, veneer, and firewood).
   d. As habitats for woodland birds, mammals, and other wildlife.
   e. As recreation resources for walkers, equestrians, picnickers, and other related outdoor activities.
   f. As visual buffers between areas of development and adjacent roads and properties.

2. Because of their resource values, all woodlands on any tract proposed for subdivision or land development shall be evaluated by the applicant to determine the extent to which such woodlands should be designated partly or entirely as greenway or development lands. Evaluation criteria shall include:
   a. Configuration and size.
   b. Present conditions (i.e., stocking, health, and species composition).
   c. Site potential (i.e., the site's capabilities to support woodlands based on its topographic, soil, and hydrologic characteristics).
   d. Ecological functions (i.e., in protecting steep slopes and erodible soils, maintaining stream quality, and providing for wildlife habitats).
   e. Relationship to woodlands on adjoining and nearby properties and the potential for maintaining continuous woodland areas.

3. The evaluation of the tract's woodlands shall be undertaken by a forester, landscape architect, horticulturist, or other qualified professional acceptable to the municipality. This evaluation shall be submitted as a report and made a part of the application for a Preliminary Plan. At a minimum, that report shall include one or more maps indicating boundaries and conditions of woodland areas accompanied by a report addressing the criteria in paragraph 2 above.

4. In designing a subdivision and land development plan for any tract, the applicant shall be guided by the following standards:
   a. Healthy woodlands exceeding one acre shall be preserved and designated as greenway areas, to the maximum extent possible. Proposed site improvements shall be located, designed, and constructed to minimize the loss or degradation of woodland areas.
   b. Subdivisions shall be designed to preserve woodlands along roadways, property lines, and lines occurring within a site such as streams, swales, stone fences, and hedgerows. Such lines and the native vegetation associated with them shall be preserved as buffers between adjacent properties and between areas being subdivided within a property. Preservation shall include ground, shrub, understory, and canopy vegetation.
   c. Disturbance or removal of woodlands occupying environmentally

sensitive areas shall be undertaken only when approved by the Board and on a limited, selective basis to minimize the adverse impacts of such actions. This shall include but not necessarily be limited to vegetation performing important soil stabilizing functions on wet soils, stream banks, and sloping lands.

    d. No clearing or earth disturbance (except for soil analysis for proposed sewage disposal systems) shall be permitted on a site before the completion of subdivision and land development agreements. The determination of sight distance clearances along roadways shall be made graphically and *not* by clearing on site prior to Final Plan approval.

E. Upland Rural-Agricultural Areas

These areas comprise fields, pastures, meadows, and former agricultural areas in early stages of woodlands succession, with fences, stone walls, tree copses, and hedgerows, typically bordered by stream valleys and upland woodlands. These constitute the Municipality's historic working landscape, dotted with historic houses, barns, and other structures. They give the municipality much of its rural character. They also contain the greatest concentration of prime agricultural soils. Because of their openness and high visibility, development in these areas is likely to be most readily seen and disruptive to the historic landscape. They sometimes provide habitat for wildlife, in conjunction with nearby woodlands and stream valleys. However, it is recognized that these areas also frequently offer the fewest constraints for development.

1. Several elements of these working landscapes lend themselves to incorporation into the municipality's Greenway network. These include prime agricultural soils and natural features that visually punctuate the landscape, such as hedgerows, tree copses, stone walls, and visually prominent places such as knolls and hilltops.

2. These areas can also accommodate development, with preferred locations being the nonprime agricultural soils and lower topographic settings where development will be visually less obtrusive. Compact clustered residential designs, with coordinated architectural and landscape architectural themes, are encouraged in highly visible locations where future development cannot be avoided (such as at the far edge of open fields).

F. Slopes

Moderately sloping lands (15 to 25 percent) and steeply sloping lands (over 25 percent) are prone to severe erosion if disturbed. Erosion and the resulting overland flow of soil sediments into streams, ponds, and public roads are detrimental to water quality and aquatic life and a potential hazard to public safety.

1. Areas of steep slope shall be preserved in accordance with Article ___ of the Zoning Ordinance and as required below.

2. All grading and earthmoving on slopes exceeding 15 percent shall be minimized.

3. No site disturbance shall be allowed on slopes exceeding 25 percent, except grading for a portion of a driveway accessing a single-family dwelling when it can be demonstrated that no other routing that avoids slopes exceeding 25 percent is feasible.

4. On slopes of 15 to 25 percent, the only permitted grading beyond the terms described above shall be in conjunction with the siting of a single-family dwelling, its access driveway, and the septic system (which should typically be designed with a long, narrow drainage field following the land contours).

5. Grading or earthmoving on all sloping lands of 15 percent or greater shall not result in earth cuts or fills whose highest vertical dimension exceeds 6 feet, except where in the judgment of the Board no reasonable alternatives exist for construction of roads, drainage structures, and other public improvements, in which case such vertical dimensions shall not exceed 12 feet. Roads and driveways shall follow the line of existing topography to minimize the required cut and fill. Finished slopes of all cuts and fills shall be as required to minimize disturbance of natural grades.

G. Significant Natural Areas and Features

Natural areas containing rare or endangered plants and animals, as well as other features of natural significance, exist throughout the municipality. Some of these have been carefully documented (e.g., by the Statewide Natural Diversity Inventory), whereas for others, only their general locations are known. Subdivision applicants shall take all reasonable measures to protect significant natural areas and features either identified by the Municipality's map of Potential Conservation

Areas or by the applicant's Existing Resources and Site Analysis Map (as required in Section 502C) by incorporating them into proposed greenway areas or avoiding their disturbance in areas proposed for development.

H. Historic Structures and Sites

The municipality's documented historical resources begin with the _____ Indians in the early eighteenth century and extend through its colonial agricultural, residential and industrial development in the late eighteenth and nineteenth centuries. Many of the municipality's historic structures and sites have been extensively researched and remain intact. The municipality's extensive historic records are maintained by its Historical Commission.

1. All subdivisions and land developments shall comply with Article ___, Historic Preservation Standards of the Zoning Ordinance.

2. Plans requiring subdivision and land development approval shall be designed to protect existing historic resources of all classes. The protection of an existing historic resource shall include the conservation of the landscape immediately associated with and significant to that resource to preserve its historic context. Where, in the opinion of the Board, a plan will have an impact on a historic resource, the developer shall mitigate that impact to the satisfaction of the Board by modifying the design, relocating proposed lot lines, providing landscape buffers, or using other approved means.

3. Township participation, review, and approval of the applicant's interaction with the Pennsylvania Historical and Museum Commission with regard to the preservation of historic resources is required for DEP approval of proposed sewage disposal systems.

I. Historic Rural Road Corridors and Scenic Viewsheds

The municipality's Open Space Plan identifies a number of historic rural roads in various parts of the municipality. All applications for subdivision and land development shall attempt to preserve the scenic visual corridors along such roads by incorporating them into greenway areas or otherwise providing for building setbacks and architectural designs to minimize their intrusion. In instances in which such designs fail to satisfactorily protect corridors, applicants will be required to provide naturalistic landscape buffers to minimize their adverse visual impacts.

The species designated for such buffers shall be selected on the basis of an inventory of tree and shrub species found in existing hedgerows and along wooded roadside edges in the vicinity of the development proposal.

J. Trails

1. When a subdivision or land development proposal is traversed by or abuts an existing trail customarily used by pedestrians and/or equestrians, the Governing Body may require the applicant to make provisions for continued recreational use of the trail.

2. The applicant may alter the course of the trail within the tract for which development is proposed under the following conditions:

   a. The points at which the trail enters and exits the tract remain unchanged.

   b. The proposed alteration exhibits quality trail design according to generally accepted principles of landscape architecture (for example: Bureau of State Parks publication *Non-Motorized Trails*).

   c. The proposed alteration does not coincide with a paved road intended for use by motorized vehicles.

3. When trails are intended for public or private use, they shall be protected by a permanent conservation easement on the properties on which they are located. The width of the protected area in which the trail is located should be a minimum of ten feet. The language of the conservation easement shall be to the satisfaction of the Governing Body upon recommendation of the Municipal Solicitor.

4. The land area permanently designated for trails for public use may be credited toward the open space requirement described in Section _____.

5. An applicant may propose and develop a new trail. If said trail is available for use by the general public and connects with an existing trail, the land area protected for said trail may be credited toward the open space requirement described in Section _____.

6. Trail improvements shall demonstrate adherence to principles of quality trail design.

7. Trails shall have a vertical clearance of no less than ten (10) feet.

8. Width of the trail surface may vary depending upon type of use to be

accommodated but in no case shall be less than three (3) feet or greater than six (6) feet.

9. No trail shall be designed with the intent to accommodate motorized vehicles.

SECTION 602. Design Process for Residential Subdivisions with Greenway Lands

A. Resource Inventory and Analysis. The tract's resources shall be delincated on an Existing Resources and Site Analysis Map, as required in Section 402C2.

B. Four-Step Design Process. Following the resource inventory and analysis, all residential subdivisions with Greenway lands shall generally follow a four-step design process as described below. Applicants will be required to document the design process as described in Section 402C3.

1. Step 1: Delineation of Greenway Lands and Development Areas

   Greenway lands and development areas shall be delineated according to the procedure illustrated below using as an example a hypothetical 50-acre subdivision parcel.

Total Tract Area	50 acres
Adjusted Tract Area (ATA)	40 acres
Minimum Greenway Requirements	
Primary Conservation Areas	
(land unsuitable for development)	10 acres
Secondary Conservation Areas	20 acres
(50% of ATA)	
Total	30 acres
Development Area (50% of ATA)	20 acres

   a. All lands deducted from the gross tract to determine adjusted tract size (i.e., floodplains, wetlands, and slopes over 25 percent), shall be delineated in their entirety as "Primary Conservation Areas," comprising ten acres in the illustration.

   b. Additional minimum acreage requirements for greenway areas consist of "Secondary Conservation Areas," to be calculated on the basis

of the standards in Section _____ of the Zoning Ordinance. In the example, a minimum of 50 percent of the adjusted tract (or 20 acres) must be Class B greenway lands.

c. Total greenway area requirements are the sum of Primary and Secondary Conservation Areas, which in the example comprise 30 acres.

d. The locations and boundaries of Primary Conservation Areas shall follow the actual boundaries of floodplains, wetlands, and slopes as indicated in paragraph 1 above.

e. The locations and boundaries of Secondary Conservation Areas shall be based on the applicant's analysis of the tract's resource features, using the design standards in Section 402C3. The applicant shall also be guided by any written recommendations provided by the municipality regarding the delineation of Secondary Conservation Areas lands, following the Site Inspection or the Pre-Sketch Conference.

f. Development areas constitute the remaining lands of the tract outside of the designated greenway areas, which in the above example consist of 20 acres, where house sites, streets, and lots are to be delineated in accordance with Steps 2, 3, and 4 below.

2. Step 2: Location of House Sites

   Applicants shall identify house site locations in the tract's designated development areas in a manner such that they fit the tract's natural topography, are served by adequate water and sewerage facilities, and provide views of and access to adjoining greenway areas (without encroaching upon them in a manner visually intrusive to users of such areas). House sites should be located no closer than 100 feet and 50 feet from Primary and Secondary Conservation Areas, respectively.

3. Step 3: Alignment of Streets and Trails

   a. With house site locations identified, applicants shall delineate a street system to provide vehicular access to each house in a manner conforming to the tract's natural topography and providing for a safe pattern of circulation and ingress and egress to and from the tract.

   b. Streets shall avoid or at least minimize adverse impacts on the greenway areas. To the greatest extent practicable, wetland crossings and new streets or driveways traversing slopes over 15 percent shall be avoided.

　c.　Street connections shall generally be encouraged to minimize the number of new cul-de-sacs to be maintained by the municipality and to facilitate easy access to and from homes in different parts of the tract (and on adjoining parcels).

　d.　A tentative network of trails shall also be shown, connecting streets with various natural and cultural features in the conserved greenway lands. Potential trail connections to adjacent parcels shall also be shown in areas where a Municipal trail network is envisioned.

4.　Step 4: Design of Lot Lines

Lot lines for the subdivision should be drawn as the last step in the design procedure. They should follow the configuration of house sites and streets in a logical and flexible manner.

SECTION 603. Greenway Design Review Standards

A.　**Prioritized List of Resources to Be Conserved.** The design of greenway lands in any subdivision or land development plan shall reflect the standards set forth in Section 601 and, to the fullest extent possible, incorporate any of the following resources if they occur on the tract (listed in order of significance):

1.　Stream channels, floodplains, wet soils, swales, springs, and other lowland areas, including adjacent buffer areas that may be required to ensure their protection.

2.　Significant natural areas of species listed as endangered, threatened, or of special concern, such as those listed in the Statewide Natural Diversity Inventory.

3.　Moderate to steep slopes, particularly those adjoining watercourses and ponds, where disturbance and resulting soil erosion and sedimentation could be detrimental to water quality.

4.　Healthy woodlands, particularly those performing important ecological functions such as soil stabilization and protection of streams, wetlands, and wildlife habitats.

5.　Areas where precipitation is most likely to recharge local groundwater resources because of topographic and soil conditions affording high rates of infiltration and percolation.

6.　Hedgerows, groups of trees, large individual trees of botanic significance, and other vegetational features representing the site's rural past.

7.　Class I, II, and III agricultural soils as defined by the USDA Natural Resource Conservation Service.

8.　Historic structures and sites.

9.　Visually prominent topographic features such as knolls, hilltops and ridges, and scenic viewsheds as seen from public roads (particularly those with historic features).

10.　Existing trails connecting the tract to other locations in the municipality.

B.　**Other Design Considerations.** The configuration of proposed greenway lands set aside for common use in residential subdivisions shall comply with the following standards:

1.　They shall be free of all structures except historic buildings, stone walls, and structures related to greenway uses. The Governing Body may grant approval of structures and improvements required for storm drainage, sewage treatment, and water supply within the greenway provided that such facilities would not be detrimental to the greenway (and that the acreage of lands required for such uses is not credited toward minimum greenway acreage requirements for the tract, unless the land they occupy is appropriate for passive recreational use).

2.　They shall generally not include parcels smaller than three acres, have a length-to-width ratio of less than 4:1, or be less than 75 feet in width, except for such lands specifically designed as neighborhood greens, playing fields, or trail links.

3.　They shall be directly accessible to the largest practicable number of lots within the subdivision. Nonadjoining lots shall be provided with safe and convenient pedestrian access to greenway land.

4.　They shall be suitable for active recreational uses to the extent deemed necessary by the Governing Body, without interfering with adjacent dwelling units, parking, driveways, and roads.

5.　They shall be interconnected wherever possible to provide a continuous network of greenway lands within and adjoining the subdivision.

6. They shall provide buffers to adjoining parks, preserves or other protected lands.

7. Except in those cases where part of the greenway is located within private house lots, they shall provide for pedestrian pathways for use by the residents of the subdivision. Consideration shall be given to providing for public access on such trails if they are linked to other publicly accessible pathway systems within the municipality. Provisions should be made for access to the greenway lands, as required for land management and emergency purposes.

8. They shall be undivided by public or private streets, except where necessary for proper traffic circulation.

9. They shall be suitably landscaped either by retaining existing natural cover and wooded areas and/or according to a landscaping plan to protect greenway resources.

10. They shall be made subject to such agreement with the municipality and such conservation easements duly recorded in the office of the County Recorder of Deeds as may be required by the Governing Body for the purpose of preserving the common open space for such uses.

11. They shall be consistent with the municipality's Comprehensive Plan and its Open Space Plan.

C. **Ownership and Maintenance.** Applicants shall demonstrate compliance with Greenway ownership and maintenance standards in Section 109 of the Zoning Ordinance.

SECTION 604. Dedication of Greenway Lands for Public Use

A. **Land Setasides for Public Recreational Use and the "Fee-in-Lieu" Alternative.** The following standards shall apply to new subdivisions. All actions by the Governing Body under this section must also be consistent with the provisions of the state enabling legislation.

1. Applicants for new residential developments involving ten or more dwelling units shall be required to set aside 5 percent of their gross tract acreage as undivided recreational land designated for public usage. Such land shall be suitable for active and/or passive recreation, with at least half the land suitable for active sports, where such facilities are required by the Governing Body.

2. In lieu of a setaside for public usage, two alternatives exist for the applicant proposing subdivision involving ten or more dwellings:

   a. The applicant may offer a setaside limited to recreational usage by the residents of the proposed subdivision. If land is set aside in this manner for private recreational use, it shall also be permanently protected through a conservation easement enforceable by the municipality and/or a land trust, prohibiting future nonrecreational (or commercial recreational) uses.

   b. The applicant may offer to pay a fee to the municipality in lieu of any recreational land setaside. Situations in which it would be appropriate for the municipality to accept such offers include cases in which the land would not provide a particular public benefit because of its small size or location. Exceptions to this rule, where public use of relatively small land areas would still be appropriate, include situations in which the land could be used to buffer or extend public parks or public schoolgrounds or could provide potential linkage in a future township trail network.

   c. The decision whether to accept a fee-in-lieu offer by the applicant shall lie with the Board, which shall also establish the amount of the fee in lieu based upon the municipality's estimated cost of acquiring land that is similar in area and attributes that would better serve public recreational needs. In appraising alternative sites, the municipality shall be guided by the site selection criteria contained in its Open Space Plan. Such estimates shall be based on discussions with realtors or appraisers familiar with land values in the locality. All such fees collected shall be deposited in an interest-bearing account earmarked for recreational land or facility provision by the municipality, and the applicant shall be informed of the use to which the fee will be put. Alternatively, the Board may establish a flat fee (based on discussions with realtors or appraisers familiar with land values in the area) for general use with subdivision applicants.

3. In Option 3 and 4 subdivisions involving fewer than five dwelling units

where, in the judgment of the Governing Body, there would be no particular public benefit accruing from a public dedication (as described above), or from a setaside for shared private recreational usage among the subdivision lot owners, the applicant may offer to place a conservation easement on certain areas of land within individual house lots where certain environmentally sensitive features are present, without conferring common access rights or privileges for the subdivision residents or the broader public. The percentage of land that is thus protected shall generally be not less than twenty percent (20%) of the gross land area of the subdivision. This land may be access-restricted not only from the public but also from other residents in the subdivision.

4. In Option 1 and 2 subdivisions with fewer than ten dwelling units, where there would be no particular benefit accruing from a public dedication (as described above), the recreational land that is part of the requirement for undivided open space shall be designated for private shared recreational usage among the subdivision lot owners.

SECTION 605. Resource Conservation Standards for Site Preparation and Cleanup

A. **Conservation Practices During Site Preparation and Cleanup**

1. Protection of Vegetation from Mechanical Injury. Where earthwork, grading, or construction activities will take place in or adjacent to woodlands, old fields, or other significant vegetation or site features, the Governing Body may require that the limit of disturbance be delineated and vegetation protected through installation of temporary fencing or other approved measures. Such fencing shall be installed prior to commencing of and shall be maintained throughout the period of construction activity.

2. Protection of Vegetation from Grading Change. Grade changes to occur at any location of the property shall not result in an alteration to soil or drainage conditions that would adversely affect existing vegetation to be retained following site disturbance, unless adequate provisions are made to protect such vegetation and its root systems.

3. Protection of Vegetation from Excavations

a. When digging trenches for utility lines or similar uses, disturbances to the root zones of all woody vegetation shall be minimized.

b. If trenches must be excavated in the root zone, all disturbed roots shall be cut as cleanly as possible. The trench shall be backfilled as quickly as possible.

c. Grading and earthmoving operations shall be scheduled to minimize site disturbance during the period November 1 to April 1 when revegetation of exposed ground surfaces is difficult, avoiding soil compaction.

4. Protection of Topsoil

a. No topsoil shall be removed from the site.

b. Prior to grading operations or excavation, topsoil in the area to be disturbed shall be removed and stored on site.

c. Topsoil removed shall be redistributed and stabilized as quickly as possible following the establishment of required grades for a project or project phase. All exposed earth surfaces shall be stabilized by hydroseeding on slopes of less than 10 percent and by sodding, hydroseeding, or rip-rap on slopes exceeding 10 percent.

d. Grading and earthmoving operations shall be scheduled to minimize site disturbance during the period from November 1 to April 1, when revegetation of exposed ground is difficult.

ARTICLE 7. SUPPLEMENTAL DESIGN STANDARDS FOR OPTION 5 HAMLETS AND VILLAGES

SECTION 700. Purposes

A. This article is established to provide opportunities for creating compact housing developments of a traditional character in the form of hamlets and villages.

B. In order to ensure that new, higher density development in the municipality will be compatible with historic village and hamlet building patterns in the rural parts of the County, and that they will reinforce the "sense of place" and neighborhood feeling experienced in traditional rural settlements, the standards herein are proposed to control the location, scale, and physical character of such new development, as well as the manner in which they would fit into the existing pattern of fields, woodlands, and developed areas.

SECTION 701. Site Design and Building Location and Design

A. The Four-Step Site Design Process for Hamlets and Villages

1. The design process for laying out hamlets and villages shall be a variation on the four-step process for conservation subdivisions, as described in Section 402C4 of this Ordinance. In hamlets and villages, where traditional streetscape and "terminal vistas" are of greater importance, Steps 2 and 3 are generally reversed, so that streets and squares are located during the second step and house sites are located immediately thereafter. The first step is to identify greenway lands, including both Primary and Secondary Conservation Areas.

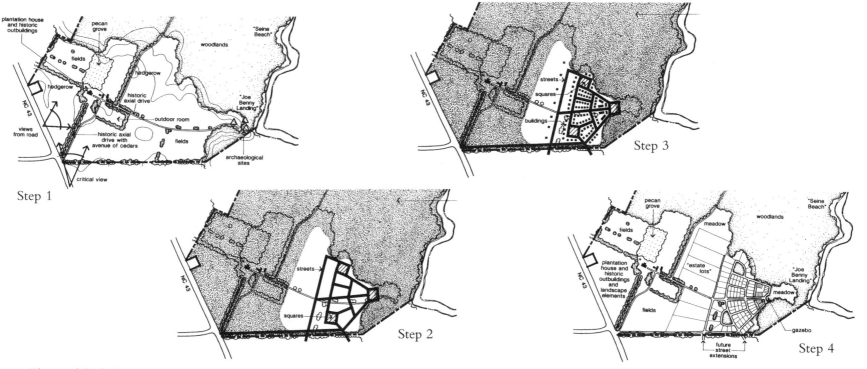

Figure 701A-1. This sequence of sketches illustrates how the four-step approach for conservation design is modified for hamlets and villages. It is essentially the same technique but with Steps 2 and 3 reversed.

B. Standards in Both Hamlets and Villages

1. All lots shall front onto a street or a green (except for flag lots, where permitted).

2. At least two-thirds of the buildings shall have pitched, gabled roofs with roof pitches between 8/12 and 12/12, and the orientation of those gable ends shall be mixed, with some facing the street and others with the ridgeline parallel to the street.

3. Readers are referred to Section 704, Illustrated Design Principles.

C. Building Design Standards for the Mixed Use/Commercial Subdistrict

1. New commercial buildings may be either traditional in their architectural character or a contemporary expression of traditional styles and forms, respecting simply the scale, proportion, and character of village shops. The massing of larger commercial buildings shall be softened in a variety of ways, including the use of projecting and recessed sections, to reduce their apparent overall bulk and volume. To harmonize with the traditional scale of commercial buildings in historic hamlets and villages, new commercial buildings shall not contain more than 10,000 square feet (above grade), and those with more than 6,000 square feet of floor space (above grade) shall be of two-story construction.

2. Buildings shall not be less than one and one half stories in height, and at least half the buildings in any single development for commercial, mixed-use, and institutional buildings shall be two stories in height, with respect to the average ground grade along the front building line.

3. Buildings shall generally be designed for multiple uses, with offices and/or residential units above, and shall generally have traditional sloping roofs with overhanging eaves. Desired roof materials include shingle (both wood and asphalt composition) and metal formed to resemble "standing seams." Roof color should be traditional (which encompasses a wide variety of hues but does not include white or tan composition shingles or shiny unpainted metal). The use of dormers and gables is encouraged to provide visual interest.

4. Exterior wall materials may include stucco, wood clapboarding (including vinyl or aluminum imitation clapboard siding), native stone, or brick of a shape, color, and texture very similar to that found in the historic villages and boroughs of the County. Specifically prohibited shall be brick that is white, tan, spray-painted, or used; except on rear walls, all forms of concrete block shall also be prohibited. In addition, concrete block and metal buildings shall also be excluded from this subdistrict.

5. Shopfront design shall be based on historic examples in the area, with large display windows having low sills and high lintels. Traditional canvas awnings without interior illumination shall be encouraged, and all signs shall be of wood or metal, preferably with dark background colors and light-colored lettering.

6. Landscaping around commercial buildings and their parking lots shall emphasize native species trees, shrubs, and flowers to reduce maintenance, help ensure longevity, and reinforce the natural spirit of the area. Species should be selected partly on the basis of their visual interest at different times of the year (spring blossoms, summer foliage, autumnal berries, and winter bark and foliage). Examples of appropriate shrub selections include viburnum, laurel, lilac, clethra (sweet pepperbush), winterberry, chokeberry, holly, and red-osier dogwood. Interesting nonnative shrub species that are recommended include caryopteris (bluebeard), pyrocantha (firethorn), winged euonymus (burning bush), and spirea. An excellent source book is Elizabeth DuPont's *Landscaping with Native Plants in the Middle Atlantic Region,* published by the Brandywine Conservancy in 1978.

D. Building Design Standards for Residential Areas

1. Single-family homes on the smaller village-scale lots (especially those less than 8,000 square feet) shall generally be designed so that approximately two-thirds are oriented with their gable ends facing the street. At least 35 percent of the houses shall have a covered front entry porch raised a minimum of 18 inches above ground level. When front porches are screened, they may be located within 10 feet of the front property line (those enclosed with windows shall observe the minimum 15 feet front setback).

2. Homes may be located at or within five feet of side lot lines if that side either has no windows or its window sills are at least 64 inches above

the finished floor elevation. Such design allows houses to be located off-center on their lots so that one side yard may be larger and therefore provide more usable outdoor space.

3. Residences housing more than one family shall be designed to emulate traditional buildings of this nature in historic settlements in the County or shall be designed to resemble large single-family residences.

4. Stucco and painted wood clapboard siding shall be encouraged, as shall pitched roofs with slopes between 8/12 and 12/12. Housing styles, shapes, and materials should be varied but within the overall theme of traditional village dwellings found in the rural parts of the County (which may also include contemporary interpretations of vernacular building forms).

5. If garages, carports, or other accessory structures designed for accessory parking of automobiles in the residential areas are front-loaded (i.e, having their large entry door facing the street), they shall generally be set back at least ten feet further from the front property line than the foremost facade of the principal building facing the front property line (stoops, porticos, open colonnades, and open porches excluded).

6. Off-street parking for multifamily residences shall generally be located at the rear of the lot in garages accessed by lanes or alleys.

SECTION 702. Street and Streetscape Design

A. Street Design

1. New streets proposed to be created as a part of any development proposal shall be integrated closely with the municipality's Official Map of existing and future streets. The Official Map shall show the realignment and redesign of certain intersections and road segments to facilitate traffic flow and improve safety.

2. Rectilinear street layouts are generally preferred, with occasional diagonal elements to enhance visual interest, although curvilinear layouts shall be acceptable when designed to interconnect and to produce terminal vistas of protected open space or prominent structures.

3. Streets shall be aligned so that their terminal vistas are of greens or other open space, or civic or institutional buildings, wherever possible. Where this is not possible, every effort shall be made to terminate those streets with buildings of above-average size and whose architecture shall be encouraged to be special in one way or another (see Section 704, Illustrated Design Principles).

4. Streets shall be interconnected as far as practicable (employing cul-de-sacs only where essential), and they may also be supplemented with back lanes or alleys. Where cul-de-sacs are deemed to be unavoidable, continuous pedestrian circulation shall be provided for by connecting sidewalks that link the end of the cul-de-sac with the next street (or open space).

5. To the greatest extent practicable, streets shall be designed to have maximum lengths of 600 feet between intersections and maximum lengths of 1,200 feet before terminating at three-way "T" intersections or angling off in a diagonal direction. (This design approach helps to reduce traffic speed, making the development more friendly to pedestrians.) Blocks greater than 600 feet long shall generally be provided with cross-block pedestrian connections at mid-block locations.

6. Streets shall be laid out to promote pedestrian circulation and ease of access from all points in the Residential Areas to the Village Mixed Use/Commercial Area.

7. Easements shall be reserved to permit streets to be extended to allow adjoining properties to be connected in the future, if so desired.

8. Collector streets shall generally connect existing municipal roads to central greens in each subdistrict.

9. The street width standards listed in Table 702A-1 take into account the need for on-street parking spaces, which generally increases as lot widths decrease.

B. Street Trees

1. The coordinated planting of deciduous shade trees within the right-of-way of all streets is a central unifying feature of development in villages and hamlets.

2. Such trees shall be 2 to 2.5 inches in diameter, measured at chest height, when planted and shall be spaced at intervals no greater than

Table 702A-1. Street Design Standards for Hamlets and Villages

	Total Lanes	Parking Lanes	Pavement Width	Shoulders	R.O.W
PRIMARY COLLECTOR					
No parking	2	0	20 feet (22 feet curbed)	4 feet grassed	50 feet
Lots >80 feet	2	0	22 feet (24 feet curbed)	4 feet grassed	50 feet
Lots 40–80 feet	3	1	28 feet (30 feet curbed)	4 feet grassed	50 feet
Lots <40 feet	4	2	34 feet (36 feet curbed)	4 feet grassed	50 feet
SECONDARY COLLECTOR					
Lots >80 feet	2	0	20 feet (22 feet curbed)	4 feet grassed	50 feet
Lots 40–80 feet	3	1	26 feet (28 feet curbed)★	4 feet grassed	50 feet
Lots <40 feet	4	2	32 feet (34 feet curbed)★	none	60 feet
LOCAL ACCESS					
Lots >80 feet	2	0	18 feet (20 feet curbed)	3 feet grassed	50 feet
Lots 40–80 feet	3	2	24 feet (26 feet curbed)	4 feet grassed	50 feet
Lots <40 feet	3	2	26 feet (28 feet curbed)★	4 feet grassed	50 feet
LANES OR ALLEYS	1	0	12 feet	2 feet grassed	20 feet
SHARED DRIVES	1	0	10 feet	3 feet grassed	N/A

★ The paved width may be reduced by 6 feet when streets are "single-loaded" (lots on one side only) or when driveways are accessed only from rear service lanes or alleys.

40 feet along both sides of each street, including arterial roads but not including rear access lanes or alleys.

3. Species shall be selected according to the following criteria:

    a. cast moderate shade to dense shade in summer;

    b. long-lived (over 60 years);

    c. mature height of at least 50 feet;

    d. be tolerant of pollution and direct or reflected heat;

    e. require little maintenance, by being mechanically strong (not brittle) and insect- and disease-resistant.

    f. be able to survive two years with no irrigation after establishment; and

    g. be of native origin, provided they meet the above criteria.

Among the species that are recommended in this ordinance are sycamore or London Plane, sweet gum, red maple, green ash, pin oak, littleleaf linden, and Village Green Zelkova. For further relevant information, readers are specifically referred to *Street Tree Factsheets* (Henry Gershold, Editor, School of Forest Resources, Pennsylvania State University, 1989).

4. Readers are referred to Section 704, Illustrated Design Principles.

C. Streetscape Standards

1. Shade trees shall generally be planted in planting strips (sometimes called "tree lawns") at least four feet wide, located between the pavement or curb and the continuous sidewalk or footpath system (which shall also be required).

2. All village streets shall be provided with sidewalks, preferably of brick, stone, or concrete paving block in commercial areas. Street lighting in villages shall utilize cast-iron posts that are decorative but not overly ornate and, in order to ensure consistency, the final decision on their style, height, color, and brightness shall rest with Township officials.

3. Sidewalks shall be constructed in villages along at least one side of all streets on which on-street parking is provided, as well as in front of civic, institutional, or community uses (however, they are not required in back lanes or alleys) They shall be constructed of brick pavers, rectangular flagstones, or concrete "paving bricks" or "flagstones." Exceptions may be made for sidewalks of poured concrete, but not for asphalt.

4. In village commercial areas and in neighborhoods where lot sizes are 15,000 square feet or less, on-street parking shall be provided in parking lanes parallel to curbs (which should also be required at such building densities to channelize runoff and to protect the paved edge from damage by parked vehicles). Parking lanes shall be encouraged to be surfaced with alternative materials, textures, or colors (such as asphalt with red-colored stone chips steamrolled in just after the asphalt is laid). Such on-street parking shall be supplemented, wherever necessary, by off-street parking areas that are screened from the street by landscaping and low fences or walls (vehicle "hood-height").

5. Buildings in the Village Mixed Use/Commercial Area shall generally be located close together with minimal side yard areas in order to form a fairly continuous row of shop fronts.

6. Readers are referred to Section 704, Illustrated Design Principles.

SECTION 703. Modifications

A. The Board may, with a positive recommendation from the Planning Commission and after a public hearing, permit by conditional use approval the modification of the provisions of this article in order to encourage a well-planned traditional town center. Applicants must demonstrate that such modifications would not substantially diminish the traditional character of the proposed development and that they would be within the spirit of this article. However, in terms of modifying any dimensional requirement (lot area, width, setbacks, etc.), such modification may not be greater than 25 percent.

B. Any conditional use to permit such a modification shall be subject to the following criteria:

1. The design and modifications shall be in harmony with the purposes and the land-use standards contained in this article;

2. The design and modifications shall generally enhance the development plan, the central core area, the streetscapes, and the neighborhoods, or at least not be any less desirable than the plan that could be created in conformance with this article;

3. The design and modifications shall not produce lots or street systems that would be impractical or detract from the appearance of the District and shall not adversely affect emergency vehicle access or deprive adjoining noncommercial properties of adequate light and air.

4. Increased residential density or intensification of nonresidential uses shall be offset by corresponding special efforts by the applicant to improve the appearance of the development through enhanced architectural and landscaping efforts.

5. The applicant shall demonstrate that the proposed modifications will produce equal or better results, from the municipality's perspective, and represent the minimum modification necessary.

C. If the Board determines that the applicant has met his/her burden, it may grant a modification of the requirements of this article. In granting modifications, the Board may impose such conditions as will, in its judgment, secure the objectives and purposes of this article.

SECTION 704. Illustrated Design Principles

A. **General.** The illustrations in this section have been selected to provide guidance to applicants, designers, local officials, and interested residents with respect to the intended ultimate visual appearance of the Hamlets and Villages. If a conflict occurs between the ordinance text and the information contained in the Illustrated Design Principles, the former shall prevail. The following illustrations and their captions are not intended to be used as regulatory language but rather as guidelines.

B. **Further Detail.** For further information and considerably more detail about these design principles, readers are referred to a sister publication entitled *Crossroad, Hamlet, Village, Town: Design Characteristics of Traditional Neighborhoods, Old and New,* published by the American Planning Association as a Planning Advisory Service report in 1999, by Randall Arendt.

C. **Organization.** The design principles are organized around the following topics and in the following order:

Context and Edge
  Understanding the Context: Respecting the Cultural Landscape
  Maintaining a Crisp Edge
  Dealing with Indistinct Edges
    Deep Meadows as Foreground Open Space
  Handling Roadside Commercial Pressures
Internal Design Issues (infilling and new sites)
  Scale of Villages
  Designing Around Existing Features
  Building on the Traditional Street Pattern
  Alternatives to the Cul-de-sac for Quieter Streets

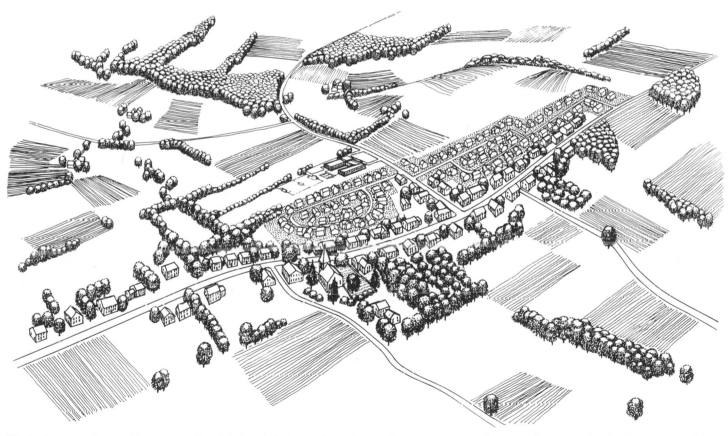

Figure 704D-1. "Filling In and Rounding Out": The stipled area shows how villages are sensitively expanded in England, adding a parallel street and a crescent overlooking new playing fields.

Figure 704D-2. UNIMAGINATIVE VILLAGE EXTENSION: The developer's first plan to enlarge the village of Waterford, Virginia, demonstrates how easy it is to unravel the traditional building pattern when one thoughtlessly applies typical suburban approaches, oblivious to the traditions of the place to which the new development would be attached.

Figure 704D-3. SENSITIVE VILLAGE EXTENSION: Fortunately, county planning staff at the time included a gifted designer, with a trained eye and a careful hand, who counter proposed a masterful little layout that picked up on Waterford's special design characteristics and tied everything together neatly while avoiding the temptation to remake the place in a more formal manner.

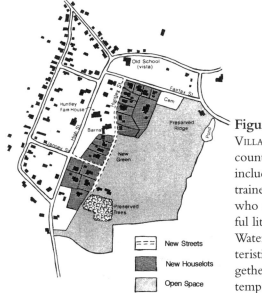

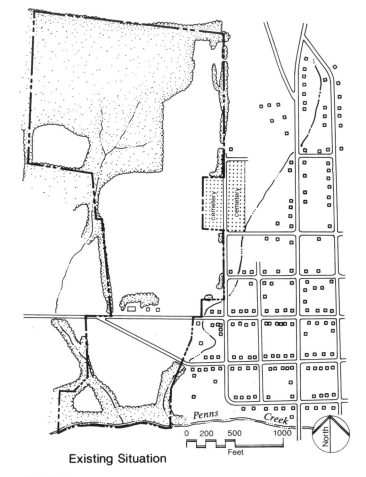

Existing Situation

Figure 704D-4. HISTORIC STREET PATTERN: The preexisting situation at New Berlin, Pennsylvania, is one of a compact and very regular village form typical of the nineteenth century.

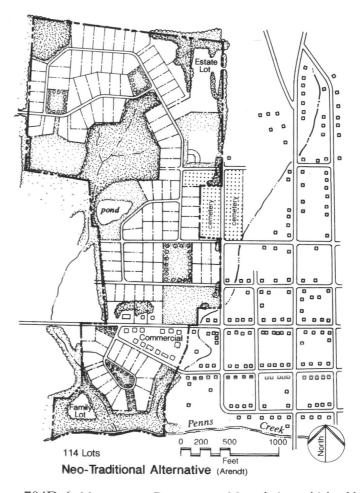

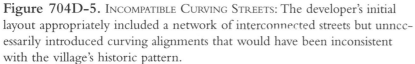

102 Lots
Developer's Proposal

114 Lots
Neo-Traditional Alternative (Arendt)

Figure 704D-5. INCOMPATIBLE CURVING STREETS: The developer's initial layout appropriately included a network of interconnected streets but unnecessarily introduced curving alignments that would have been inconsistent with the village's historic pattern.

Figure 704D-6. MAINTAINING REGULARITY: My redesign, which added 14 incentive lots to the total, squared off the street extensions, and occasionally introduced angular alignments. Several of the open spaces were also positioned to provide terminal vistas and pedestrian connections.

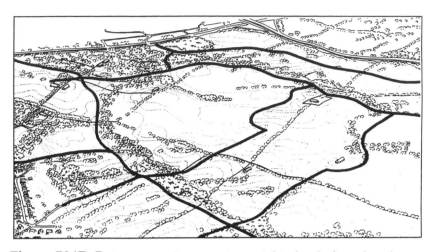

Figure 704D-7. Retaining Country Lanes: This sketch, from the *Bluegrass Design Book,* shows how some of the old country lanes were deliberately not designated to be widened to accommodate the increased traffic projected to flow through this expansion area to Lexington's Urban Growth Area. (*Source:* UDA Architects)

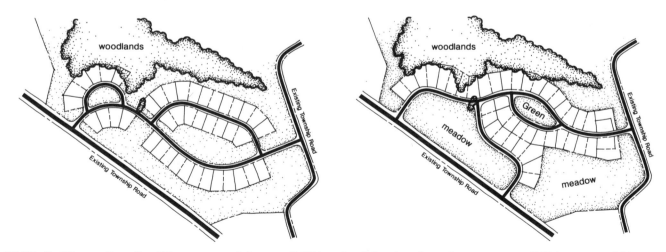

Figure 704D-8. "Fanny First" vs. "Foreground Meadows": This pair of sketches shows how a group of 42 houses could be arranged on a site bordering a rural highway so that the 300 to 500 feet of existing meadow could be preserved to buffer the homes from the traffic and mitigate their visual impact on the community's scenic character. The conventional approach results in a "fanny first" design wherein the view from the road is one of sliding glass doors and pressure-treated decks with little backyard privacy unless the roadside is bermed, which would again diminish the area's rural character.

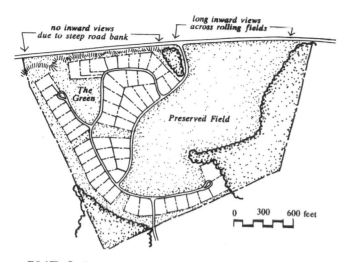

Figure 704D-9. ROADSIDE VIEWSHED PROTECTION: Conditions at this site enabled some of the homes to be located quite close to the existing township road without visual impact or privacy loss because of the deep road cut along that edge of the property. Where the land is visible from the road, a deep "foreground meadow" is provided.

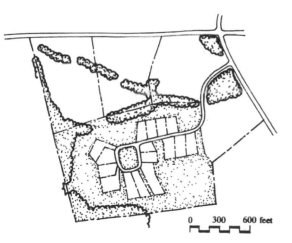

Figure 704D-10. ROADSIDE VIEWSHED PROTECTION: The public viewshed can also be protected by arranging "country properties" or "conservancy lots" (minimum ten acres) along the road, occupying part of the greenbelt open space required of new hamlets.

Figure 704D-11. "YIELD PLANS" TO DETERMINE DENSITY: Under the Growing Greener program, conventional "Yield Plans" like this, demonstrating the feasibility of 18 two-acre lots in the two-acre district, are no longer allowed to be built. One of the five alternative options permitted is the village or hamlet approach shown in Figure 704D-12.

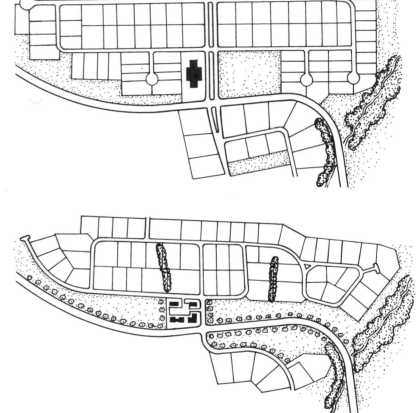

Figure 704D-12. Village Design Under "Growing Greener": This alternative layout illustrates how lot yield could be doubled as a strong incentive for developers to produce layouts following certain hamlet design principles, including 70 percent of the unconstrained land remaining as permanent open space.

Figure 704D-13. Roadside Greenbelt Design: My redesign (bottom) shows how lots can literally be turned around to present their most attractive sides to the public thoroughfare, increase their backyard privacy, and create a parkway effect along the preexisting rural road bordering the property.

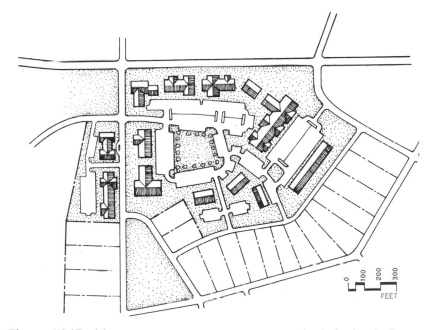

Figure 704D-14. Internal Parking Courtyards: This little sketch illustrates a good way of providing parking in new village mixed-use areas that for viability reasons typically must be located along busy roads. The internal parking courtyard screens the parking lot, but shops are designed with signs and display windows facing both the highway and the parking area.

Figure 704D-15. Walking Radius: The five minute walking radius in this village encompasses much less land than a one-mile radius, illustrating how close new development must be to existing centers for new residents to be able to walk easily to downtown shops, services, schools, churches, and libraries. A bikeway along the river would extend that distance greatly, enabling far more residents to frequent central facilities without driving. (*Source:* GBQC Architects)

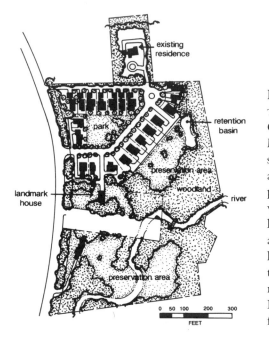

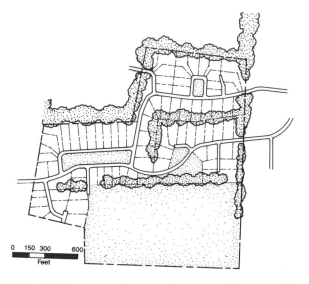

Figure 704D-16. BLENDING THE ELEMENTS: Westwood Common in Beverly Hills, Michigan, is a little gem designed by William Gibbs, who artfully blended hamlet design principles and broader conservation objectives. Of particular note are the hamlet green, abutted on two sides by house lots without any street between them, and the large natural area down by the Rouge River, perfect for informal recreation and wildlife.

Figure 704D-18. DESIGNING AROUND LANDSCAPE FEATURES: Rural landscape features can either be designed across or designed around. Those who wish to take advantage of the mature landscaping and buffering opportunities offered by existing hedgerows can also win the respect of community residents who sometimes take such features quite seriously.

Figure 704D-17. DESIGNING ACROSS LANDSCAPE FEATURES: Nothing appears to be wrong with this picture until one examines the next figure, which makes it evident that the first designer completely ignored the preexisting pattern of trees and hedgerows.

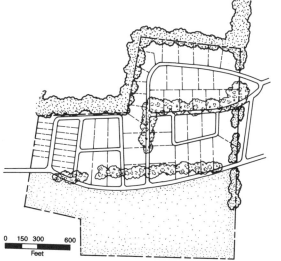

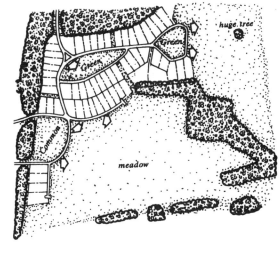

Figure 704D-19. NATURAL FEATURES AS TERMINAL VISTAS: When streets are aligned so that the terminal vista is of open space features, either human-made (greens or commons) or natural (meadows, large trees in the distance, etc.), a sense of spaciousness is introduced as a counterpoint to the enclosed feeling created by parallel rows of buildings on small lots.

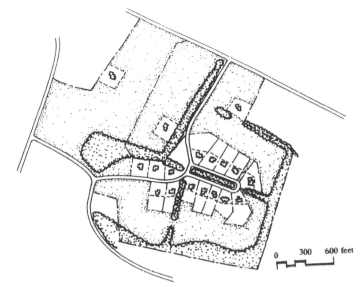

Figure 704D-20. HEDGEROWS AS LAYOUT DETERMINANTS: This layout respectfully follows the existing pattern of hedgerows and woodlands, giving structure to the street system, with large conservancy lots protecting the public viewshed from the main road bordering the property.

Figure 704D-21. HEDGEROW TREES AS STREET TREES: The large trees lining the sidewalk at Tioga, near Gainesville, Florida, are from an old hedgerow on the site, illustrating the "instant landscaping" effect that can be achieved when construction is conducted very carefully outside the "drip lines" defining the root zone.

Figure 704D-22. THE ESPLANADE: When it was purchased for development, this area was entirely wooded. However, the perceptive eye of designer-developer Luis Diaz noticed two lines of trees larger than their neighbors, and research confirmed that they had originally lined a country lane on the property. Clearing away the smaller trees left the original tree rows intact and gave Diaz the idea of using this remnant landscape feature to frame a walkway connecting the community meeting house and park with the retail district at his new Town of Tioga, near Gainesville, Florida.

Figure 704D-23. IRREGULAR STREET PATTERN: The traditional street pattern of villages that grew more by common sense than by deliberate design includes many irregular block shapes and intersections but provides the basic interconnectedness that makes it easier for vehicles to move about.

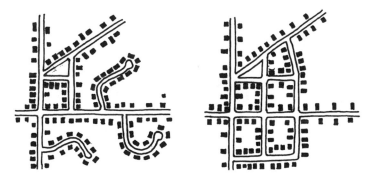

Figure 704D-24. "LOOSE ENDS" VS. TIGHT-KNIT: Examples of the "unravelling" effect of not paying attention to the basic pattern and form of older settlements can be seen at the edges of most older communities, where local officials are not trained to recognize inappropriate layouts and prohibit them through better ordinance standards. The preferred approach, shown at the right, is no more difficult to create.

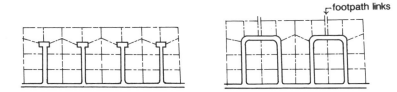

Figure 704D-25. JOINING CUL-DE-SACS INTO LOOPS: Pairing cul-de-sacs to form loop streets offers a sensible and workable alternative, ensuring slow vehicle speed and maintaining low traffic volumes.

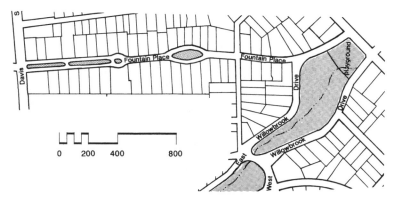

Figure 704D-26. MEDIANS, OVALS, AND "SINGLE-LOADED" STREETS: Central medians planted with trees, a small circle with a fountain, and a larger oval all serve to calm traffic in this wonderful 1920s neighborhood in Burlington, North Carolina, which also includes a streamside park bounded by single-loaded streets (instead of this landscape feature being hidden behind two rows of houses, as is typically the case).

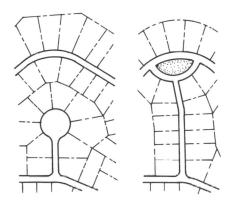

Figure 704D-27. CRESCENT VS. CUL-DE-SAC: Driving speed is cut and through traffic is discouraged with this alternative to the cul-de-sac, involving a small crescent and several stop signs. But developers will frequently choose the cul-de-sac unless regulations prohibit them except where they support a larger design objective (such as greater open space provision or extensive pedestrian linkages).

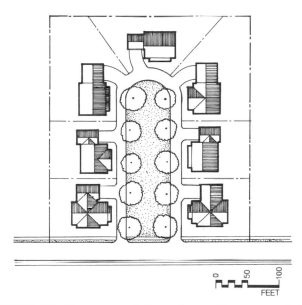

Figure 704D-29. "LOOP LANES": Loop lanes offer a practical alternative to the cul-de-sac and also provide neighborhood green space and an opportunity to install a "rain garden" to capture stormwater runoff close to its source.

Figure 704D-28. PROJECTING GAZEBO: The traffic-calming gazebo projecting into the street at Newpoint in Beaufort, South Carolina, was approved by county engineers only after the developer demonstrated that it would not interfere with emergency vehicles.

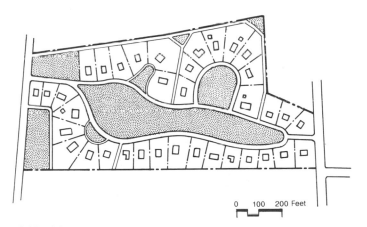

Figure 704D-30. CENTRAL PARKLAND: Narbrook Park in Narberth, Pennsylvania, is a period piece blending substantial open space with graceful informality. Several homes front directly onto open space with no intervening street.

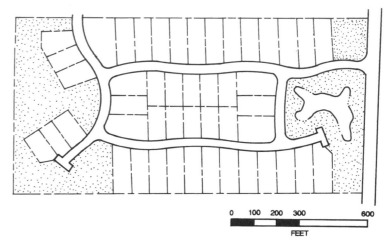

Figure 704D-31. COMPOSITE DESIGN: When cul-de-sacs are inevitable they should generally be required to be planted with trees and connected by footpaths. The "eyebrow" or crescent is another way homes can be accessed off a quiet street. In this redesign I have also fit house lots into the old hedgerow pattern of "outdoor rooms" and have terminated one vista with a neighborhood park.

Figure 704D-33. "TURNING-T's": Turning-T's provide for three-point turns and are appropriate in very low traffic situations.

Figure 704D-32. PLANTING ISLANDS: Shade trees planted within cul-de-sac islands help fill the vast "celestial space" that exists at the ends of these truncated streets.

Figure 704D-34. "TWEETENS": This entrance to a mid-block footpath at Druid Hills in Atlanta is very low key, but all the neighborhood residents know where the entrances are and use them frequently during their evening strolls. They are known locally as "tweetens," perhaps a blend of "betwixt" and "between."

Figure 704D-35. FOOTPATH LINKS TO THE PARK: These pedestrian ways at Radburn link every house with the internal open space network of greens and commons.

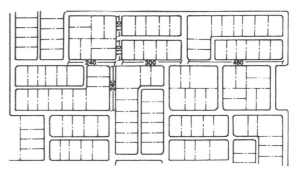

Figure 704D-37. SHORTER BLOCK LENGTH TO CALM TRAFFIC: Even in a rectilinear system, streets can be shortened and terminated at three-way intersections to slow vehicle speed and discourage through traffic while still respecting the principle of interconnectedness.

Figure 704D-36. MID BLOCK SIDEWALK CONNECTIONS: Mid-block sidewalks make it much easier for children to navigate around their neighborhoods. They make so much sense that it is hard to understand why every community does not simply require developers to provide them.

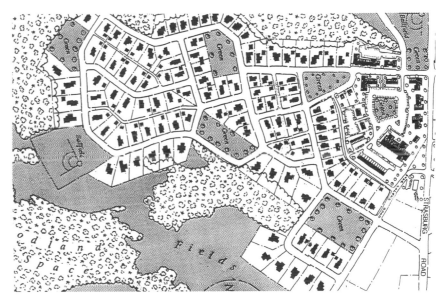

Figure 704D-38. GREENS AS "TERMINAL VISTAS": Sometimes a greater number of smaller greens provides a better result than fewer larger common areas. Another goal of mine was to provide terminal vistas of open space, helping to relieve the otherwise tight feeling created by the village lots.

Figure 704D-39. NEIGHBORHOOD PARKWAYS: The linear park I proposed on this seemingly featureless site follows dark areas on aerial photos indicating seasonally saturated soils and provides a logical greenway linking neighborhoods and even adjacent subdivisions into a community-wide trail network. Regulations must address these opportunities if local officials want to ensure that developers will pay attention to such features.

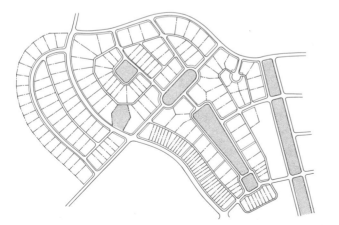

Figure 704D-40. MULTIPLE GREENS: The concept of multiple greens is nicely demonstrated at Celebration, Florida. These greens also terminate views.

Figure 704D-41. HALF-ACRE COURTHOUSE GREEN: Greens need not be huge to be effective, as this half-acre common in front of the county courthouse in Edenton, North Carolina, demonstrates.

Figure 704D-42. LARGE NEIGHBORHOOD GREEN: This green at Celebration encompasses about 30,000 square feet and is more than adequate for the several dozen homes in its immediate vicinity. It approaches the recommended upper size limit for neighborhood use.

Figure 704D-43. SQUARES AND CRESCENTS: About a dozen homes face directly onto each of the two differently shaped greens at McDonnell, near Davidson, North Carolina, increasing livability and elevating property values. (*Source:* Wentling Architects)

Figure 704D-45. IMPORTANCE OF SHADE TREES TO MODULATE SCALE: The large central green at Prairie Crossing will gradually become more human in scale as more shade trees are planted and mature.

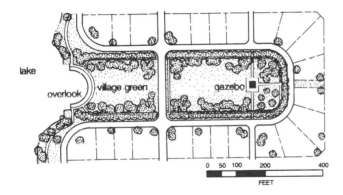

Figure 704D-44. FORMAL GREEN: Prairie Crossing's central green is rather formal, with a gazebo at one end and a lake overlook at the other, providing a refreshing counterpoint to the more rural aspects of the overall development plan. The gazebo also terminates vistas from two side streets.

Figure 704D-46. PLAINS INTO PARKS: The transformation of this two-block site in Bozeman, Montana, from a piece of flat featureless ground to a delightful urban park is principally the result of extensive planting and maintenance of shade trees over decades.

Figure 704D-47. CookIE CUTTER EXPANSION: Expanding villages in a conventional way with standard suburban lots is typically required in most zoning codes, which produce a coarsely grained pattern of "wall-to-wall" house lots with no community open space.

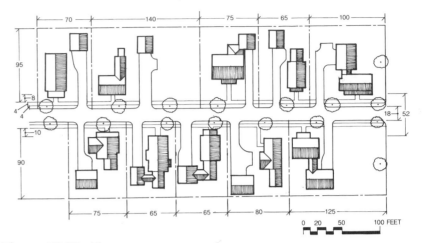

Figure 704D-49. LITERALLY MADE TO MEASURE: The tape measure is one of the conservation planner's best tools, extending everyone's understanding about the dimensions of traditional streetscapes. Measured drawings such as this one from Brunswick, Maine, help people put the density issue in perspective. The neighborhood here supports 20 to 25 people per acre. (*Source:* Steven Moore)

Figure 704D-48.
CONTRASTING NEIGHBORHOOD OPEN SPACES: Scaling back the size of new lots to be more in keeping with the older ones in the village enables the community to grow gracefully and with neighborhood greens and playing fields that the original settlement had never provided. One is a formal square with homes fronting onto it, while the other is an informal ball field behind people's homes.

Figure 704D-50. NARROW LOTS AROUND GREEN: These homes in Celebration occupy lots just 45 feet wide at a density of close to eight dwellings per acre, in a neighborhood particularly popular with empty-nesters, single-parent households, and young couples. Streets encircling such greens are always "single-loaded," but efficiency loss is offset by narrower lots and high sales prices.

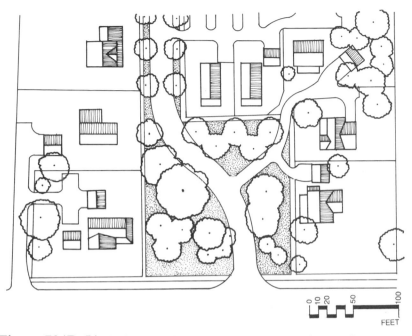

Figure 704D-51. A CURVING DIAGONAL: Entering Wyndcrest Village in Sandy Spring, Maryland, on the diagonal, through a parklike "outdoor room," is an ingenious idea by Duany Plater-Zyberk. The curving street cuts across and through the "square" formed by the houses bounding it.

Figure 704D-52. FRAMING THE VIEW: The gable ends of these two traditional houses frame the view and terminate the vista at Wyndcrest's entrance.

Figure 704D-53. HOUSES FRONTING ONTO GREENS: The visual significance of the 9,000-square-foot parklet at Fairview in Portland, Oregon, is magnified by its positioning at the end of a principal street. Houses fronting onto this small open space sold faster and at premium prices, perhaps because the street does not run right past their front doors. (*Source:* Richard Holt)

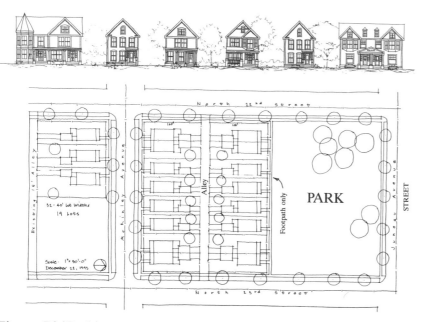

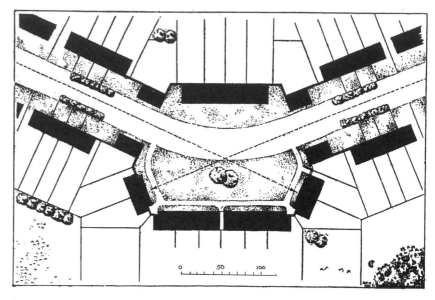

Figure 704D-54. More Houses Fronting Onto Greens: Locating houses at the edges of parks enables developers to reduce street costs, provided garages are located to the rear and are accessed by back lanes, as shown in this project from Milwaukee. (*Source:* Wentling Architects)

Figure 704D-55. Unwinian Vistas Across Parklets: Greater visual interest is created when the street bisecting a housing group is curved so that some of the buildings stop the view and produce a sense of enclosure. This sketch is from Raymond Unwin's classic 1909 treatise *Town Planning in Practice*.

Figure 704D-56. Garden City Court: The housing group shown here, which is similar to the one at Wyndcrest (Figure 704D-57), is a recurring element in some of England's "Garden Cities." (*Source:* Unwin)

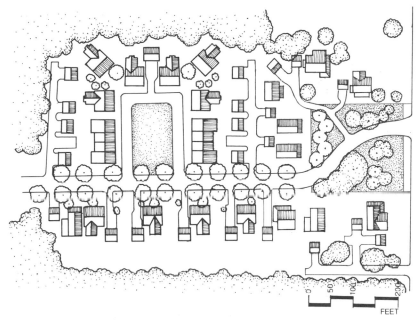

Figure 704D-57. MIXING SINGLES AND TOWNS—I: The greenlet at Wyndcrest measures only 5,000 square feet, yet it creates just enough of a visual feature to establish a special feeling.

Figure 704D-58. MIXING SINGLES AND TOWNS—II: Pictured here is one of the two townhouses containing four single-family dwellings that frame the greenlet at Wyndcrest, plus two of the detached homes occupying the far end of this mixed-type housing group.

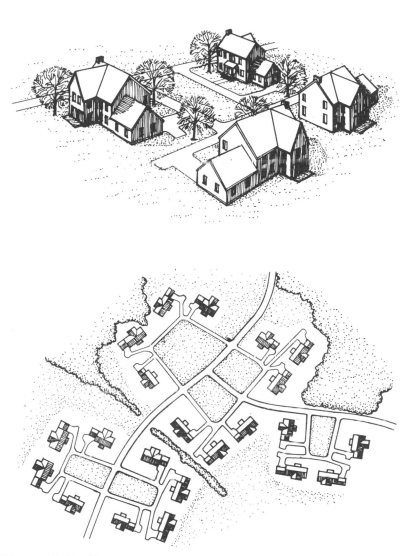

Figure 704D-59. MULTIPLE ADJACENT GREENLETS: When several greenlets are combined, a sense of greater openness can be achieved, which might be advantageous in some rural communities.

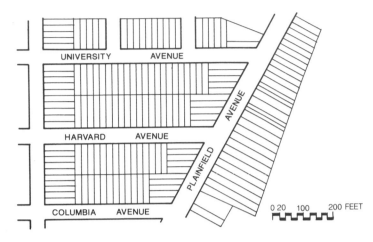

Figure 704D-60. Combining Strip-Lots: There is historical precedent for dividing residential areas into narrow strips of land so that buyers may purchase them in multiples of two, three, or four, enabling a greater variety of house sizes to be accommodated on the same block. This example of 20-foot-wide strips is from Metuchen, New Jersey, in the 1920s.

Figure 704D-62. Trees Make the Street: Streetscapes such as this beautiful one in Bozeman are possible to create almost everywhere in America. In the vast unwooded expanses of the Great Plains, cities such as Bozeman, Missoula, Grand Forks, Omaha, and many others possess surprisingly wonderful "urban forests" that outshine those in most cities located in the more verdant eastern and midwestern states—testimony to what can be accomplished with foresight and determination to create greener neighborhoods.

Figure 704D-61. Blending House Types: A feature of many older neighborhoods is the sympathetic relationship of single-family, semi-detached, and multifamily homes, as in this example from Lexington, Kentucky's Ashland Park section.

Figure 704D-63. Neighborhood Freeway Design: The combination of excessively wide streets and the absence of shade trees is an absolutely "deadly" combination, despite engineers' claims that wider streets are safer and that trees constitute "fixed deadly objects."

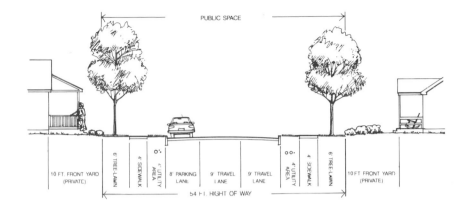

Figure 704D-64. TIGHT STREETSCAPES WITHOUT TREES: The chief exception to the rule that shade trees are an essential component of the proper residential streetscape is the occasional situation in which the street cross-section is very tight, as in many European villages and places like this in Bethel, Delaware. However, trees would not be inappropriate, only somewhat less essential.

Figure 704D-66. UNDERSTANDING RELATIONSHIPS THROUGH CROSS-SECTIONS: This streetscape cross-section shows the importance of scale relationships between opposing buildings, porches and sidewalks, positioning of street trees between curbs and sidewalks, etc.

Figure 704D-65. EVEN TIGHTER BUILDING RELATIONSHIPS: Another exception to the street tree rule occurs when the street is abolished, as in this recent co-housing project in Aspen, Colorado.

Figure 704D-67. THREE-LANE STREET: This local access street in Harbortown, in Memphis, is scaled for three lanes, providing for one full parking lane or two semi-full parking lanes. Homes on these 30-foot lots are accessed via back lanes. Streets such as this are sometimes called "queueing streets" and are excellent traffic-calming devices for local access street situations. Note the terminal vista (gazebo in square).

Figure 704D-68. Boulevards for Grace and Volume: This boulevard in Wyomissing, Pennsylvania, is capable of conducting substantial numbers of vehicles safely, efficiently, and in an attractive way, adding value to the surrounding properties (which might have otherwise been negatively affected by the thoroughfare).

Figure 704D-70. Cul-de-sac Sidewalk: The absence of code requirements for sidewalk continuity can lead to absurd results, as shown in this photo from Chattanooga. This may be the country's only example of a sidewalk designed to resemble a cul-de-sac.

Figure 704D-69. Street Tree Positioning: It makes one sad to realize that every street in every subdivision approved during the past 50 years could look as good as this one in Boise had the local codes only required developers to plant shade trees every 30–40 feet between curbs and sidewalks. In this location they cast shade onto both street and footpath, help to narrow the perception of street width (especially important with two travel lanes and two parking lanes), and provide a psychological barrier sheltering pedestrians from vehicles.

Figure 704D-71. The "Build-Up" Line: The concept of a "build-up" line can help to ensure a certain measure of scale along new village streets, whose ability to cohere visually would be compromised by inappropriately scaled ranch houses.

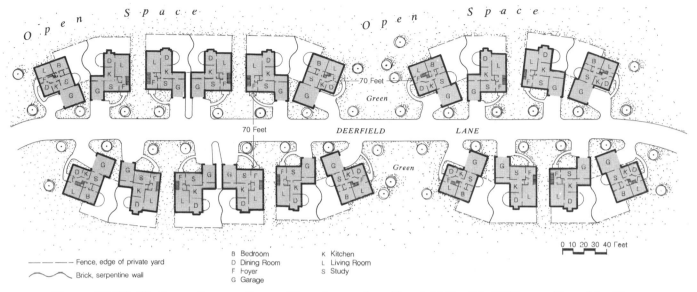

B Bedroom	K Kitchen
D Dining Room	L Living Room
F Foyer	S Study
G Garage	

— — — Fence, edge of private yard

〰〰 Brick, serpentine wall

Figure 704D-72. FRONT SETBACK RANGE: These homes from Deerfield Knoll in Willistown Township, Chester County, Pennsylvania, illustrate how streetscape variety can be enhanced by building within a modest range of front setbacks, instead of adhering strictly to a regimental "build-to" line.

Figure 704D-73. GARAGE DOORS FLUSH WITH HOUSE: It is certainly possible to build attractive homes on narrow lots (40 to 50 feet wide) with garages that do not protrude forward, even in neighborhoods without alleys or rear lanes, as illustrated in this 2,400-square-foot model from Fox Heath by Hovnanian Homes in Perkiomen Township, Montgomery County, Pennsylvania.

Figure 704D-74. SNOUT HOUSES: Designs with projecting garages are becoming known as "snout houses."

Figure 704D-76. ELEGANCE AT 22 FEET WIDE: Another local builder in Carmel has demonstrated that narrow homes can look great if the garage is located to the side or rear.

Figure 704D-75. SNOUT HOUSE ROW: Sometimes the snoutish design idea becomes the controlling concept for an entire neighborhood of snouts, elevated to a kind of bad art form in Carmel, Indiana.

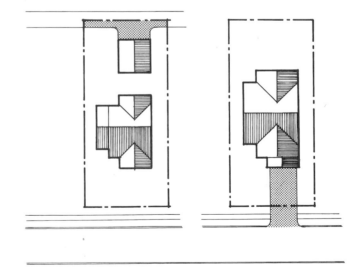

Figure 704D-77. ALLEY PAVING COMPARISON: The total amount of paving required for back lanes can sometimes be slightly less than that required for front driveways. (*Source: New Urban News*)

Figure 704D-78. SIDE-LOADED GARAGES: Homes with side-loaded garages present an acceptable face to the street, especially when the space above the garage is utilized as another room.

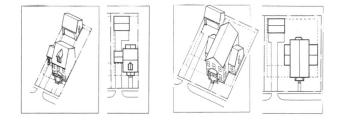

Figure 704D-79. DEEP SETBACKS FOR FRONT-LOADING GARAGES: Several positions for front-loaded garages on lots both narrow and wider. (*Source:* UDA Architects)

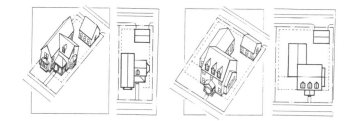

Figure 704D-80. ALLEY-LOADED GARAGE PLACEMENT: Several positions for alley-loaded garages on lots both narrow and wider. (*Source:* UDA Architects)

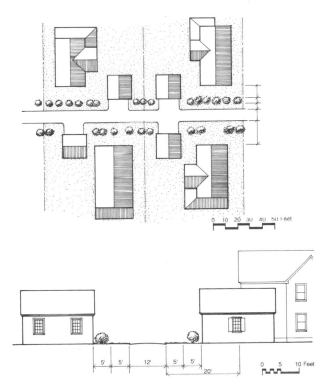

Figure 704D-81. ALLEY LAYOUT AND SCALE RELATIONSHIPS: This plan and cross-sectional view of an alley illustrates spatial relationships. Opposing garage doors should generally be between 30 and 35 feet apart (more in areas where snow removal is an issue). Experience in some new villages also suggests a need for off-street parking spaces between the garage doors and the alley or lane.

Figure 704D-82. IMPROVING ALLEY APPEARANCE: Alleys incorporating gentle curves, street trees, and dog-leg ends, as this one does at Tioga New Town, produce the most pleasing appearance, which is important to potential buyers.

Figure 704D-84. "EMERALD NECKLACE": The stormwater management system at Harbortown in Memphis has been designed as a landscaped crescent of open space with continuous trails linking various neighborhoods together and providing a relaxing counterpoint to the formality of the community's many fine squares and greens. Some of these greenway parks abut streets for an entire block or two, opening vistas from the public thoroughfares into these attractively landscaped drainageways.

Figure 704D-83. DRAINS FOR GAMES: Stormwater detention basins can sometimes be made to be quite broad and shallow, with grassy surfaces suitable for active recreation after the collected runoff has drained away, as shown in this example from Draper, Utah.

Figure 704D-85. AQUIFER RECHARGE: At Village Homes in Davis, California, landscaped footpaths run through the green corridor onto which nearly every house's backyard abuts. Deep infiltration trenches located within these greenways are backfilled with stone and gravel and are instrumental in recharging the underlying aquifer with neighborhood runoff.

Figure 704D-86. Village Center Design: The main shopping street at Haile Village, near Gainesville, Florida, with its two-story buildings, shade trees, and narrow cross-section, has a pleasant scale.

Figure 704D-88. Building New Town Greens—II: A new green is emerging, phoenix-like, in Grand Forks, North Dakota, on the site of a building that burned during the great flood of 1997.

Figure 704D-87. Building New Town Greens—I: This green anchoring one end of the main shopping street in Winslow on Bainbridge Island, Washington, was provided by the developer, who was able to achieve his density objectives with new mixed-use buildings occupying less than all of his site. Officials interested in promoting similar projects in their communities should combine increased code flexibility with certain minimum open space requirements for such semi-public areas in new developments.

Figure 704D-89. Enclosed Spaces and Rear Parking: This aerial perspective sketch of a village center shows how the civic space is enclosed by shops, offices, and apartments, behind which is located the off-street parking, supplemented by parallel curbside parking. (*Source:* Victor Dover)

Figure 704D-90. FLATS ABOVE SHOPPING CENTER: New rental housing has been provided above a new shopping center in Vail, Colorado, to provide living accommodations for store employees earning low wages. The same could be done in almost every community in the country, especially those with college students (who would constitute a ready market for such flats and who some-times cause problems when renting homes in established neighborhoods).

SUGGESTED FURTHER READING

Arendt, Randall. 1989. "Patterns in the Rural Landscape," *Orion Nature Quarterly,* Vol. 8, No. 4, pp. 22–27.

———. 1992. "Open Space Zoning: What It Is and Why It Works," *Planning Commissioners Journal,* No. 5, pp. 4–8.

———. 1993. *Open Space Developments in Sussex County, Delaware.* Georgetown: Sussex Conservation District.

———. 1996. "Creating Open Space Networks," *Environment and Development,* American Planning Association, Planners Advisory Service, May/June.

———. 1996. *Conservation Design for Subdivisions: A Practical Guide to Creating Open Space Networks.* Washington, DC: Island Press.

———. 1996. *Open Space Design Guidebook for the Albemarle-Pamlico Estuarine Region.* Raleigh: North Carolina Association of County Commissioners.

———. 1997. "Basing Cluster Techniques on Development Densities Appropriate to the Area," *Journal of the American Planning Association,* Winter, pp. 135–143.

———. 1998. "Beyond Clustering," *Civil Engineering News,* January, pp. 48–54.

———. 1999. *Crossroad, Hamlet, Village, Town: Design Characteristics of Traditional Neighborhoods, Old and New.* Chicago: American Planning Association, Planning Advisory Report.

———. 1999. "Growing Greener," *Planning Commissioners Journal,* No. 33, Winter, pp. 7–14.

Arendt, Randall, et al. 1994. *Rural by Design: A Handbook for Maintaining Small Town Character.* Chicago: Planners' Press.

Brown, Lauren. 1976. *Wildflowers and Winter Weeds.* New York. W.W. Norton.

Bruce, Hal. 1976. *How to Grow Wildflowers and Wild Shrubs in Your Garden.* New York: Alfred A. Knopf.

Corbett, Michael N. 1981. *A Better Place to Live.* Emmaus, PA: Rodale Press.

Corbett, Michael, and Judy Corbett. 1999. *Designing Sustainable Communities: Learning from Village Homes.* Washington, DC: Island Press.

Cox, Jeff. 1991. *Landscaping with Nature.* Emmaus, PA: Rodale Books.

Diehl, Janet, and Thomas Barrett. 1988. *The Conservation Easement Handbook.* Washington, DC: Land Trust Alliance.

Dobson, Andrew, ed. 1991. *The Green Reader: Essays Toward a Sustainable Society.* San Francisco: Mercury House.

Dupont, Elizabeth. 1978. *Landscaping with Native Plants in the Middle Atlantic Region.* Chadds Ford, PA: The Brandywine Conservancy.

Fabos, Julius Gy, and Jack Ahern. 1996. *Greenways: The Beginning of an International Movement.* Amsterdam: Elsevier Science B.V.

Fazio, James R., ed. 1999. "Resolving Tree–Sidewalk Conflicts," *Tree City USA Bulletin.* Nebraska, NE: National ArborDay Foundation.

Flink, Charles A., and Robert Searns. 1993. *Greenways: A Guide to Planning, Design, and Development.* Washington, DC: Island Press.

Halpern, Daniel, and Dan Frank, eds. 1996. *The Nature Reader.* Hopewell, NJ: Ecco Press.

Harker, Donald F., and Elizabeth Ungar Natter. 1995. *Where We Live: A Citizen's Guide to Conducting a Community Environmental Inventory.* Washington, DC: Island Press.

Jarvis, Frederick D. 1993. *Site Planning and Community Design.* Washington, DC: Home Builder Press.

Kaplan, Rachel, Stephen Kaplan, and Robert Ryan. 1998. *With People in Mind.* Washington, DC: Island Press.

Lacy, Jeff. 1991. "Clustered Home Values Found to Appreciate More," *Land Development,* Vol. 3, No. 3.

Leopold, Aldo. 1976. *A Sand County Almanac.* New York: Ballantine Books.

Little, Charles. 1990. *Greenways for America.* Baltimore: Johns Hopkins University Press.

———. 1992. *Hope for the Land.* New Brunswick, NJ: Rutgers University Press.

Livingston County Planning Department. 1995. *The Greenway Preservation Guidebook for Local Communities.* Howell, MI: Livingston County Planning Department.

———. 1996. *Open Space Planning: Techniques, Design Guidelines, Case Studies, and Model Ordinances.* Howell, MI: Livingston County Planning Department.

Lyle, John Tillman. 1999. *Design for Human Ecosystems: Landscape, Land Use, and Natural Resources.* Washington, DC: Island Press.

MacLeish, William H. 1994. *The Day Before America.* Boston: Houghton Mifflin.

Martin, Laura C. 1986. *The Wildflower Meadow Book: A Gardener's Guide.* Charlotte, NC: East Woods Press.

McHarg, Ian. 1991. *Design with Nature.* New York: John Wiley & Sons.

Mitchell, John H. 1984. *Ceremonial Time: Fifteen Thousand Years on One Square Mile.* Garden City, NJ: Anchor Press/Doubleday.

National Park Service. 1993. *Economic Impacts of Protecting Rivers, Trails and Greenway Corridors: A Resource Book.* Washington, DC: National Park Service, Rivers, Trails and Conservation Assistance Section.

Ndubisi, Forster. 1999. *Approaches to Ecological Planning.* Baltimore: Johns Hopkins University Press.

Nelessen, Anton. 1994. *Visions for a New American Dream: Process, Principles and an Ordinance to Plan and Design Small Communities.* Chicago: Planners' Press.

Noss, Reed F., Michael A. O'Connell, and Dennis D. Murphy. 1997. *The Science of Conservation Planning: Habitat Conservation Under the Endangered Species Act.* Washington, DC: Island Press.

Peattie, Donald Culross. 1935. *An Almanac for Moderns.* New York: G.P. Putnam's Sons.

———. 1948 (reprinted 1991). *A Natural History of Trees of Eastern and Central North America.* Boston: Houghton Mifflin.

Peck, Sheila. 1998. *Planning for Biodiversity: Issues and Examples.* Washington, DC: Island Press.

Petit, Jack, Debra Bassert, and Cheryl Kollin. 1995. *Building Greener Neighborhoods: Trees as Part of the Plan.* Washington, DC: American Forests and Home Builder Press.

Pitz, D. Andrew, et al. 1994. *Design and Management Handbook for Preservation Areas.* Media, PA: Natural Lands Trust.

Small, Stephen. 1992. *Preserving Family Lands.* Boston: Landowner Planning Center.

Steiner, Frederick. 1991. *The Living Landscape: An Ecological Approach to Landscape Planning.* New York: McGraw-Hill.

Teale, Edwin Way. 1951. *North with the Spring.* New York: St. Martin's Press.

Thompson, George F., and Frederick R. Steiner. 1997. *Ecological Design and Planning.* New York: John Wiley and Sons.

Urban Land Institute. 1991. *The Fields at Long Grove.* Project Reference File Series, Vol. 21, No. 10, April–June.

————. 1993. *Farmview.* Project Reference File Series, Vol. 23, No. 7, April–June.

————. 1994. *Hawksnest.* Project Reference File Series, Vol. 24, No. 10, April–June.

Westover, Peter. 1994. *Managing Conservation Land: The Stewardship of Conservation Areas, Wildlife Sanctuaries, and Open Spaces in Massachusetts.* Belmont, MA: Massachusetts Society of Municipal Conservation Professionals.

Wilson, Alex, et al. 1998. *Green Development: Integrating Ecology and Real Estate.* New York: John Wiley and Sons.

Wilson, Edward O. 1992. *The Diversity of Life.* Cambridge, MA: Harvard University Press.

Yaro, Robert, Randall Arendt, Harry Dodson, and Elizabeth Brabec. 1988. *Dealing with Change in the Connecticut River Valley: A Design Manual for Conservation and Development.* Cambridge, MA: Lincoln Institute of Land Policy.

About the Author

Randall Arendt is a land-use planner, site designer, author, and lecturer, and an advocate of conservation planning. A *magna cum laude* graduate of Wesleyan University and a St. Andrews Scholar at the University of Edinburgh, he is vice president of conservation planning at the Natural Lands Trust in Media, Pennsylvania. He coauthored the award-winning volume *Dealing with Change in the Connecticut River Valley: A Design Manual for Conservation and Development* and is the principal author of *Rural by Design: A Handbook for Maintaining Small Town Character.* His most recent book, *Conservation Design for Subdivisions: A Practical Guide to Creating Open Space Networks,* was published by Island Press in 1996. An elected member of the Royal Town Planning Institute in London, Mr. Arendt has lectured in 45 states and 5 Canadian provinces and has designed conservation subdivisions in 16 states.

INDEX